Teaching Text Structures

A Key to Nonfiction Reading Success

Research-Based Strategy Lessons With Reproducible
Passages for Teaching Students to Comprehend Articles,
Textbooks, Reference Materials & More

Sue Dymock and Tom Nicholson

■SCHOLASTIC

New York • Toronto • London • Auckland • Sydney
Mexico City • New Delhi • Hong Kong • Buenos Aires

Dedication

We'd like to dedicate this book to Professor Robert Calfee who, with his research team at Stanford University, was able to take the complex and sometimes impenetrable research on text structure and turn it into workable, elegant designs that teachers could easily use to make their teaching more effective.

To contact the authors directly, e-mail Sue Dymock at sdymock@waikato.ac.nz and Tom Nicholson at T.Nicholson@massey.ac.nw.

Credits

Text credits: "Lake Living," "Stair Masters," "Alutiiq Nation," "Animal Homes," "Survival Tactics," "Amazing Animals," "Animal Messages," "Toys From the Solomon Islands," "From Grower to Seller—9,000 Miles," "Hunting the Horned Lizard," "Going for Green," "War: Who Wants to Remember It?" "The Freeway Debate" © Learning Media Limited, Wellington, New Zealand. / "Swimming: Then and Now" was first published by Learning Media Limited in *Choices*, on behalf of the Ministry of Education © Tessa Duder 1995; "Making Ice Cream" was first published by Learning Media Limited in *School Journal*, on behalf of the Ministry of Education © Jill MacGregor 2003; "Picking Up Rubbish" was first published by Learning Media Limited in *School Journal*, on behalf of the Ministry of Education © Gerry Brackenbury 1996; "Why Do I Blush?" was first published by Learning Media Limited in *School Journal*, on behalf of the Ministry of Education © Julia Wall 2006; "Volcanoes: Indonesia's Deadly 3" was first published in *The School Magazine* © John Malone. / "Fueling the Future," "Hatred's Horrors," "The Fight to Have a Voice," "Heart of A Champion," "Warming Up," "Get Fit," "Koala Chaos" are reprinted from *Scholastic News*. Copyright © 2005 by Scholastic Inc. Reprinted by permission.

Interior photo and illustration credits: pages 5, 6, 18, 21, 25, 26, and 236 courtesy of the authors; page 58: Larry Lee Photography/Corbis; page 59: (top) Simon Phipps/iStockphoto, (bottom) Jim Jurica/iStockphoto; page 61: (top) Kevin Connors/Morguefile, (bottom) Mary Altaffer/AP Photo; page 62: Henny Ray Abrams/Agence France Press/Newscom; page 64: (top) Dale Robbins/iStockphoto, (bottom) Mike Mergen/AP Photo; page 65: (top) Macduff Everton/Corbis, (bottom) Reuters/Sukree Sukplang; page 67: George F. Mobley/National Geographic Image Collection; page 68: David Sanger Photography/Alamy; page 70: Hulton-Deutsch Collection/Corbis; page 71: map by Jason Robinson; page 72: Ira Nowinski/Corbis; page 99: (top) Trish Punch/iStockphoto, (bottom) Gabriela Schaufelberger/iStockphoto; page 100: (top) iStockphoto, (bottom) Bettmann/Corbis; page 102: EcoPrint/Shutterstock; page 103 (top) Nigel J. Dennis, Gallo Images/Corbis, (bottom) Andy Rouse/StockImage/Age Fotostock; page 105: (top) Nature's Images, Inc./Photo Researchers, Inc., (bottom) Dante Fenolio/Photo Researchers, Inc; page 106: (top) iStockphoto, (bottom) Lorraine Swanson/Shutterstock; page 108 (top) DLILLC/Corbis, (bottom) David Ward/Dorling Kindersley/Getty Images; page 109: rainlady/iStockphoto; page 110: (top) Geoffrey Kuchera/iStockphoto, (bottom) illustration by Nathan Hale; page 112: © Popperfoto/Classicstock.com; page 113: Reuters/Jerry Lampen; page 114: Reuters/Ian Waldie; page 130: Roger Ressmeyer/Corbis; page 131: (top) Stacey Newman/iStockphoto, (bottom) Sean Justice/Corbis; page 134: Jaroslaw Wojcik /iStockphoto; page 137: (top) W. Stone/UN Photo; (bottom) illustration by Brian LaRossa; page 158: (top) Anna Milkova/iStockphoto, (bottom) Shawano Cleary/AP Photo; page 159: (top, left) Pablo Corral V/CORBIS, (top, right) Index Open, (bottom) Photos.com; page 161: Flip Schulke/Corbis; page 162: Photodisc; page 164: UPI Bettmann/Corbis; page 165: Bettmann/Corbis; page 166: Dave Nagel/Taxi/Getty Images; page 168: Jeremy Woodhouse/Photodisc/Getty Images; page 169: James Gerholdt/Peter Arnold, Inc.; page 183: (top) NASA Goddard Space Flight Center, (bottom) map by Brian LaRossa; page 184: Kike Calvo/V&W/Newscom; page 186: Isabel Massé/iStockphoto; page 188: Jill Gocher/Asia Images/Getty Images; page 189: illustration by OPS, LLC; page 190: Corbis; page 208: Stephen Mallon/Corbis, (inset) Mary Kate Denny/PhotoEdit ; page 209: Andres Balcazar/iStockphoto; page 211: (top) Dave Nagel/Taxi/Getty Images, (bottom) Amy Myers/Shutterstock; page 214: Clint Scholz/Shutterstock; page 215: (top) map by Ka-Yeon Kim, (bottom) Stock Connection USA/Newscom; pages 228–229: Photodisc; page 231: Alan Traeger/Veer; pages 232–234: Alex S. MacLean/Veer; page 234: (inset) David Wall/Alamy

Cover photo credits: City Street © Dmitry/Mourgefile.com, Bulldozer and Native American © Kenn Kiser/Mourgefile.com, Sunflowers © Wun Ee/Mourgefile.com, Map © Michelle Kwajafa/Mourgefile.com, Tiger © William Attard McCarthy/Mourgefile.com

Every effort has been made to acquire permission to use the materials in this book.

Editor: Mela Ottaiano
Cover design: Brian LaRossa

ISBN-13 978-0-545-01103-7
ISBN-10 0-545-01103-5

Contents

Introduction

By the time our students enter high school most of the instructional reading material they encounter is expository. Students must cope with a heavy diet of nonfiction material not just in short articles but also in whole textbooks. Exposition is the most challenging text young readers will encounter. In fact, research suggests that all students, at times, struggle with content area reading material. Richard Vacca (1998, p. 608), in reference to exposition, states, "What I learned in my early days as a teacher was that average and above-average students . . . also struggled with [expository] texts." This does not need to be the case.

This book provides you with everything you need to enable your students to comprehend the common—yet complex—expository texts they encounter throughout the school day, including:

- the theories that support teaching text structure awareness

- practical teaching strategies

- prepared lesson plans with completed diagrams (graphic organizers) on expository text structure awareness (Note: The "answers" placed in the diagrams are suggestions. You may wish to add your own ideas as well, and those of your students.)

- reproducible versions of the articles

- reproducible graphic organizer templates to distribute to students (Note: The templates show the basic text structure. Students can use these to fill in the key details about each article. This enables readers to "see" the structure the writer has followed. And, if readers know what to look for as they read, their comprehension is enhanced.)

Chapters 1 and 2 are where you'll find the theoretical background. In Chapter 1, we define reading comprehension, and discuss research-based strategies readers use to comprehend expository text and reasons why some students have trouble comprehending this type of text. Chapter 2 discusses the nature of expository text, explains research-based ways to teach it, and describes the main types of expository text that students encounter in school. The chapter outlines strategies on how to teach expository text structure awareness by using the CORE model of instruction.

Chapters 3 to 9 are the "how to" chapters of the book. These chapters aim to help you teach students not just how to comprehend expository text but how writers structure exposi-

tory text. Each chapter includes articles published for readers in grades 4 through 6 that are typical of material found in content area reading as well as articles students encounter during reading periods. The articles focus on science and social studies topics. Within each chapter, the articles increase in difficulty. Some of the articles at the end of the chapters, although originally intended for Grade 6 readers, may present challenges to your students. This is typical of expository text. It is often impersonal, the vocabulary challenging, and the text structure may not be familiar. We highly recommend beginning with the easier articles, regardless of the reading level of your students. The easier articles, which most grade-level students will be able to read and comprehend will give them good preparation for the more challenging articles.

Chapters 3, 4, and 5 focus on descriptive text structures. Chapter 3 focuses on the web structure, which looks like a spider web, with lines that branch out from a central hub. Articles with this structure are about one topic. For example, in an article about spiders, subtopics that branch out from the main topic might include what the spider eats, its habitat, its enemies, and what it looks like. Chapter 4 is about the matrix structure. The matrix is like a weave pattern where lines appear in a criss-cross fashion. While articles with this structure often describe the attributes of objects, animals, people, and places, as a web does, the matrix goes a step further. It *compares and contrasts* these objects, animals, people, or places. For example, rather than describing the attributes of one thing, such as spiders (e.g., diet, habitat, enemies, physical characteristics), the matrix text structure compares and contrasts two or more insects (e.g., spiders and cockroaches) and notes differences in such things as their diet, habitat, and so on. Chapter 5 explains what we call a list structure. This is the simplest of structures. The list structure is similar to a shopping list—the order of the items is not important. In a list of the physical characteristics of a beaver, for example, it does not matter which characteristic comes first.

Chapters 6, 7, and 8 contain sequential structures. Overall, the sequence structure is like a flowchart. All arrows go in the same direction and the elements are linked. Time (or

Articles and Structures Included in This Book

Title	Primary Structure	Secondary Structure
Lake Living	Web	Sequence
Stair Masters	Web	
Fueling the Future	Web	
Alutiiq Nation	Web	
Hatred's Horrors	Web	
Animal Homes	Matrix	
Survival Tactics	Matrix	
Amazing Animals	Matrix	
Animal Messages	Matrix	
Swimming: Then and Now	Matrix	
Making Ice Cream	List	Sequence
Picking Up Rubbish	List	Web
Toys From the Solomon Islands	List	
From Grower to Seller	Linear String	
The Fight to Have a Voice	Linear String	
Heart of A Champion	Linear String	Continuum, Web
Hunting the Horned Lizard	Linear String	Web
Warming Up	Cause-Effect	
Why Do I Blush?	Cause-Effect	
Volcanoes: Indonesia's Deadly 3	Cause-Effect	
Going for Green	Problem-Solution	Linear String
Get Fit	Problem-Solution	
Koala Chaos	Problem-Solution	List
War: Who Wants to Remember It?	Argument/Persuasion	
The Freeway Debate	Argument/Persuasion	

another order) is a key element in sequential structures. You cannot mix up the order of the events. Chapter 6 has the more common sequential structure—the linear string pattern. In a linear string, one thing comes after the other but each step does not cause the next to happen. Chapter 7 focuses on cause-effect text structures. A cause-effect article proceeds in a step-by-step fashion but differs from the linear string in that each step in the process causes the next step to happen. Visually, this kind of information can be represented as "falling dominoes" or as a "branching tree." Problem-solution text structures are in Chapter 8. Time is a factor in problem-solution texts. The time it takes to solve a problem can be a matter of minutes, days, or possibly years. Problem-solution articles can be represented with several different patterns.

Argument/persuasion texts are in Chapter 9. Most students are skilled at orally presenting a case for a fast food meal or why their bedtime should be extended. However, they typically do not read argument/persuasion text until high school. We think students should be exposed to this text type prior to this so they are better prepared when they *need* to read it. In high school, students often engage in debates, and write and read essays, editorials, and other persuasive texts. Argument texts attempt to persuade the reader to come to a particular point of view. Chambliss and Calfee (1998) explain that an argument/persuasion text makes a claim and then presents evidence to support the claim. In Chapter 9, one article presents an argument for and against remembering wars and one presents an argument for and against building freeways.

Following the principle of KISS (Keep it Simple, Sweetheart) we recommend that you focus on one text structure at a time. You may need to spend several weeks on one structure, depending upon the students. In general, younger readers will need more time than older readers to gain a good understanding of the text structure being taught, but this will vary from class to class, and grade to grade. We suggest that you cover all different types of nonfiction text, since research suggests that learning about one type of text (e.g., web) will not extend to other types of texts (e.g., matrix, cause-effect, persuasion). We also recommend teaching the simpler text structures before the more complex ones, so the web structure should be taught before the matrix structure. With the matrix, students must have two or more topics in mind, compared to the one web topic. Readers must also consider the similarities and differences between the objects. With the sequential structures, the linear string should be taught before cause-effect or problem-solution text structures.

We have taught text structure awareness to teachers and students at all grade levels for more than a decade. At the end of the seminars or lessons, we often see the "aha" factor. Text structure awareness brings coherence to the text and structure to the "sea of words." Structure is the key to comprehension.

CHAPTER 1

Reading Comprehension, the "Fourth-Grade Slump," and Expository Text

When I ask teachers about their most serious concerns in literacy instruction, they invariably say—and this is especially true if they teach fourth grade or higher—"Well, if you think my kids have trouble with stories, you should come and see what we do with our social studies and science class. That's where the real trouble begins." (Pearson, 1996, p. 268)

Every day teachers encounter students who are experiencing difficulty comprehending written text, even though the students are bright, enthusiastic, and keen to learn. English is the first language for some, for others it is their second or third. Some of these students are, in other respects, ahead of the curve. According to the National Assessment of Educational Progress (NAEP) fourth grade readers fall into three equal-size groups: proficient readers, grade-appropriate readers, and below fourth grade readers (National Center for Education Statistics, 2004). Readers in the bottom third are clearly experiencing reading difficulties, but proficient and grade-appropriate readers also experience difficulty comprehending written text. Good story readers may find content area reading challenging. We know that at times, *all* students, good and not-so-good readers, struggle with text. As Vacca (1998, p. 608) puts it, "What I learned in my early days as a teacher was that average and above average students—kids who were most like me in high school, promising students who sometimes worked hard and sometimes didn't—also struggled with texts."

One of the aims of this chapter is to discuss why readers have trouble with comprehension. We also discuss the phenomenon known as the "fourth-grade slump." The chapter begins by defining reading comprehension and identifying its components. This chapter also provides an overview of the skills and strategies needed to comprehend written text.

What Is Reading Comprehension?

To define reading comprehension would be to define reading. This is very complex. Comprehension is where the "meanings of words are integrated into sentences and text structures" (Juel, 1988, p. 438). Put another way, it is "the process by which, given lexical (i.e., word) information, sentences and discourses are interpreted" (Gough & Tunmer, 1986, p. 7).

Reading comprehension is the result of several stages. It does not just happen. In the diagram below, we have outlined these steps. First, students must decode the print. Second, students must find the meanings of the words in their mental lexicons (or dictionaries).

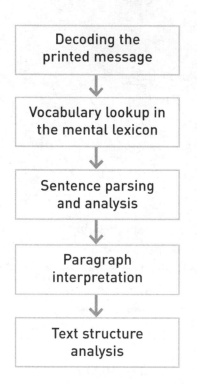

Third, students must parse the sentences in the text—that is, analyze to discern their meanings. Fourth, students must figure out the main idea of each paragraph. Fifth, they must understand the structure of the text as a whole. In this book, we have focused on the fifth step: understanding the text as a whole.

Research by cognitive scientists indicates that in addition to decoding, having a large vocabulary, and using comprehension strategies, *knowledge* is also fundamental to reading comprehension (National Reading Panel, 2000). Reading comprehension requires students to have a lot of background knowledge, and students who have this knowledge find learning easier. As a result, readers who have a lot of knowledge continue to grow more knowledgeable. That is, the rich get richer (Stanovich, 1986).

Phil Gough and Bill Tunmer (1986) were the first to put forward a bold but "simple view" of reading comprehension. They wrote that there are two equally important components to reading. The first component is decoding. Decoding is the ability to read words accurately and quickly. The second component is language comprehension. This is the ability to comprehend spoken language. Gough and Tunmer (1986) argue that reading comprehension is the product of decoding and language comprehension. Most students enter school with the ability to understand language but lack the ability decode.

Students who cannot decode are not "readers." On the other hand, some students develop excellent decoding skills but they don't comprehend what they have decoded (Dymock, 1993). Students who lack language comprehension are also not "readers." A true reader has good decoding *and* good language comprehension skills.

There are different levels of understanding of a text, from very cursory to overly detailed. Cursory understanding is demonstrated in the joke about the student who said he had read the novel *War and Peace*. His teacher asked what the book was about and he replied, "Russia." An example of overly detailed learning is the student who remembers many of the details in a kind of "mind dump." The student shows no understanding of the big picture, no sense of coherence. The student has not thought about the text in terms of its structure, only in terms of words and sentences.

In this book we want to provide you with a key set of useful comprehension strategies for making sense of expository text. This kind of text material—which is so very different from narrative texts—becomes more common by Grade 4. Because these texts are not stories, they provide a whole new challenge to students who are required to read and understand them.

Comprehension Strategies Defined

According to Harris and Hodges (1995, p. 39) a reading comprehension strategy is "a systematic sequence of steps for understanding text." Pearson, Roehler, Dole, and Duffy (1992, p. 169) suggest that strategies "refer to conscious and flexible plans that readers apply and adapt to particular texts and tasks." Pearson et al., continue (1992, p. 169), "Strategies emphasize conscious plans under the control of the reader." A good reader will make conscious "decisions about which [comprehension] strategy to use and when to use it." While some strategies are used across different text types, other strategies are specific to a particular text structure. For example, narrative (or story) text structure awareness is not a strategy used when reading nonfiction texts. For the reader who is interested in narrative text structure, see Calfee and Patrick (1995), Dymock (in press), Dymock and Nicholson (1999, 2001), and Nicholson (1999).

Good Readers Use Reading Comprehension Strategies

Good readers use a number of reading comprehension strategies (Dymock & Nicholson, 1999; National Reading Panel, 2000; RAND, 2002; Pressley, 2000, 2002, 2006a; Sweet & Snow, 2003). As Pressley puts it, (2000, p. 554), "Self-regulated use of comprehension strategies is prominent in the reading of exceptionally skilled adult readers." Whether reading the newspaper, a novel, or a scientific article, good readers use a small number of comprehension strategies to enhance their understanding.

For example, in the case of narrative text, proficient readers are aware that the novel they are reading adheres to the structure of narratives. They know that there will be a problem, characters will respond to the problem, do something about the problem, and there will be an outcome to the problem. Good readers know that in addition to the plot, the story will also have a theme, characters, and a setting. Because good readers are aware of the structure of narratives they know what to look for when they read and their comprehension is enhanced.

In the case of expository text, proficient readers use different comprehension strategies than for narrative. For example, imagine a good reader preparing for a science test on volcanoes. She reads an article about the Mt. St. Helens eruption in 1980. She recognizes that the events leading up to the eruption were sequential and that this is reflected in the structure of the article. The good reader will recognize that time is a factor in the text, and that each step follows the previous step. She knows that there is a set order of events in a sequential text. This good reader studies an article that compares and contrasts the environmental effects caused by the Mt. St. Helens eruption and the 1995 Mt. Ruapehu eruption in New Zealand. She recognizes that the structure of the article may be analyzed using a matrix and that time is not a factor as it was in the previous article. A good reader can immediately spot the difference in structure between this text (compare-contrast) and the previous text (sequence). In a comparison-contrast text, the good reader will recognize that there are two subjects (e.g., Mt. St. Helens and Mt. Ruapehu) and that there are several points of comparison (e.g., effects on animals, plants, air, streams, rivers, and lakes). Having an awareness of the different structures writers use to put together text enables the reader to bring order to the sea of words.

Five Key Comprehension Strategies

Pressley (2002, 2006a), and Brown (2002) call for the teaching of a small number of strategies. According to Brown (2002, p. 344), teachers should "teach a few research validated comprehension strategies well." We agree. Due to the mind's limited capacity we recommend that teachers focus on several key comprehension strategies.

We recommend teaching five research-based comprehension strategies to enhance comprehension of expository text. They are text structure awareness, making connections to background knowledge, creating mental images, summarizing, and questioning.

Comprehension Strategy 1 Expository text structure awareness (Block & Pressley, 2002, 2007; Brown, 2002; Calfee & Patrick, 1995; Dymock, 1999, 2005; Dymock & Nicholson, 1999, 2002; Meyer, Brandt & Bluth, 1980; National Reading Panel, 2000; Ogle & Blachowicz, 2002; Pearson & Duke, 2002; Williams, 2005). Expository text structure awareness is an awareness of the structure the writer has used to put together the text. We strongly believe that students need to be taught how to pay attention to text organization and structure, particularly exposition. Students need to know how expository text is structured. It is very different from the narrative text structure that students have been exposed to from an early age. Narratives follow one structure; exposition has many. Beginning in third and fourth grades, social studies and science textbooks play an increasingly larger role in the curriculum. Because little time has been spent teaching nonfiction writing forms, students begin to encounter difficulty handling this type of text. From several decades of research (refer to Chapter 2) we know that text structure awareness aids comprehension. The teacher plays an important role in developing a student's awareness of expository text structures. Ogle and Blachowicz (2002, p. 264) say it is "important that we provide guidance so that students can learn to identify and use these writing patterns [e.g., cause-effect, problem-solution, description, linear string, etc.] for their own reading."

Research suggests that teachers need to teach each of the main expository text structures. Williams (2005) reported that training students to read one kind of text (e.g., web structure) did not transfer to other structures, nor does it mean that students can somehow intuitively teach themselves about compare-contrast, problem-solution, cause-effect, or other kinds of expository structures.

Chapter 2 details the characteristics of expository text, discusses research that supports teaching students the structure of expository text, and provides tips on how to go about teaching this type of text. Chapters 3 through 9 contain lesson plans on teaching expository text structure awareness.

Comprehension Strategy 2 Making connections to background knowledge (Brown, 2002; Calfee & Patrick, 1995; Pressley, 2002). Knowing a lot about American history helps the reader understand American historical texts. Knowing a lot about climate will help the reader when reading articles on global warming. Readers who know a lot about the civil rights movement will have an advantage when reading about the life of Martin Luther King, Jr. Background knowledge plays an important role in reading comprehension. According to Chambliss and Calfee (1998, p. 54) "Effective instruction *connects* to students' knowledge." The CORE model of teaching, which is discussed in Chapter 2, recommends that teachers "connect" students to what they are reading by building background knowledge. Teachers can connect students to both the text structure (e.g., cause-effect, matrix, web) the writer has followed, and content. Connecting to background knowledge occurs at the beginning of the lesson, but teachers should continue to connect to, and build, background knowledge throughout the lesson. Building on the combined knowledge of the entire class is a powerful way to build background knowledge.

Comprehension Strategy 3 Creating mental images (Brown, 2002; Pearson & Duke, 2002; Pressley, 2002, 2006a, 2006b; Pressley & Block, 2002). One type of imaging is when readers visualize objects, people, places, or events. This type of imaging is usually associated with narratives. Another type of imaging is when the reader organizes the information into a graphic form that illustrates the relationship between ideas and concepts. This type of visualizing is usually associated with exposition but it is also used with narratives (e.g., story graphs). According to Calfee and Associates (1984, p. 82) "structure is the key to comprehension—to comprehend a passage is to create a mental structure." When learning about expository text structures (refer to comprehension strategy 1) it is helpful for students to literally see how texts are structured. This can be achieved by diagramming the text. The diagrams enable the reader to visualize the structure. A web diagram is used for descriptive texts about one topic (e.g., whales). A matrix is used to represent matrix or compare-contrast text types. A timeline is used to represent continuum texts, a type of sequential text. These diagrams represent the top-level structure—that is, the "big picture"—of a text. For example, in the figure below, compare the excerpt about moving a house (Newman, 1995, p. 32) with the diagram that summarizes it. The diagram is visual and memorable, whereas the text is verbal and more difficult to remember. The advantage of the visual diagram is that it breaks the excerpt into smaller chunks that are easier to remember. Over time, readers who have had a lot of experience diagramming expository text structures should be able to create a visual representation of the text in their minds as they read.

Text and Visual Representation of an Excerpt

When Mr. and Mrs. Fisher bought a kiwifruit orchard, it didn't have a house on it. Instead of building a new house on the orchard, they decided to buy a big old house and move it there. It didn't take long to find one they liked.

The house movers took only a few days to cut the house up into large pieces and load them on their trucks. Then the trucks traveled all night to the orchard. (By traveling at night, they didn't hold up other road users.)

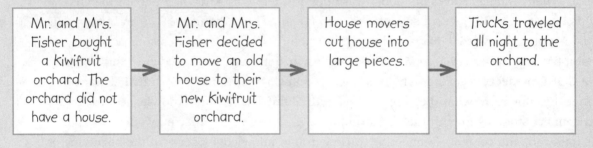

Comprehension Strategy 4 Summarizing (Calfee & Patrick, 1995; National Reading Panel, 2000; Pressley & Block, 2002). Research shows that knowing how to summarize text has a positive effect on reading comprehension. Block and Pressley (2003, p. 117) define summarizing as, "the ability to delete irrelevant details, combine similar ideas, condense main ideas, and connect major themes into concise statements that capture the purpose of a reading for the reader."

Brown and Day (1983) suggest the following rules for summarizing:

- Delete trivial or irrelevant information
- Delete redundant information
- Provide a superordinate term for members of a category
- Find and use generalizations the author has made
- Create generalizations when the author has not provided them

Summarizing is embedded within what we refer to as comprehension strategy 1, expository text structure awareness, and is part of the CORE model of teaching. After the reader has identified the structure (e.g., linear string, web, matrix, etc.) that the writer has used, the reader then diagrams the structure. If the article is a descriptive web structure (e.g., an article that describes the characteristics of Texas) the reader needs to identify the subtopics. In doing so, trivial and redundant information will be discarded. In a Texas article, subtopics may include Texan cities, Texan history, features of the Texan economy, and favorite outdoor activities of Texans. Texan cities, history, etc. are the relevant superordinate terms for the article on Texas. The reader places the subtopics in a web structure as shown in the figure at right, then locates information for each subtopic, and adds it to the diagram. After the article is diagramed the reader is able to see a visual representation of the topic (Texas), subtopics (history, outdoor activities, economy, and cities), and details about the subtopics. This diagram helps the reader to summarize the article. The organization stage of the CORE model of instruction, which is discussed in Chapter 2, shows students how to go about identifying the subtopics and supporting information. This process of homing in on the key points in a structured way is the essence of summarizing.

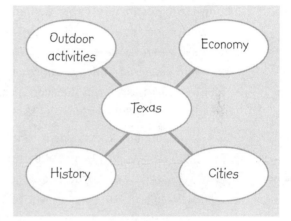

Comprehension Strategy 5 Questioning (Calfee & Patrick, 1995; Block & Pressley, 2007; Dymock & Nicholson, 1999; National Reading Panel, 2000; Pressley & Block, 2002). Generating questions before and during reading aids text comprehension. Prior to reading expository text, good readers will consider the text structure the writer has followed. An article titled "The Monarch Butterfly" can follow one of several text structures. The article may simply describe the monarch butterfly (e.g., a web structure) or it could discuss its life cycle (e.g., sequential structure). Good readers know that writers follow one of many patterns, so prior to and during reading, good readers will generate questions related to the text structure. Once good readers have identified the text structure, they continue to generate questions. While reading a descriptive article on the monarch butterfly, good readers will generate questions such as: "What are the subcategories or topics?" If "diet" is a subcategory, good readers will be generating questions about what the butterfly eats.

In the CORE model (see Chapter 2), questioning is a key component of each lesson. We use questions to **connect** to prior knowledge, we use questions to **organize** the text structure, and we use questions to **review** and **extend** the text. Questioning is not an add-on to each lesson, it is a basic part of each lesson plan.

Difficulties Comprehending Written Text

There are many reasons why students experience reading comprehension difficulties. For example, students may have difficulty decoding (Gough & Tunmer, 1986; Nicholson, 2006), a key component of reading comprehension. Vocabulary also plays a role (Anderson & Freebody, 1981; Stahl & Nagy, 2000). The number of words a reader knows provides a relatively accurate reflection of his or her ability to comprehend the text. According to Perfetti, Marron, and Foltz (1996), "The role of vocabulary [in reading comprehension failure] is obvious enough. A failure to understand words in text will cause problems in understanding the text" (p. 142). As students progress through school they encounter more complex expository text that demands good vocabulary knowledge. Imagine a 12-year-old student preparing for a test on earthquakes. A student who knows the meaning of words such as *tectonic plate, fault line, seismic waves, tremors, tsunamis, seismometer, seismograph, epicenter, magnitude, energy,* and *Richter scale* will be in a much better position to do well than a student to whom the words are unknown or are "getting in the way" (Nicholson, 1984, p. 449; 1989). As Nagy (1988, p. 1) puts it:

> Vocabulary knowledge is fundamental to reading comprehension; one cannot understand text without knowing what most of the words mean. A wealth of research has documented the strength of the relationship between vocabulary and comprehension. The proportion of difficult words in a text is the single most powerful predictor of text difficulty, and a reader's general vocabulary knowledge is the single best predictor of how well that reader can understand text.

Nagy and Scott (2000) report that the reader needs to know the meaning of 90 to 95 percent of the words in the text for adequate comprehension. A reader who knows 90 percent of the words in the text can use this knowledge to learn the remaining 10 percent. If the reader knows fewer than 90 percent of the words in the text, comprehension is at risk. Picture the 10-year-old student in a science class who is reading the article "Warming Up" found in Chapter 7. Comprehension will be a challenge if the meaning of words such as *global warming, indigenous, vanishing, opposite, natural, causes, surrounds, fossil fuels, releases, carbon dioxide,* and *atmosphere* are unknown.

Vocabulary knowledge is important for comprehension but it is only one component of reading nonfiction texts. Comprehension will still be at risk for students with good decoding skills but who lack knowledge of text structure (Calfee & Patrick, 1995). Readers who are unable to make links to their own background knowledge, or who lack background knowledge also struggle with comprehension. Australian or Pakistani readers will have little difficulty understanding an article that includes words and phrases such as *wicket, over, three runs from two balls, six runs from four balls, gone for a duck,* and *stumped.* These terms and phrases are associated with cricket, a sport played in Australia, Pakistan, and a number of other countries. Because most Americans have little or no knowledge of the game of cricket, American readers will have great difficulty understanding the article.

What many otherwise good readers lack is knowledge of text structure. They can read the words but they can't see the design of the text. Many students will not develop text structure awareness without explicit teaching. Research suggests that a lack of explicit comprehension instruction is one of the causes of poor comprehension (Calfee & Drum, 1986; Pressley, 2006a, 2006b; Stanovich, 2000; Sweet & Snow, 2003). Vacca (1998) argues that many readers experience comprehension difficulties because they have never been shown how to handle the "conceptual demands inherent in texts." We suggest that the lesson plans in this book based on the CORE model are an excellent way to tackle these conceptual demands.

After decades of research on reading comprehension and particularly the benefits of comprehension strategy instruction, one might expect that the kind of effective comprehension strategies that we recommend are being taught in classrooms today. Research shows, however, that the explicit teaching of comprehension is far from the norm. Durkin (1978– 1979) and her team of researchers visited 30 classrooms of 9 to 12 year olds in order to determine how, when, and how often teachers engaged in explicit teaching of reading comprehension. She found that of the 11,587 minutes observed, only 45, or less than 1 percent of the reading period, were spent teaching comprehension strategies. Durkin reported that teachers mentioned enough for students to work on the task. They gave and checked assignments. They also questioned students about what they had read. However, reading comprehension strategies were not taught.

Twenty years later, despite decades of research, Pressley, Wharton-McDonald, Mistretta-Hampston, and Echevarria (1998) report that little has changed. They found a scarcity of comprehension instruction in Grades 4–5. They report that "We were struck by the almost complete absence of direct instruction about comprehension strategies" (p. 172). It is not surprising then that many students experience problems comprehending written text, especially the more complex expository text. As one student put it, with reference to the material in her social studies textbook, "I don't really remember this too well; I don't know why. We always learn about this and I always forget. It's so important. Something like one of the colonies was too strong and something happened and they got into a war over it, and it was going on for a while and that's just one of the things. I don't know why I don't remember. It's pretty embarrassing" (quoted in Beck, McKeown, Hamilton & Kucan, 1998). One aim of this book is to help teachers reduce or eliminate embarrassing moments attributable to a lack of reading comprehension strategies.

The "Fourth-Grade Slump" and Expository Text

According to Chall (1983) and others (Duke, 2000; Neuman, 2006) most of the text material students encounter during their initial stages of reading is narrative in structure. Narrative texts are familiar to young readers. Before they even enter school, students have listened to stories at the dinner table, when traveling in the car, and at bedtime. After reading primarily narrative texts in Grades 1–3, students are suddenly confronted with an increasing amount of nonfiction, with which they are unfamiliar. It is not surprising that students encounter, at about age 10, what Chall (1983) called "the fourth-grade slump," a phenomenon that often happens when students are making the difficult transition between learning to read to reading to learn.

Some readers have trouble because they lack decoding fluency and automaticity, the ability to recognize words quickly and accurately (Chall & Jacobs, 2003). Vocabulary knowledge also has an effect on students' ability to decode and comprehend more difficult text that is beyond their immediate experience (Nagy & Scott, 2000). Students may not have

sufficient background knowledge. But a major reason, in our experience, is that the students encounter more text that is expository in structure and they don't know how to handle it. The form is unfamiliar to them, it's very complex, and many students become lost when they encounter it.

Chall (1983, p. 68) puts forward the argument that "some are able to read the stories in their 'readers,' but not their content textbooks, which contain a more extensive vocabulary and concept load and require more background knowledge." Texts at the Grade 4 level begin to contain what Chall (1983, p. 21) refers to as "unfamiliar, bookish, abstract words, and a higher proportion of long and complex sentences." Compare the following three excerpts. The first passage, written for Grade 1 readers, describes how snowflakes form. The second, written for Grade 4 readers, compares and contrasts unwanted items found in food. The third passage, written for Grades 6–8 readers, discusses research by a Canadian scientist on how to survive in freezing temperatures. The Grade 1 excerpt has short sentences (5–12 words), the vocabulary is simple, and all but one word have one and two syllables.

> Drops of water are inside clouds. The drops of water get cold. The drops of water freeze. They become little bits of ice. The bits of ice get bigger as more water freezes on them. The little bits of ice stick together and get heavy. They fall from the clouds as snowflakes. ["It's snowing," 2005.]

The Grade 4 article is more challenging. Sentences are longer (19–23 words), more complex, and the vocabulary is more difficult. There are several three- and four-syllable words.

> Cockroaches, flies, rat droppings, pieces of metal or glass—these are just some of the mysterious things that are often found in food. When someone finds something weird in their food, scientists try to solve the mystery of how it got there using science and technology. It's important that scientists solve these mysteries so people don't get hurt from eating things like glass or metal. [Thomas, 2002, p. 20.]

The following excerpt demonstrates the more sophisticated words that readers in Grades 6–8 face as they progress through school. The article on how to survive in freezing temperatures also has longer and more complex sentences than the snowflake article.

> Giesbrecht heads the Laboratory for Exercise and Environmental Medicine at the University of Manitoba, in Winnipeg. For 18 years, he has studied human responses to work and exercise in low-temperature conditions. Giesbrecht doesn't limit his studies to data collected by other researchers. Canada's guru of goose bumps has jumped into frozen lakes, taken ice-cold Jacuzzis, and injected more than a gallon of ice water into his veins. [Wulsin, 2004, p. 6.]

We believe that the fourth-grade slump can be overcome, and even prevented. For some, this can be achieved by improving decoding skills (Gough & Tunmer, 1986; Nicholson, 2006). For many others, however, it will be text structure awareness training and the CORE model of teaching. We hope this book provides you with a better understanding of how to teach text structure awareness to strengthen your students' comprehension skills.

CHAPTER 2

Teaching About Nonfiction Texts—and the CORE Model of Instruction

My 6th grade daughter slumped over her social studies textbook. Suddenly she straightened upright, slammed down her pencil, and complained loudly, "I can't even understand this stuff!" A good reader, she typically labored to comprehend the exposition in her social studies, science, and mathematics instructional materials. Her frustration with her own failure to comprehend reflects a common problem. Readers frequently struggle to understand expository writing, which is often impersonal, typically nonfictional, systematic explication of information. Indeed, recent data collected on young adults aged 21–25 suggest that the majority of adults never learn how to comprehend even slightly complex expository texts. (Chambliss, 1993, p. 319.)

In this chapter we focus on nonfiction text structures and how to teach them. We discuss the difference between narrative and expository texts, the various terms used to describe types of expository text, and explain why we have broken these terms down into just a few key descriptors.

We also discuss research on teaching about expository text and we explain the CORE approach to teaching about text structures. This approach takes into account research about being strategic in reading. It involves not just diving into the text when you present it to the class but instead building bridges between your students' own knowledge of the world and the new material that is presented in the text material they are to read.

Narrative and Expository Text: What Is the Difference?

Texts can be either narrative or expository. Calfee and Patrick (1995) recommend teaching these different structures separately. While young students often have this intuitive sense of narrative structure, many students are unsure of the difference between narrative and expository text. The important thing to share with them is that expository, or nonfiction, texts are not stories. An article about monkeys, for example, is not a story. A comparison between the Tate Art Gallery in England, the Louvre in France, and the Museum of Modern Art in New York, for example, is not a story. And while a biography sometimes may seem like a story, it is not.

Narrative text is a story. Narratives have a theme, a setting, a plot, and characters. Events in many narratives build toward a high point, or climax, and a resolution.

Characters can be described in terms of their features and personality or, they can be compared and contrasted in a matrix structure. For example, the plot of a story can be summarized as a list of episodes. This can be done by simply writing a list of what happened, 1, 2, 3, etc., one thing after another. Or, the main events can be shown on a large sheet of paper or a whiteboard using the story graph technique. A story graph looks like a graph on which the Y axis represents levels of action or emotion, from low to high, and the X axis represents time, from the start of the story to the finish. In a story graph you can write in the main events in the whole story, writing in the points either high or low on the Y axis to show levels of action or emotion. Begin with the first event and move along the X axis until you cover all the events in the story. You can also use a matrix for comparing characters. For practical examples of the structure of narrative text, refer to Calfee and Patrick (1995), Dymock and Nicholson (1999; 2001).

Although there are other terms in the literature that refer to nonfiction text, such as informational text (Duke, 2000, 2004) and transactional text (Rosenblatt, 1978), in this book we use the term **expository** text. Calfee and Patrick (1995) reason that expository text does "everything but tell a story" (p. 83). Exposition informs, argues, and explains (Chambliss & Calfee, 1998). Calfee, Henry, and Funderburg (1988, p. 132) explain that "a passage is expository if it describes an event, person, or thing, presents a time sequence for a factual event, or gives a logical set of directions or steps, and makes an argument or attempts to persuade." According to Weaver and Kintsch (1991) exposition primarily communicates information. Finally, exposition, according to Chambliss and Calfee (1998, p. 33), "is an invention, an artifact, a construction." Unlike the familiar narrative text, exposition is not "natural."

Expository text seems in some ways to be a more inclusive term than other terms that are used. Our rule of thumb is the same as that of Calfee and Patrick (1995)—expository text is anything that does not tell a story.

Types of Nonfiction Texts—and a Plethora of Terms

Categorizing types of nonfiction text types can be confusing when there are so many terms used by authors and publishers. Terms include *recount, description, compare-contrast, collection, enumeration, procedure,* etc., but our feeling is that many of these terms can be expressed through a few key words. We have chosen these terms because they bring to mind a picture of the structure of the text. Please see the Text Structures and Related Terms chart (pages 23 and 24).

Text Structures and Related Terms

Terms and images used in this book	Rationale	Examples	Related terms found in other published material
Web	A web text focuses on one topic. The information about that topic is grouped in ways that make sense. Descriptive categories, typically four or five, are connected to the central topic like the lines in a spider web. For more complex web texts, each subtopic can have subtopics of its own.	• an animal: physical characteristics, habitat, diet, enemies, and "other things" • robot: who invented it, why it was made, how it works, other machines	• Description
Matrix	A matrix refers to text material that involves comparison and contrast of descriptive information. Texts of this type focus on the similarities and differences between things. The matrix structure enables the reader to compare two or more things.	• crocodiles and alligators • brown bears and polar bears • lives of Martin Luther King, Jr., Nelson Mandela, and Mahatma Gandhi	• Comparison • Compare-contrast • Venn diagram: often used to compare and contrast
List	Although the terms collection and enumeration (Meyer, 1975; Dickson, Simmons, & Kameenui, 1998) refer to information that is presented in an unrelated way, we prefer to call this text type a list. In a list, there is no reason why one set of information would go before or after another.	• a "jobs to do" list • China's main imports and exports • shopping list • country information: population, products, geography, languages, etc.	• Collection • Enumeration

Terms and images used in this book	Rationale	Examples	Related terms found in other published material
Sequence	Sequence suggests a flowchart or sequence of steps. It is imperative that the information is listed in the order in which it occurs. In this book sequence is represented in a few sub-types: linear string, cause-effect ("falling dominoes" or "branching tree"), continuum, and problem-solution.	• how the body reacts when blushing • how to put together a model boat • how to milk a cow • how exercise improves a body's health • important events in the life of Eleanor Roosevelt • how to get from home to school	• **Recount/biography:** recounts the details of an event or a person's life • **Explanation:** tells how things work • **Procedure:** instructions on how to do something • **Instructions:** has the same meaning as procedure • **Cause-effect:** shows how one thing causes another to happen • **Antecedent-consequent:** has the same meaning as cause-effect • **Continuum:** has the same structure as recount but gives dates and events together in a timeline • **Problem-solution:** states a problem and then describes a solution • **Response:** a term similar to problem-solution
Argument and Persuasion 	For	Against
---	---
			While examples of argument and persuasion texts may not be widespread in the nonfiction books and articles that students read in school, discussion and debate are very much a part of all classroom reading and writing programs. For this reason, we feel it important that the argument/persuasion structure is explained to students. They need to increase their awareness of and ability to analyze this structure more and more as they encounter it in newspapers, magazines, advertisements, and on the Internet.	The writer tries to persuade the reader. The reader has to decide if the arguments are persuasive or not. We consider both sides of the case and make a decision. • Should we build a freeway through the inner city? • Should the country go to war?	• **Argument:** these are discussion texts that usually present information for and against an idea • **Persuasion:** these are the same as argument texts

Research on Text Structure

Text structure refers to "how the ideas in a text are interrelated to convey a message to a reader" (Meyer & Rice, 1984, p. 319). Dickson, Simmons, and Kameenui (1998, p. 242) write that "text structures are more abstract, less visual presentations of text that involve organizational patterns of text written to convey a purpose (e.g., to persuade, describe, compare-contrast, or entertain with a story). Text structure relates to the way in which sentences, paragraphs, and the entire text have been organized, whether in a novel, an editorial, an article on global warming, or a chapter in a social studies textbook on the history of the Pacific Northwest.

While ideas about expository text structure go back to Greek oratory, it was during the 1970s and 1980s that a great deal of active cognitive research into text structures took place (Calfee & Chambliss, 1987). Meyer (1975, 1981) was one of the first researchers to classify expository texts into different design structures, such as cause-effect, compare-contrast, problem-solution, and lists. Although a complete text is made up of sentences and paragraphs, Meyer's work focused on the structures of texts as a whole, as macro-structures.

Meyer, (1975, 1981) argued that there are three levels at which expository text can be analyzed. At the sentence level (also referred to as microproposition or microstructure) the focus is on sentence coherence. It is the most basic level to find specific and supporting details.

The gist or main idea of the passage is represented in the middle of the hierarchy, at the paragraph, or second level. At this level the concern is with the relationship between ideas that are represented by paragraphs.

The top-level structure, or third level, relates to the organizing principles of the text. Top-level structures are the highest-order elements, and they refer to the global form of the text. The top-level structure is central to the organization of a text (Meyer, Brandt & Bluth, 1980).

Research studies by text structure analysts such as Bonnie Meyer were very important in understanding the structural components of texts. However, the analyses of text that were made were often very detailed, taking pages to describe even a very short text (Calfee & Chambliss, 1987). For large texts a simpler approach was needed. This simplicity was achieved by researchers at Stanford University in a professional development package called Project Read (Calfee & Patrick, 1995). In Project Read it was argued that a good text has a focus and a simple design to convey that focus (Calfee & Chambliss, 1987). Good writers have a clear focus and use a simple text design. In contrast, less skilled writers put many ideas onto a page without a sense of order or plan. Similarly readers who lack good comprehension skills recall the text in a disordered way, as a jumble of ideas. This is why an understanding of text structure is so important, especially for nonfiction text.

Why Teach Expository Text Structure Awareness?

As discussed in the previous chapter, many students experience problems comprehending expository text for many reasons. Some students get lost in the words and can't see the big picture (Dymock, 1998; Dymock & Nicholson, 1999). Content area reading is often technical, the topic is unfamiliar, vocabulary is new, and text materials differ from the narrative form with which they are familiar. It might be that Grades 4–6 students find expository materials hard to comprehend because there is a scarcity of nonfiction text in the lower primary grades. Susan Neuman (2006) found little expository text in basal readers, a key source of reading material in primary grades. Smith (1991) found that only 15 to 20 percent of Grade 1, 3, and 5 basal readers had nonfiction content. Duke (2000) also found a scarcity of nonfiction text in Grade 1. So it will come as no surprise then that many Grades 4–6 readers are unaware of the top-level structure the writer has used or that well-written expository text even adheres to a structure at all.

Readers who understand the many expository text structures, and who use this knowledge as they read, will remember more of the important information in the text (Meyer et al., 1980, Meyer Young, & Bartlett, 1993; Pearson & Duke, 2002). Readers who have text structure awareness know that authors structure expository text in a number of ways. Readers who have text structure awareness build a representation of the text by following the top-level structure (Meyer & Poon, 2001). Good readers are aware of the patterns writers use to compose text, and they use this knowledge to comprehend. Chambliss and Calfee (1998, p. 29) write that "Decades of research and centuries of experiences suggests that text structure—the organization of sentences, paragraphs, and the total discourse—has a powerful effect on comprehensibility." Smolkin and Donovan (2002, p. 151) agree. They state, "As comprehension research has shown repeatedly, awareness of text structure aids reading comprehension."

Dickson, Simmons, and Kameenui (1998) analyzed seven secondary and 10 elementary school studies that investigated the relationship between text organization and reading comprehension, and found that text structure awareness has a positive impact on comprehension, particularly in terms of identifying and recalling the most important information in the text (e.g., information at the top-level). They also found that good readers had a better understanding of text structure than poor, and good readers used this knowledge to comprehend text.

Common Expository Text Types

Grade 4 is about the time students experience a dip in comprehension that is often referred to as the "fourth-grade slump." At this juncture, students begin to face increasing volumes of expository text, which is unfamiliar to many of them. And the many different text types only add to their confusion. Often, multiple text structures are covered in various content lessons. In science, students may be reading a chapter that describes stem cells, their characteristics, uses, and ethical issues associated with this kind of research. The text material is a web structure. In social studies, students may encounter a list of features of New York City. In health, students might read about the problems and solutions associated with obesity. So, it is not surprising that readers struggle to comprehend expository writing.

Drawing from Meyer's (1975, 1981) work, Calfee and Associates (1984), Calfee and Curley (1984), and Calfee and Patrick (1995) divided the main text patterns that students encounter in school into two groups, descriptive and sequential. These two groups represent six top-level structures or writing plans authors use to organize their ideas. Chambliss (1993a, p. 325) defines descriptive text as text that "presents the static characteristics of an object (somewhat analogous to a snapshot)." Sequential texts are affected by time. She defines sequence text as text that "presents events progressing over time (roughly similar to a movie)."

In our own reading of Grades 4–6 reading material, we have found that the most common text types are list, web, matrix, and linear string. Sequences are mostly of the linear string variety, such as a step-by-step description of how to do something, or how things happen. Sequence texts that follow a cause-effect or problem-solution pattern are less common.

Descriptive Text Structures

Descriptive patterns focus on the attributes of something. Time is not an element in descriptive texts.

Web

The web is a descriptive pattern about one thing. In a web, the information about a person or animal or object is grouped into a small number of related categories. There may be

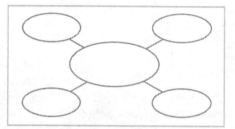

many bits of information that can be grouped together. For example, in an article on raccoons, the information can be put into broad categories (e.g., diet, habitat, physical characteristics, enemies). The diagram at left shows a web pattern. See Chapter 3 for web articles and lesson plans.

Matrix

The matrix compares and contrasts two or more topics. For example, the author may be comparing the features of two European cities, or five elementary schools in Boston, or polar, black, and brown bears. The diagram at left shows a matrix (compare-contrast) pattern. Refer to Chapter 4 for matrix articles and lesson plans.

List

A basic descriptive pattern is the list. Calfee and Chambliss (1987) consider the list to be the most "primitive of the patterns" (p. 364). With the list there are few, if any, links between the elements. Examples of list patterns include a grocery list, a list of countries where English is the dominant language, a list of state flowers, or in science, a list of the attributes of penguins. On a list, it doesn't matter what goes first. The diagram at left shows the list pattern. Refer to Chapter 5 for list articles and lesson plans.

Sequential Text Structures

Sequence texts present a series of events, from first to last. Time is an important element in sequence structures.

Linear String

The linear string pattern is a common sequential pattern. It is similar to the list pattern but a significant difference is that the elements are linked by time. In a string pattern there is a chronological description of events (e.g., the sequence involved in baking bread, or harvesting carrots, or the events leading up to World War II). A sequence can also refer to the steps to follow in working out a math problem. The diagram at right illustrates the string structure. Refer to Chapter 6 for string articles and lesson plans.

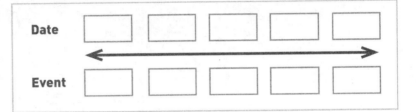

Continuum

The continuum sequence pattern is more common in a biography or a historical text where dates and events that happened on those dates are linked together. The continuum template (a timeline) is shown at right:

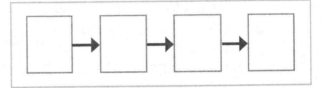

Cause-Effect: Falling Dominoes

Here, two or more ideas or events interact with one another. For example, the text may cover the causes and effects of environmental disasters (e.g., the Exxon Valdez environmental disaster in Alaska, or the Chernobyl disaster). While this pattern does appear in Grades 4–6 reading material, it is more common in high school history, science, and health classes. The diagram at right is used to show cause-effect text structures. Refer to Chapter 7 for cause-effect articles and lesson plans.

Cause-Effect: Branching Tree

In this type of sequence design, an event has several consequences. The template for a branching tree design is shown at right.

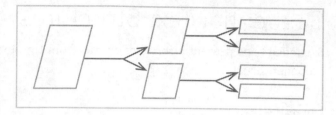

Problem-Solution

Problem-solution texts describe a problem and suggest one or more solutions to the problem. The author may also offer possible outcomes to the "solved" problem. Time is an element in problem-solution texts. First the problem is explained, solutions to the problem are considered, and over time, the problem is either solved, partially solved, or is not solved. The time it takes to solve a problem varies, and some problems may never be fully solved (e.g., the problems associated with global warming, or alcohol abuse, or air pollution, or school bullying). Problem-solution articles and lesson plans are in Chapter 8. Problem-solution texts can be presented using one of the diagrams at left.

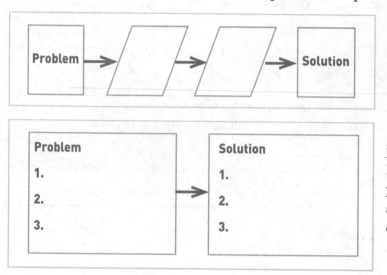

Argument/Persuasion Text Structures

Argument/persuasion texts usually make a claim and then provide arguments to support or oppose the claim. In the case of advertisements, the text may only give arguments in favor, but most discussion texts give arguments on both sides. A simple way to represent the structure of argument text is to have a diagram, such as the one at left, that enables you to list arguments for and against. Refer to Chapter 9 for argument/persuasion articles and lesson plans.

For	Against

Signal or Cue Words

Writers often use signal or cue words to highlight the structural organization of the text. We suggest asking students to look for these signal words when reading expository text. Identifying signal words makes it easier to decide on the relevant structure. Research suggests that signals have a positive impact on text recall, particularly for less-able readers. Meyer and Poon (2004) and Calfee and Curley (1984) identified signal words and phrases for six text structures. The following table contains these signal words.

Signals for Six Basic Expository Text Structures

Structure	Signals
Descriptive: Web	for example • which was one • this particular • for instance • specifically • such as • attributes of • that is • namely • properties of • characteristics are • qualities are • marks of • in describing
Descriptive: Matrix	not everyone • but • in contrast • instead • act like • however • in comparison • on the other hand • whereas • in opposition • unlike • have in common • share • resemble • the same as • different • difference • differentiate • compared to • while • although • as well as • not only • but also
Descriptive: List	and • in addition • also • include • moreover • besides • first • second • third (etc.) • subsequent • furthermore • at the same time • another
Sequence: Linear String	afterward • later • finally • last • early • following • to begin with • to start with • then • as time passed • continuing on • to end • years ago • in the first place • before • after • soon • more recently • not long after • on [date] • before
Sequence: Cause-effect	as a result • because • since • for the purpose of • caused • led to • consequence • thus • in order to • this is why • if/then • the reason • so • in explanation • therefore • because • so that • nevertheless
Sequence: Problem-solution	**Problem:** question • puzzle • perplexity • enigma • riddle • issue • query • need to prevent • the trouble; **Solution:** answer • response • reply • rejoinder • return • comeback • to satisfy the problem • to set the issue at risk • to solve these problems

Lesson Design and the 3 Cs

We recommend that teachers follow the three Cs when designing lessons: Coherence, connectedness, and communication (Calfee, 1994). The three Cs stem from research carried out by cognitive psychologists that emphasizes the importance of preparing students to read text (Calfee, 1994; Calfee & Patrick, 1995). Preparation means that students are asked to bring their background knowledge to the text, to think about what the text will be about, to use visual designs to organize the text information, to reflect on the text and its message, and to transfer what has been learned to new text material (Pressley, 2006a).

Calfee (1994) suggests that teachers follow three principles when designing lessons. The first guiding principle in lesson design is **coherence**, or KISS, "keep it simple, sweetheart." Due to constraints of short-term memory, lessons should focus on one thing at a time. By following the principle of KISS, knowledge and performance can be enhanced. The lessons in Chapters 3 to 9 try to "keep it simple."

Connectedness is another guiding principle for designing lessons. Connectedness is the link between what the reader knows and what is being learned, the link between prior knowledge and new knowledge. Teachers can build on the reader's knowledge base by focusing on what the reader knows, rather than on what the reader does not know. Students do have a great deal of knowledge about the world—they just might not have knowledge about the topic the teacher is focusing on. A key is to build on what students *do know*.

The third principle is **communication**, in particular the distinction between natural and formal language. Most students enter school with a good grasp of natural language—language they use to communicate with their parents, sisters, brothers, and other family members. This language is highly implicit, interactive, and personal. Language in written text is "formal language."

The formal language typically found in expository text is highly explicit. The following excerpt from "Fueling the Future" (Scholastic, 2005), written for Grade 4 students, illustrates the type of formal language found in expository text. "Many people believe carbon dioxide and carbon monoxide cause global warming. Another alternative fuel made from corn, called ethanol, is being used by people across the US to fill up their cars. Ethanol is made by breaking down the sugar found in corn. Ethanol can be blended with gasoline to create a cleaner type of fuel. About 30 percent of all gas used in the US last year was blended with ethanol." Clearly, this language is very different from the natural language associated with talk, "What's for dinner?" "Chicken, rice, and salad." "How was school?" "Boring." In natural language, sentences or phrases are short, vocabulary is familiar, and words are often less than three syllables. In the excerpt above, sentences are longer (e.g., up to 21 words), vocabulary is challenging (e.g., *ethanol, alternative, global warming, carbon dioxide, carbon monoxide*), and there are many three-syllable words (e.g., *dioxide, monoxide, ethanol, gasoline*). Teaching students how to handle this formal type of communication is one of the functions of schools.

The CORE Model of Instruction

The CORE model of instruction (Connect, Organize, Reflect, Extend) provides an excellent framework for lesson design (see figure below). The lessons in Chapters 3 to 9 all follow the CORE model of teaching. We have found it to be a really helpful way to plan lessons because it connects to students' background knowledge, teaches them how to look at text the way an architect looks at the design of a house, teaches them to visualize the information, teaches them to think about the meaning and reflect on it, and teaches them to transfer lessons learned to new text material.

The CORE model of instruction (Calfee & Patrick, 1995) directs teachers towards more interactive, flexible, and reflective teaching. Rather than follow a locked-in, step-by-step lesson plan, the CORE model begins with connecting students to the topic using questioning strategies that stimulate thought. Teachers can connect students to the text structure, the content, or both. During the "connect" stage of the lesson students' background knowledge can be built upon. Drawing on background knowledge is an important strategy for comprehen-

The CORE Model of Instruction

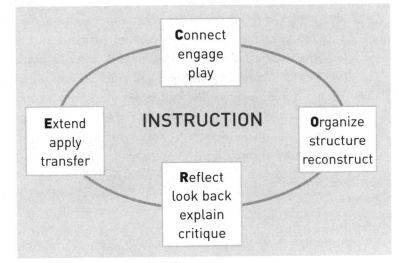

(Calfee & Patrick, 1995, p. 63)

sion. A key element of the "connect" section of the CORE model is asking the right questions. Asking questions that relate to the text is also an important strategy for comprehension. Questions can either promote thinking or stifle it. We discourage yes-or-no questions, unless followed by "why?" for the CORE model encourages "real questions." Real questions:

- Connect
- Call for complex answers, rather than yes or no
- Encourage dialogue
- Call for real listening

During the organize part of the lesson, the teacher, together with the students, diagrams the article. There is a lot of discussion of the content of the text, the vocabulary, and how to summarize the ideas in the text. Vocabulary and summarization are important strategies for comprehension. Another important comprehension strategy is to put the text ideas into a picture format (e.g., web, matrix, linear string, etc.). The diagram should be large enough for the students to see. Overhead transparencies, whiteboards, smart boards, or large sheets of paper are all suitable for organizing the content of the article into a web, matrix, linear string, etc. Because the CORE model is flexible, teachers can continually return to the connect stage and the organize stage.

Reflect provides an opportunity to "look back" and review content, structures, and strategies. It is an opportunity to reflect on the message of the text, the main point of the article, through questioning techniques that enable the student to step back from the task and discuss what has happened. "What type of text did we read today? How do we know it was a matrix text structure?" "Let's return to the beginning of the lesson—to the list of things we knew about cockroaches before we read the article. What do we know now that we did not know before? Do you view cockroaches differently, now that you have read the article?"

Extend activities, as explained by Calfee, Chambliss, and Beretz (1991), "are productive activities by individuals and groups to promote acquisition and transfer of lesson concepts and procedures" (p. 84). Reflection and extension are linked. Extension provides an opportunity for transfer—to apply the present structure to a new situation. Extension provides an opportunity for meaningful practice. After diagramming a descriptive web article on the beaver, students could work in pairs, or individually, to diagram a descriptive web on a different animal. Or students could find out more information on the beaver by searching the Internet or going to the library. Or after reading an article on castles and learning about their construction, purpose, security, rooms, etc., students could develop a matrix by comparing the castle to an office building or a hotel, or to something similar in the animal world, such as a beehive or a termite tower.

———————○———————

Although there is a plethora of terms in the literature to describe different types of expository texts, we suggested using a few key terms. We believe that research on text structure supports the teaching about the design of texts to help students gain better comprehension of nonfiction material. We recommend that comprehension lessons be kept simple. Our lesson plans follow the CORE model, which combines students' background knowledge with ideas for capturing the nonfiction material in a suitable text structure. The lesson plans focus not only on capturing the key information in nonfiction text but offer ideas for going beyond the text and applying what has been learned to new topics of study.

CHAPTER 3

Teaching Descriptive Structures: Web

The descriptive web structure is a very common structure that resembles a spider web (Calfee & Patrick, 1995). It has a center and a number of threads that form a network of lines. A key thing to remember about a web is that it has just one topic. This is the center of the web. The threads link to subtopics that help explain the main topic. Each subtopic has supporting details and these give strength to the web.

For example, a student would use a web diagram to analyze an article about one main topic, such as fish (see diagram at right).

The value of the web structure is that it simplifies the material that is being described without dumbing it down. It does not contain all the details of the article but it highlights the key details associated with each subtopic. The human mind is designed to handle just four or five chunks of information at a time and the web is an ideal way to set out the main chunks in a descriptive text.

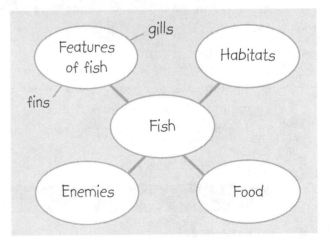

An Example of How the Web Structure is Commonly Used in Classrooms

John, a sixth-grade student, begins his school day with science. Today the class reads and discusses an article on primates. After science John attends his language arts, mathematics, and other classes. John's music class, which has been studying Mozart has been given an article to read that describes Mozart's childhood, adult life, and his symphonies. During social studies, as part of a unit on World War II, students read and discuss an article on the Holocaust. John's school day concludes with health. The focus of the lesson is junk food and the article he has been asked to read is titled, "Junk Food Battles." As diverse as these articles are, they have one important thing in common: text structure. All of them are descriptive and follow the web pattern.

The question is whether John recognized the descriptive structure of the articles, and that they followed the web pattern. Did he know to look for subtopics, and that there would be information, within the article, on each supporting topic?

If John does struggle to comprehend these texts, he is far from alone, but the good news is that John and students like him can learn comprehension strategies (Pressley, 2002; Sweet & Snow, 2003). Comprehension strategy instruction has a positive effect on comprehension (Pearson & Duke, 2002). How teachers go about teaching comprehension strategies is also important. This chapter will help you teach students how to identify, diagram, and comprehend descriptive web text structures. It is important to break down the text for students (diagram the text) and to work with them over an extended period of time, withdrawing support as students become increasingly skilled at applying the strategy.

Web Articles

This chapter includes five articles that follow a web structure, and companion lessons. Each lesson follows the CORE model of teaching. At the end of each chapter you will find the articles and diagram templates to photocopy and distribute to students to use in small groups or in a whole class setting. The table below provides an overview of the articles included in this chapter, giving you a quick guide to the content and grade level of the articles.

When selecting additional articles to teach web text structure awareness it is best to begin with an easier text. When students have an understanding of the strategy then it is appropriate to move to more challenging texts. When introducing the web text structure to students in grades 4, 5, or 6, we recommend beginning with "Lake Living."

Summary of Web Articles

Title	Topic	Content Area	Grade Level
Lake Living	Beavers	Science—Mammals	4
Stair Masters	Competition climbing stairs in very tall buildings	Social Studies—Sports	4
Fueling the Future	Finding alternative sources for fuel	Science—Environment	4
Alutiiq Nation	Native Alaskans	Social Studies	5
Hatred's Horrors	The Holocaust	Social Studies—Holocaust Survivors	5/6

How to Teach the Web Structure

The lessons in this chapter follow the CORE (Connect, Organize, Reflect, Extend) model outlined in Chapter 2:

Connect is the link between what the reader knows and what is being learned. As readers progress through school, they constantly face written information that is new. It is up to the teacher to assist students in making the link between the known and the unknown. This is achieved through questioning strategies that encourage thinking.

Organize includes both the principle of KISS (keeping the lessons simple) and a method of diagramming the text structure.

Reflect is an opportunity to look back and review content, structures, and strategies.

Extend is an opportunity to apply the lesson content to a new topic, or to expand on the existing topic. It is also an opportunity for meaningful practice.

Build Knowledge Prior knowledge is an important factor in text comprehension. The pre- and during-reading discussion provides an opportunity to help students connect to the text. Remember to encourage them to think about a question while reading the article. Discuss the web text structure.

Model How to Diagram the Text Structure Diagramming the web structure enables students to see how the text is constructed and helps them visualize the text to remember it better. The completed web can also be used to guide discussion.

Research suggests that the text structure strategies need to be explicitly taught and modeled long-term at all grade levels (Block & Pressley, 2002; Calfee & Patrick, 1995; Gaskins, 2003; Pressley, 2006b; RAND, 2002; Sweet & Snow, 2003). If your students have not done text structure work before, you will need to prepare them for this way of thinking. This is where modeling comes in. Your students will need to see how the web structure works and practice diagramming the web (and later, the other structures) so that they will become confident before tackling the articles. First explicitly teach and model the text structure. Then use the following steps for each lesson. (Note: Because this may be your students' first experience analyzing text structure, we have included a simple introductory activity to get the lesson going. You may want to create your own examples when introducing the subsequent structures.)

Using Each Lesson

Step 1 Introduce the article to students. Hand out copies of the article to everyone in the class.

Step 2 Make a copy of the lesson plan (and article) for yourself and use this to introduce the article to the class.

Step 3 Complete the "Connect" part of the lesson.

Step 4 Make copies of the web structure template and break the class into small groups. Give one copy to each group.

Step 5 Give each group 10–15 minutes to complete the web.

Step 6 Call the class together to "Organize" as a group. Make a big copy to use for this activity by putting the structure template onto a transparency or whiteboard.

Step 7 Ask each group to report back on one subtopic until you can complete the web on the transparency or whiteboard.

Step 8 Follow the lesson plan for "Review."

Step 9 Follow the lesson plan for "Extend."

Lessons

Lake Living

Rationale Introduce this lesson by explaining that students will read an article that has a special structure called a web—like a spider web. There's a topic in the middle and different subtopics that connect to the hub of the web. In "Lake Living," the main topic is the beaver. Subtopics include the beaver's dam and lodge, and its physical characteristics, general characteristics, and diet. Let students know that before they read the article, you will start with an easy example of how a web structure works.

Summary After reading this article the reader will have an understanding of the phrase, "as busy as a beaver." The beaver spends its time either creating a dam for his lodge (home) or maintaining it. The busy beaver has four front teeth. These teeth, which never stop growing, are used to gnaw away at trees and branches. Beavers move trees and branches to the site where they build the dam and the lodge.

CORE Teaching Ideas

Connecting to the Structure (Introduction)

TEACHER:	Pets. What comes to your mind when I say the word *pets*?
STUDENTS:	Dogs. Cats. Fish. Rabbits. Hamsters. I have a snake for a pet. Pets are a lot of fun. Our dog likes to chase sticks. My dog licks my hand. Our dog loves to swim. My cat likes to sit on my lap.
TEACHER:	What do pet owners need to do for their pets?
STUDENTS:	Feed it. I fed our rabbit carrots. We feed our fish flaky fish food—but not every day otherwise they will die. We feed our dog every morning and then a little at night. I have to walk our dog every day after school but I always keep her on the lead. I clean our fish bowl every couple weeks, or when Mom tells me to!
TEACHER:	Great! How would you describe your pet to someone who has never seen a dog, or cat, or rabbit, or fish?
STUDENTS:	My pet has a tail and paws. Mine has wings and a beak. Cats have fur and dogs have hair.
TEACHER:	What sorts of things does your pet like to do?
STUDENTS:	Run. Eat. Sleep. Chase sticks.
TEACHER:	Pets are a lot of fun. I have recorded your ideas on the whiteboard. [Note: The information can be recorded and then reorganized into subtopics. In this case, you can organize the information into subtopics as students share their ideas. The subtopics do not have a heading as in the following diagram.]

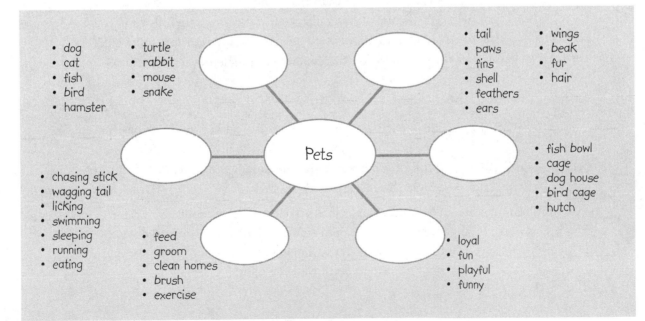

Discuss possible subtopics, such as types of pets, pet homes, and owner responsibility. Add the subtopics to the diagram (see below). Then explain that the diagram is a web structure that describes pets. It is called a web because it is shaped like a spider web. This diagram describes one thing—pets, and it has six subtopics.

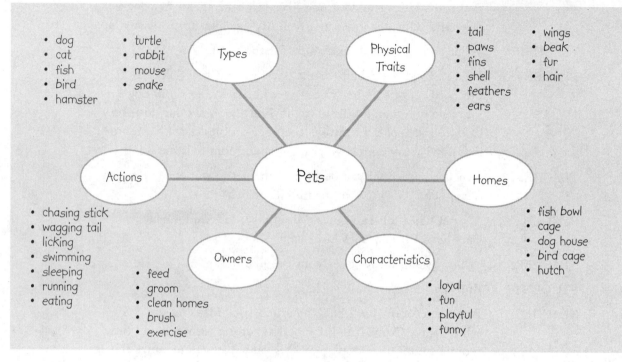

TEACHER: Today we will be reading an article that follows a web structure. There is a main topic, and there are subtopics. This is one of several structures that writers follow. If you are able to identify the structure the writer has followed, it will help you understand the article.

Connect to the Content (Before reading)

TEACHER: This article is about the beaver. The article describes the beaver's lodge (home), both inside and outside. Can you think of other subtopics the author might include in an article that describes the beaver?

STUDENTS: What the beaver looks like. What the beaver eats. The beaver builds a dam so the author might describe what the dam looks like. The beaver works hard so the writer may describe how it builds a dam.

TEACHER: Well done. These are very good answers. Let's read and find
             out. As you read, remember to think about the subtopics.
             [Note: Comprehension is enhanced if students have
             a purpose for reading.]

Organize (After reading) Put the word "beaver" in the middle of the whiteboard, on
a large sheet of paper, or an overhead transparency. Ask students for the subtopics, which
include the lodge (inside), lodge (outside), dam, diet, physical characteristics, and interesting
facts. Place the subtopics around the word "beaver," the main topic.

Return to each subtopic one by one. The first sentence under the heading "The Dam"
describes the beaver's teeth so the first subtopic to focus on is "physical characteristics." The
Fact File also includes several of the beaver's physical characteristics and some interesting
facts, the second subtopic. The third subtopic to work on is the beaver's "dam."

Reflect Reflect on the lesson. What type of text did we read today? What are the characteristics of this type of text? Review the characteristics of beavers. Explain to students that
having a good understanding of how writers go about structuring a text helps you understand and remember it better.

Extend Students may want to find out more about beavers. If necessary, provide guiding
questions, such as "Which states do beavers live in?" "Are they endangered?" Students can
use the Internet, encyclopedia, and other reference books from the library. As they add new
information to the web, students should use a different colored pen or whiteboard marker to
highlight what is *not* in the article.

Students may notice that "Lake Living" also contains the linear string sequence structure, which follows a first-to-last pattern (see Chapter 6). This article explains the sequence
a beaver follows to build a dam. Ask students to reread the first page of the article. When
building a dam, what is the first thing the beaver does? *(gnaws tree until it falls over)* What
happens next? *(drags trees to nearest stream)* Then what?

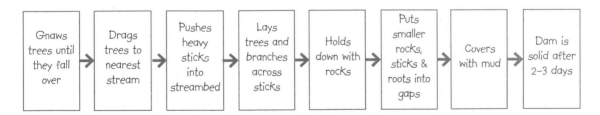

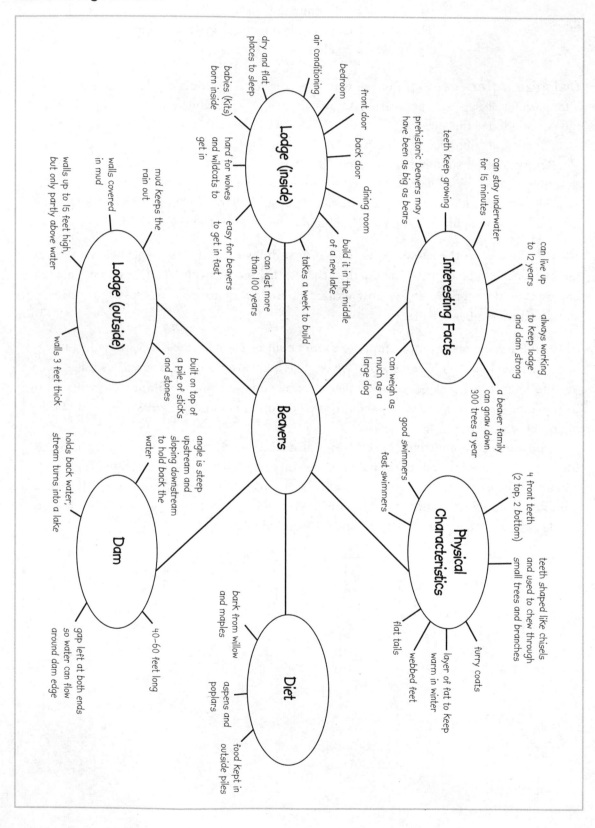

Lodge (inside)
- dry and flat places to sleep
- air conditioning
- bedroom
- front door
- back door
- dining room
- babies (kits) born inside
- hard for wolves and wildcats to get in
- easy for beavers to get in fast
- build it in the middle of a new lake
- takes a week to build
- can last more than 100 years

Lodge (outside)
- walls covered in mud
- mud keeps the rain out
- walls up to 15 feet high, but only partly above water
- walls 3 feet thick
- built on top of a pile of sticks and stones

Interesting Facts
- can stay underwater for 15 minutes
- teeth keep growing
- prehistoric beavers may have been as big as bears
- can live up to 12 years
- always working to keep lodge and dam strong
- a beaver family can gnaw down 300 trees a year
- can weigh as much as a large dog

Beavers

Dam
- holds back water; stream turns into a lake
- angle is steep upstream and sloping downstream to hold back the water
- 40–60 feet long
- gap left at both ends so water can flow around dam edge

Physical Characteristics
- good swimmers
- fast swimmers
- 4 front teeth (2 top, 2 bottom)
- teeth shaped like chisels and used to chew through small trees and branches
- layer of fat to keep warm in winter
- furry coats
- webbed feet
- flat tails

Diet
- bark from willow and maples
- aspens and poplars
- food kept in outside piles

Stair Masters

Rationale This is a descriptive text about one thing. The subheadings of the article clearly indicate the web pattern used in writing the article: features of stair racing, history of stair racing, people that race, stair races around the world, the Empire State Building stair race. An important strategy to explain to students is to look at the subheadings of the article. These provide key clues as to the categories of the web.

Summary Most people would not dream of taking the stairs to get to the top of the Empire State Building. However, many do it for the challenge. "Stair Masters" are people who race up the stairs of tall buildings. This article focuses on the Empire State Building run-up where men and women compete to race to the 86th floor by way of the stairs. The races are staggered, so that men and women run separately. The first race was in 1978. People of all ages run the race. Other stair races happen around the world wherever there are tall buildings. There have been races in the United States, New Zealand, Australia, Malaysia, and Canada.

CORE Teaching Ideas

Connect to the Content (Introduction)

TEACHER:	This article is called "Stair Masters." Why is that?
STUDENTS:	Is it because the article is about people who are good at walking up stairs?
TEACHER:	Yes, you are very close. It is about people who run up the stairs of tall buildings.
STUDENTS:	Why would they do that?
TEACHER:	Well, some people like to run up stairs. It's good exercise.
STUDENT 1:	We live in an apartment building on the 3rd floor and we have stairs.
STUDENT 2:	We have stairs in our house. I always forget something and have to walk back up the stairs. I hate it. Why would anyone want to run up the stairs of a tall building?
TEACHER:	Well, why do people like to climb mountains? They just want to get to the top. Some people run up mountains to do it as quickly as they can. That's what a race is all about. It is to see how fast you can run.

Connect to the Structure (Before reading)

TEACHER:	Before we read the article, think about the structure. What kind of structure do you think the text will be?
STUDENTS:	We're not too sure.

TEACHER:	Well, remember what we learned about the web structure. A web is about one thing. This article is about one thing, "stair masters." When you look at the subheadings and the illustrations, what particular topic is the article about?
STUDENTS:	Well, it seems to be mainly about the Empire State Building run-up.
TEACHER:	Why would they choose the Empire State Building?
STUDENT 1:	Because it's one of the tallest buildings in the world.
STUDENT 2:	Yes, but it also mentions stair races in other places like Canada and Australia. So isn't the article comparing different races around the world?
TEACHER:	Well, if you look just at that part of the article, the chart with the heading "Stair Races Around the World," then it does seem to be comparing more than one thing, but is this what the whole article is about?
STUDENTS:	Not really. It's mostly about the race that happens in the Empire State Building.
TEACHER:	Exactly. This is the main clue to the structure. Ask yourself, what is the article mostly about? Read the subheadings of the article and you get good clues about categories for the web. What do you get?
STUDENTS:	Empire State Building run-up, History of the race, People who run the race, Races in other places, Facts about the Empire State Building, Fastest times.
TEACHER:	That's great. I am writing your categories on the board as you speak. This looks like a great example of web structure. Now read the article and find supporting details to go with each category. Let's focus on the first category: the race. What does the article say?
STUDENTS:	It says men and women race separately. They run up 1,576 stairs from the lobby to the eighty-sixth floor. And the winners get a trophy.
TEACHER:	That's great. I am writing these points down. Now we will tackle the next category, the history of the race.
STUDENT 1:	The first race was in 1978. Fifteen people were in it.
STUDENT 2:	In 2001 there were 154 runners in the race, from 15 different countries. So the race got a lot more popular.
TEACHER:	Absolutely. People love to compete.

STUDENT 3: The table "Recordholders" mentions five races since 1978. The best women's time is Belinda Soszyn of Australia. She did it in 12 minutes. The record for men is 9 minutes.

TEACHER: Great. Now let's look at the people who have run the race. What details are there?

STUDENTS: The first winner was Gary Murke. He just wanted to see the view from the top. The oldest competitor was Chico Scimone from Italy. He ran the race when he was 89. It says it was his eleventh time in the race! Philip Florie was 60 years old when he ran the race. It was his first time at stair racing. He was a security guard in the Empire State Building. Paul Crake from Australia set the men's record in 2001. He had a lot of experience. He had competed in mountain races around the world. He trains by running up stairs and cycling.

TEACHER: Phew—that's a lot of information. How can we shorten it a bit?

STUDENTS: Just write down a few points like "all ages," "different countries," "the view at the top," and "set records."

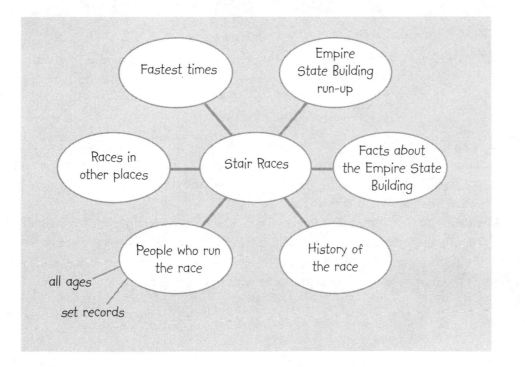

TEACHER: Excellent, now let's do the other headings.

Organize (After reading)

TEACHER: I have listed the subtopics you have suggested on the board, and the details. Let's review them.
- Empire State Building run-up
- Facts about the Empire State Building
- History of the race
- People who run the race
- Races in other places
- Fastest times

Reflect

TEACHER: This is an interesting article about people who compete to run up the stairs of tall buildings. What sort of structure does it have?

STUDENTS: A web structure.

TEACHER: Can you remember the main categories without looking back?

STUDENTS: The race up the Empire State Building, the history of the race, the competitors, the fastest times, other countries that hold similar races.

TEACHER: That's great. How is the the web structure useful?

STUDENTS: You can summarize the article in just one diagram. It gives you a structure for your writing. And it's easy to remember.

TEACHER: Excellent.

Extend Students can find out more about stair racing on the Internet. One piece of information that comes up in an Internet search for "Empire State Building Run-up" is that the 30th race occurred in February 2007. You'll also find that participation in the race is by invitation only from the New York Runners Club.

Ask students to find out more things. What is the current record time? Who holds the record? When is the next Empire State Building race? What other races are going on around the world? Are there any disadvantages to stair racing? What if you are claustrophobic? Ask students to report back at the next lesson with any new information they find.

Stair Masters Answers

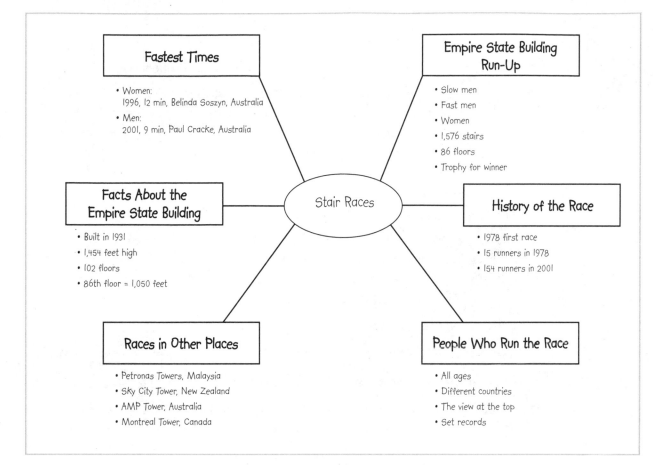

Fastest Times

- Women:
  1996, 12 min, Belinda Soszyn, Australia
- Men:
  2001, 9 min, Paul Cracke, Australia

Empire State Building Run-Up

- Slow men
- Fast men
- Women
- 1,576 stairs
- 86 floors
- Trophy for winner

Facts About the Empire State Building

- Built in 1931
- 1,454 feet high
- 102 floors
- 86th floor = 1,050 feet

Stair Races

History of the Race

- 1978 first race
- 15 runners in 1978
- 154 runners in 2001

Races in Other Places

- Petronas Towers, Malaysia
- Sky City Tower, New Zealand
- AMP Tower, Australia
- Montreal Tower, Canada

People Who Run the Race

- All ages
- Different countries
- The view at the top
- Set records

Fueling the Future

Rationale This article is about one topic—how to create new energy for the future—which makes it a web structure. The article has four subtopics: old energy sources, new energy sources, advantages of new forms of energy, and concerns about old forms of energy. These are the main categories needed for the web.

Summary "Fueling the Future" discusses why we need to find alternative energy sources to oil, coal, and natural gas. The article explains that 60 percent of the Earth's natural resources, including oil, coal, and natural gas, have been destroyed. These resources generate electricity and provide fuel for transportation, but they also pollute. The challenge is to find alternative sources of energy before the natural resources have been used up. The article discusses alternative sources such as wind, sun, ethanol, bio-diesel, and even turkey bones!

CORE Teaching Ideas

Connect to the Content (Introduction)

TEACHER: How did you get to school today?

STUDENTS: I rode the bus. Mom drove me. I walked to school.

TEACHER: Yes, many children walk to school but there are a lot of children who ride the bus or drive a car to school or work. Most buses and cars use a valuable natural resource—gas or diesel—which is produced from oil. Oil is running out but it also harms the environment. What do you think we should do about this?

STUDENTS: Everyone should walk to work or school. We could all ride bikes. But what if it is raining or snowing? I think scientists should develop new ways of powering cars and buses.

TEACHER: Yes—and scientists are working on this. What could be used for alternative fuel?

STUDENTS: The sun? Wind?

TEACHER: You're right, we do use the sun and wind to generate electricity.

Connect to the Structure (Before and during reading)

TEACHER: Today we are reading a descriptive article titled, "Fueling the Future." This article discusses alternative sources of fuel. As you read the article, underline the different sources of fuel that are discussed.

Organize (After reading)

TEACHER: What new transportation fuels were discussed?

STUDENTS: Corn was used to make fuel for cars. Turkey bones were used. Fuel was also made from vegetable oil.

TEACHER: What have we been using to power cars?

STUDENTS: Gas. Diesel.

TEACHER: What are the disadvantages of gas and diesel?

STUDENTS: Well, we are running out of gas. One day it will be all gone. Oil is a natural resource. You can't make it. And gas pollutes.

TEACHER: Let's organize this information. What structure does this article follow?

STUDENT: It's a web structure.

TEACHER: Can you explain why?

STUDENT: The article focuses on one thing—finding sources of fuel for the future. And the information can be grouped into subtopics. One subtopic is the new sources—like corn.

Draw a web structure on the whiteboard. Put Fueling the Future in the middle of the web. Explain that the information in the article can be grouped into categories. Ask students to give you some possible categories, such as Fuel sources that we use today, New or alternative energy/fuel sources, Advantages of the new fuels, Concerns about existing fuels. Place the subtopics in the web, as shown below.

Return to each topic and discuss the relevant information for each subtopic. Add the information to the web.

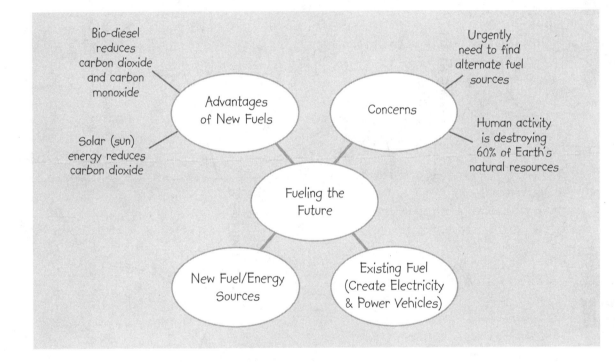

Reflect After diagramming the article suggest that students think again about its structure. Why is it a web? *[It is about one topic.]* Remind students why it is important to not only identify the structure the writer has used but also to actually diagram the structure. Explain to students that good readers are able to identify the structure the writer has followed and that they use this knowledge to help them comprehend. Diagramming the structure enables the reader to "see" the structure. Could the web be improved by grouping the new fuel sources in a different way (e.g., natural sources—sun and wind; recycling of people-made products—garbage, turkey parts, etc.)?

Extend Suggest to students that they research some of the alternative fuel sources mentioned in the article. For example, can they find information on both the advantages and disadvantages of using wind power?

Fueling the Future Answers

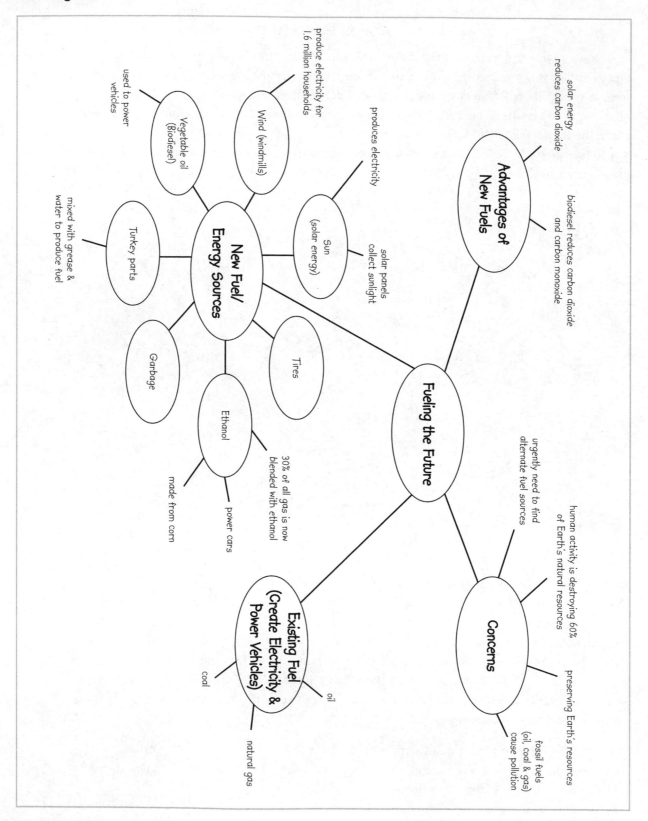

Advantages of New Fuels
- solar energy reduces carbon dioxide
- biodiesel reduces carbon dioxide and carbon monoxide

Fueling the Future

New Fuel/Energy Sources
- Wind (windmills)
  - produce electricity for 1.6 million households
- Sun (solar energy)
  - produces electricity
  - solar panels collect sunlight
- Vegetable oil (Biodiesel)
  - used to power vehicles
- Turkey parts
  - mixed with grease & water to produce fuel
- Garbage
- Tires
- Ethanol
  - 30% of all gas is now blended with ethanol
  - power cars
  - made from corn

Concerns
- urgently need to find alternate fuel sources
- human activity is destroying 60% of Earth's natural resources
- preserving Earth's resources
- fossil fuels (oil, coal & gas) cause pollution

Existing Fuel (Create Electricity & Power Vehicles)
- oil
- coal
- natural gas

Alutiiq Nation

Rationale This article takes the form of an interview with Dr. Sven Haakanson who is an Alutiiq and works as an ethnographer at the Alutiiq museum. The article is partly about his work at the museum but it is mostly about the Alutiiq people themselves. In this sense it fits into a web structure where the main topic is the Alutiiq Nation. A guide to the structure of the web is to look at the subheadings of the article, which suggest several categories that relate to the Alutiiq people, such as location, how they used to live, the effects of colonization, and the efforts being made to preserve the language and culture.

Summary "Alutiiq Nation" is a descriptive article about an indigenous people from Alaska. Like many indigenous peoples, the Alutiiq people experienced a dramatic change in their way of life when their land was colonized. The article describes the old way of life and the efforts now being made to preserve the culture and continue the language.

CORE Teaching Ideas

Connecting to the Structure (Introduction)

TEACHER:	This nonfiction article follows a web structure. Will someone explain what a web structure is?
STUDENTS:	It's a structure for presenting information about one topic. The topic of this article is the Alutiiq.
TEACHER:	How does a web structure work?
STUDENTS:	If the topic was Mexican people then the article would cover things like location, geography, population, history, language, way of life, and products that come from Mexico.
TEACHER:	That's it. That's how a web structure works. In the center is the main topic and around the center, connected to it, are subcategories that each give details about some relevant aspect of the topic. So what information is likely to be in this article about the Alutiiq?
STUDENTS:	We haven't read it yet so how can we know?
TEACHER:	You could skim the first few lines and maybe look at some of the subheadings.
STUDENTS:	Well, the Alutiiqs are from Alaska. They are trying to make sure their language survives.
TEACHER:	Yes, exactly. Dr. Haakanson helps to promote and preserve the language and the culture. They have a museum that focuses on educating people about the Alutiiq culture.

Connect to the Structure and the Content (Before reading)

TEACHER: Now as you read the article, try to put the information into categories that are easy to remember. What is the first paragraph about?

STUDENTS: It's about the museum, what it does, where it's located.

TEACHER: Right, now look at the other subheadings in the article. What do you think they are going to talk about?

STUDENTS: The headings are not that clear but the main subtopics will probably be Homeland, History, Traditional way of life, Effects of colonization, Attempts to preserve the culture and language.

TEACHER: That's excellent. I'll put these categories on the board. As you read, try to keep in mind that you will be taking details from the article and placing them into the different subtopics.

Organize (After reading)

TEACHER: Let's recap. What kind of structure is it?

STUDENTS: A web structure.

TEACHER: Is this the correct structure for this article?

STUDENTS: Yes—because it is about one topic, the Alutiiq Nation.

TEACHER: You added some new categories into the web. What were they?

STUDENTS: Interesting things that needed their own category.

TEACHER: Such as?

STUDENTS: We added "ceremonies" because they had mask dancing and story telling, and "work" because they had different jobs for women and men.

TEACHER: That's excellent.

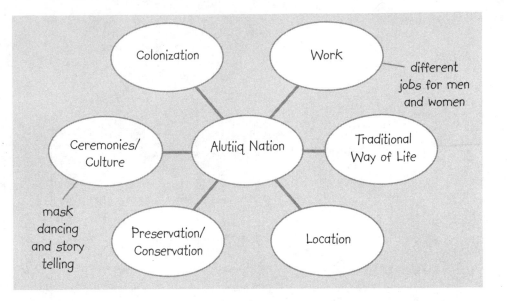

Reflect After finishing the diagram of the web structure, ask students to reflect on the web. What were the main subtopics? Ask students to picture the web in their minds. Can they remember the main categories without looking back to the web?

Ask students to consider what might have happened if the Russians or Americans had not colonized the land of the Alutiiqs. Would history be different? Would it be a good thing for the Alutiiq people to still have their old way of life? Why? *(Students might consider that it would have been better if the Alutiiq people had been given a choice about whether to change their way of life. They might have become a fishing nation that could sell its produce and still retain the old ways in today's world.)*

Invite students to retell the article, using the subheadings as an organizing structure. Remind students of the purpose of the web: to organize the information in the article into five or six chunks so it is easier to remember.

Extend The web structure lesson enabled students to summarize a lot of information in an organized way, but as an extension, students might seek more information about the people who live in Alaska. Where did people like the Alutiiqs come from? Why did they decide to live in such a cold place? What is their life like in the 21st century? Or, students could extend their knowledge of indigenous people by studying other people around the world who have had their lands colonized.

Alutiiq Nation Answers

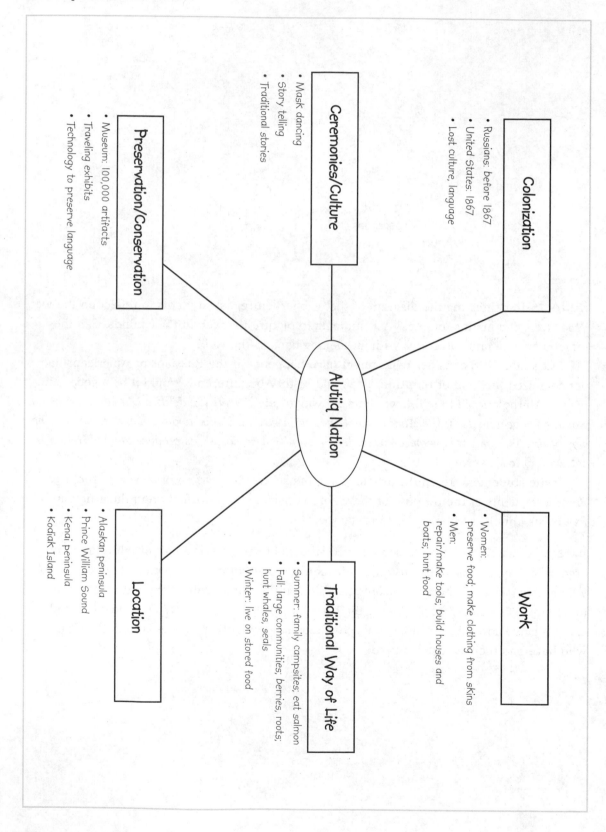

Colonization
- Russians: before 1867
- United States: 1867
- Lost culture, language

Ceremonies/Culture
- Mask dancing
- Story telling
- Traditional stories

Preservation/Conservation
- Museum: 100,000 artifacts
- Traveling exhibits
- Technology to preserve language

Alutiiq Nation

Work
- Women: preserve food; make clothing from skins
- Men: repair/make tools; build houses and boats; hunt food

Traditional Way of Life
- Summer: family campsites; eat salmon
- Fall: large communities; berries, roots; hunt whales, seals
- Winter: live on stored food

Location
- Alaskan peninsula
- Prince William Sound
- Kenai peninsula
- Kodiak Island

Hatred's Horrors

Rationale This article has a web structure because it is about only one thing: the Holocaust. The article might initially confuse students because the title mentions "stories" told by three survivors. You'll need to explain to students that the article gives information, it does not tell a story.

Summary This article describes the Holocaust in Europe during World War II. The word *Holocaust* is from the Greek *holos* meaning "whole" and *caust* meaning "burn." The general meaning of the word is slaughter or destruction on a mass scale. The specific meaning of "the Holocaust" refers to 1939–1945, when there was systematic imprisonment and killing of millions of Jews and others by the Nazis. This took place in Germany and in other countries that the Nazis had conquered and occupied during that period of time.

CORE Teaching Ideas

Connecting to the Structure and Content (Introduction)

TEACHER: Let's review what a web structure is. Who can tell us?

STUDENTS: A web is about just one thing. The design of the web is like a spider web. Each part of the web has a main category. Each category is a main idea with details listed under it.

TEACHER: That's great—an excellent definition. The article today is called "Hatred's Horrors." It is about the Holocaust—a time of mass killing and destruction of Jews. This happened during World War II. What do you think this article will say?

STUDENTS: We went to a museum once and saw an exhibition about the Holocaust. During the second world war the Jews were rounded up by the Nazis and sent to concentration camps where many of them were killed.

TEACHER: Yes—that's exactly what happened. It happened a long time ago but sometimes the term *Holocaust* is used to refer to the mass killing of one particular people by another group of people.

Organize (Before and during reading)

TEACHER: As we read about the Holocaust, think about how you can put the information into categories. One clue is to look at the main headings. What are they?

STUDENTS: Nazi Occupation, Life in Auschwitz, and Life After the Holocaust.

TEACHER: Yes—these are possible categories. As we read, try to think of other possible categories like the reasons for the Holocaust, the features of the Holocaust, and the locations in which Jews were killed.

Organize (After reading)

TEACHER: Now we are going to diagram the article. What did we agree was the structure?

STUDENTS: It's a web structure. It's about one thing, the Holocaust.

TEACHER: Yes, let's put this as the title in the middle of the web. I've listed the main headings from the article on the board. Can you suggest some other categories?

STUDENTS: Causes; Features of the Concentration Camps; Locations of the Camps; Treatment of Jews; Effects; Survivors.

TEACHER: That's a great start. Let's add these categories to the structure. Then we can put relevant details with each category.

Reflect After completing the web structure with the class, ask students to reflect on the structure. Remind students that the article, "Hatred's Horrors" is about one thing, the Holocaust during 1939–1945. Point out the value of the web diagram. It breaks the article up into just a few main categories to make it easier to remember what the article is about. Ask students to close their eyes and picture the web. Ask them if they can see in their minds each category. What are the categories? Ask students to recall the details under each category.

As a comprehension activity, ask students to answer the following questions:

- What were the causes of the Holocaust? *(hatred, bigotry)*

- What were the features of the concentration camps? *(Jews were killed or forced into hard labor, had to wear a uniform, starved from not enough food, had shaved heads, and had tattooed numbers on their arms.)*

- What happened to survivors after the war? *(Some emigrated to new countries like the United States, got jobs, and raised families.)*

- How were Jews treated? *(They were put into ghettoes, had few rights, they wore special badges, and they could not shop for food.)*

- Where were concentrations camps located? *(in Germany and in other countries that the German Nazis conquered)*

- What were the effects of the Holocaust? *(Millions of Jews were killed, and two out of three in Europe.)*

Extend After completing the article, students might want to research the Holocaust in more detail. They can read about this topic in encyclopedias and on the Internet. Suggest that they look up the United States Holocaust museum Web site, www.ushmm.org. This Web site compares the term "holocaust" to the term "genocide," which has a similar meaning but came to be used after World War II. (Note: Please keep in mind that Internet locations and content can change over time. Always check Web sites in advance to make certain the intended information is still available.)

When adding new information gathered by students to the web, make sure to use a different color so that it is clear to everyone that the information is not from the original article.

Hatred's Horrors Answers

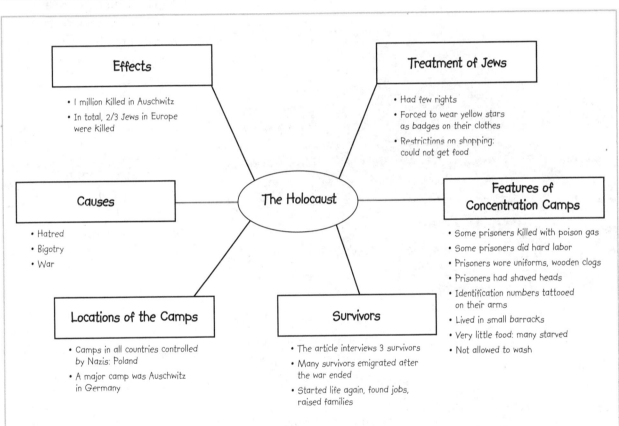

Lake Living
by David Hill

Would you like to own a house?
Would you like to own a house with a swimming pool?
Would you like to own a house *in* a swimming pool?

You could if you were a beaver! Beavers are good swimmers. To keep themselves safe from wolves and wildcats, they build a home, called a lodge, in the middle of a lake. But first, they have to make the lake!

The Dam

A beaver's four front teeth (two at the top and two at the bottom) are shaped like **chisels**, and they keep growing all the time. They use their teeth to chew through small trees and branches. They gnaw away at a tree until it falls over, then they drag it to the nearest stream. Sometimes, they can even dig a canal to a tree so that they can float the log to a stream.

Now the family of beavers starts building a dam across the stream. They push heavy sticks into the streambed with their front paws. They lay trees and long branches across these sticks and hold them down with rocks.

Next, they push smaller rocks, sticks, and roots into the gaps and cover them with mud. After two or three days, the dam is quite solid. The dam has a steep upstream side

Fact File

- A grown-up beaver can weigh as much as a large dog. **Prehistoric** beavers may have been as big as bears!

- Beavers live for up to 12 years.

- They have furry coats and a layer of fat to keep them warm in the water. Their webbed feet and flat tails make them fast swimmers. They can stay underwater for up to 15 minutes.

- A beaver can chew through a tree 16 inches wide in one night. A family of beavers may **gnaw** three hundred trees in a year.

- A beaver dam is often 40 to 60 feet long. Some are as long as a football field.

- One beaver lodge that was found in North America may have been a beaver home for a thousand years!

Teaching Text Structures © 2007 by Dymock & Nicholson. Scholastic. 58

and a sloping downstream side so that it's strong enough to hold back the water.

The beavers leave a gap at each end so that sudden floods can flow around the edge of the dam.

The dam has turned part of the stream into a lake. Now the beaver family can build their lodge.

The Lodge

The lodge will have a front door, a back door, a dining room, a bedroom—and air conditioning! Most lodges are built in the middle of a new lake so that enemies can't easily reach them. It takes a family of beavers about a week to build a lodge.

First, the beavers make a big pile of branches and rocks. This pile may be 15 feet high,

the top of the pile rises above the surface of the lake, and its walls are often three feet thick. Then the beavers cover these outside walls with mud. The mud dries hard and stops rain from getting in.

Two underwater tunnels lead into the lodge. The beavers can easily enter or escape this way, but the tunnels are built so that their enemies can't get in. Narrow gaps in the roof let fresh air into the lodge.

Inside, above the water, there are dry, flat places where the beavers eat and sleep. Baby beavers (called kits) are born here.

Beavers don't just build houses with trees. They eat trees too. Mostly, they eat small aspens and poplars, but they also like the bark from willow and maple trees. They keep this food in piles that float outside the lodge. At dinnertime, the beavers swim out through one of the tunnels, chew off a branch or

some bark, and take it back inside the lodge to eat.

After they've made their lake and their home, the beavers work to keep the dam and the lodge strong. Some lodges last for over a hundred years. Slowly, dirt, leaves, and twigs sink to the bottom of the lake, and it becomes shallow. After many years, it isn't a lake anymore—it's a swamp. After many more years, the swamp turns into a flat green field. By then, the beavers will have moved away to find a new stream and new trees. Then another dam and lodge will appear. No wonder people sometimes say that a hard-working person is "as busy as a beaver."

word wise

- **prehistoric:** belonging to a time very long ago

- **gnaw:** to keep chewing or biting on something

- **chisel:** a tool with a short, sharp end

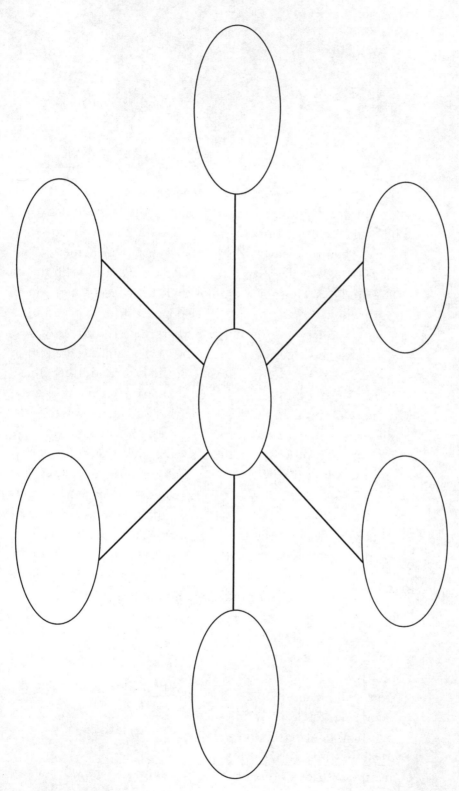

Stair Masters

by Patrick Morgan

The Empire State Building in New York is one of the tallest buildings in the world. How long does it take to run all the way up? Every year, more than one hundred people find out when they take part in the Empire State Building Run-Up.

The Challenge

To race up the stairs of the Empire State Building.

Teaching Text Structures © 2007 by Dymock & Nicholson, Scholastic, 61

The Race

The competitors race in three groups: the fast men, the slow men, and the women. Each group runs separately, and the person with the fastest time in each group wins. The runners race up 1,576 stairs from the lobby to the eighty-sixth floor.

The fastest man and the fastest woman each win a trophy.

The History of the Race

The first Empire State Building Run-Up took place in 1978. Fred Lebow, who lived in a **walk-up**, figured that if he walked up the stairs every day, why not run a race up them all? His idea caught on, and now there are stair races all over the world.

Fifteen runners competed in the first race up the Empire State Building. In 2001, 154 runners from 15 countries took part in the race.

Recordholders

Year	Runner	Time	Note
1978	Gary Muhrcke, USA	12 minutes, 33 seconds	First men's champion
1978	Marcy Schwamm, USA	16 minutes, 4 seconds	First women's champion
1996	Belinda Soszyn, Australia	12 minutes, 19 seconds	Women's recordholder
2001	Paul Crake, Australia	9 minutes, 37 seconds	Men's recordholder
2001	Chico Scimone, Italy	35 minutes, 5 seconds	Oldest runner (89 years old)

word wise

- **walk-up:** an apartment building without an elevator

- **flight:** a series of steps between one floor of a building and the next

Who Races up the Empire State Building?

Gary Muhrcke, who won the first race in 1978, couldn't wait to see the view from the top. It was his first visit to the Empire State Building.

"Everyone knows the Empire State Building, but not everyone has the chance to say they've run up eighty-six **flights**. That's nearly my age!" said Chico Scimone from Italy.

At 89 years old, he was the oldest competitor in the 2001 race, and he completed the run-up in 35 minutes, 5 seconds. It was his eleventh time in the race.

"I was worried I wouldn't finish, but I did it," said Philip Florie. "It was a challenge. I'm over 60 years old, and I wanted to prove I could do it." This was Philip's first attempt at racing up the stairs (he usually takes the elevator), and he finished in 21 minutes, 54 seconds.

He didn't have to travel far for the race—he works as a security guard in the building.

Paul Crake from Australia set a new record in 2001. His goal was to finish in less than 10 minutes, and he ran in 9 minutes, 37 seconds. "At the start, there was a lot of pushing and shoving, but then I settled in," Paul said. He climbed two stairs at a time. Paul has competed in stair races and mountain races in the United States, Europe, Asia and Australia. He trains by running up stairs and hills and does a lot of cycling.

Fact File

- Building the Empire State Building was a challenge. It was the tallest building in the world when it was finished in 1931. It was built in just one year and 4 days.

- Total height to the top of the radio mast: 1,454 feet

- Height of the building: 1,250 feet (102 Floors)

- Height of the 86th floor (observation deck): 1,050 feet

- Number of elevators: 73.

Race	Building height	Number of stairs
Empire State Building, New York	1,454 feet	1,576
Petronas Towers, Kuala Lumpur, Malaysia	1,483 feet	2,058
Sky City Tower, Auckland, New Zealand	1,076 feet	1,081
AMP Tower, Sydney, Australia	1,001 feet	1,550
Montreal Tower, Montreal, Canada	544 feet	850

Stair Masters

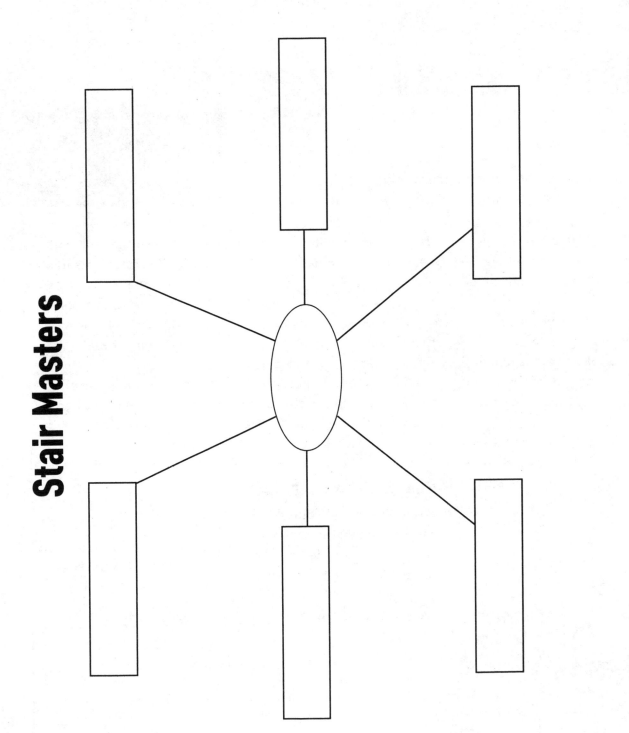

Teaching Text Structures © 2007 by Dymock & Nicholson, Scholastic. 63

Fueling the Future

by Paul Coco

People across the country are working to find newer and cleaner fuels and energy

WORKING WIND A wind farm in Southern California helps to create electricity.

Earth Day is April 22—a great time to think about how we can protect our planet in the future. Experts say finding new ways to bring fuel and power to people around the world is one of the most important steps toward preserving Earth's resources for years to come.

For example, can you imagine riding in a school bus that runs on fuel used for cooking? Or what about living in a home that is heated by turkey parts?

Finding new energy sources is more important than ever. According to a recent report, human activity is destroying about 60 percent of Earth's natural resources.

In an effort to protect those resources, some scientists are using sun and wind for energy. Others are using organic materials, such as corn and even animal parts to make cleaner fuels.

Fuel for Transportation

Fossil fuels—oil, natural gas, and coal—are used to create power for electricity or refined into gasoline to power cars, trucks, and buses. Fossil fuels can cause harmful pollution.

Recently, a group of college students from Vermont wanted to promote cleaner forms of fuel. They traveled across the U.S. in a bus fueled by biodiesel, a fuel made from vegetable oil. On the trip, the students filled the tank with cooking oil used at restaurants.

"Biodiesel greatly reduces carbon dioxide and carbon monoxide," says Stephen Swank, 22, one of the students.

Many people believe carbon dioxide and carbon monoxide cause global warming.

Another alternative fuel made from corn, called ethanol, is being used by people across the U.S. to fill up their cars. Ethanol is made by breaking down the sugar found in corn. Ethanol can be

word wise

- **organic:** (or-GAN-ik) adjective. To do with or coming from living things.

- **fossil fuel:** (FOSS-uhl FYOO-uhl) noun. Coal, oil, or natural gas, formed from the remains of prehistoric plants and animals.

Teaching Text Structures © 2007 by Dymock & Nicholson, Scholastic, 64

blended with gasoline to create a cleaner type of fuel. About 30 percent of all gas used in the U.S. last year was blended with ethanol.

The search for new kinds of fuel has led to even stranger ideas. One company is developing a process to make **organic** fuel from animal parts!

ORGANIC FUELS Corn can be turned into liquid fuel. Fuel can also be made from turkey parts.

Changing World Technologies (CWT) mixes turkey parts with grease and water. The mixture is heated to about 1,000 degrees and put under great pressure, which breaks down the turkey parts. CWT also uses tires and garbage to make cleaner fuel.

"If we take plastic, tires, and [turkey] bones and turn that into fuels, much less fossil fuel will need to be dug up out of the ground," says Brian Appel, who heads CWT.

Help From the Sun and the Wind

Some houses across the U.S. are powered by solar energy, or energy from the sun. Solar panels placed on the roofs of these homes collect sunlight and turn it into electricity, without waste or pollution. This electricity is used to heat and light homes, even when it is dark outside.

Some lawmakers in Los Angeles, California, want solar panels installed on about 30,000 rooftops by 2017. That much solar power would help reduce the amount of carbon dioxide in the air.

Like the sun, wind is another source of energy. Wind turbines, or windmills, are being used to turn wind power into electricity in more than 30 states. In states such as Minnesota, Iowa, California, and Texas, large numbers of windmills are built close together to form wind farms. As of this year, windmills created enough electricity to power about 1.6 million U.S. households.

"We need to think about using cleaner types of energy," Swank says. "Working on the problem now will reduce the harm people cause the earth."

Recycling Waste
Animal droppings are used to make paper

What do you get when you boil elephant poop, cut it, and press it flat? If you guessed sheets of paper, you are correct.

Companies in Asia, Africa, and Australia are recycling animal waste to make paper products. The Thai Elephant Conservation Center in Lampang, Thailand, is one place selling the poopy paper. The average elephant drops more than 100 pounds of poop each day, which can be made into about 115 sheets of paper.

To make the paper, workers wash and boil the poop for five hours. It is then dried, cut, and pressed into different types of paper. Best of all, no trees need to be cut down to make the paper.

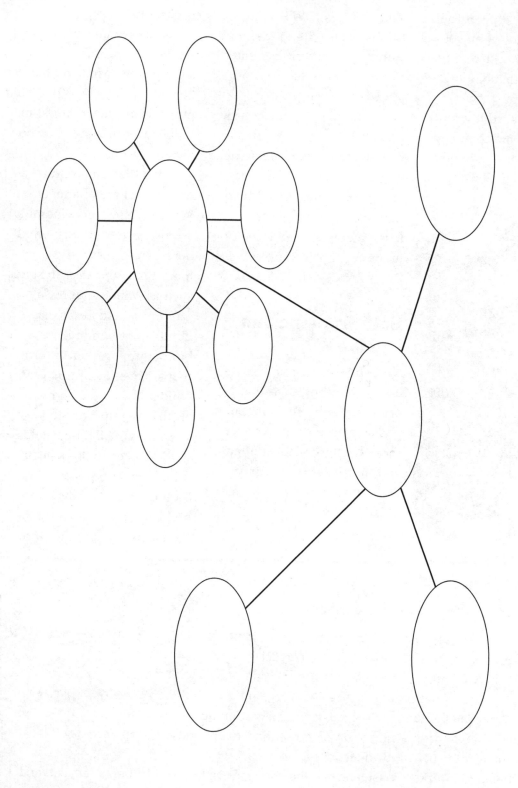

Alutiiq Nation

Interview by Sarah Wilson

Dr. Sven Haakanson, Jr., is an Alutiiq who grew up in Old Harbor, an Alutiiq village on Kodiak Island, Alaska. He works as an ethnographer at the Alutiiq Museum on Kodiak Island, preserving and promoting the Alutiiq culture. In this interview, Sven discusses his work.

What does your job involve?
I teach people about the Alutiiq culture through the Alutiiq Museum and its different programs. To promote the museum and raise funds, I also spend a lot of time traveling in Alaska, the rest of the United States, and even Europe.

Each day is a new challenge. I care for the museum, but I also ensure that the Alutiiq community is happy with the way their culture is represented. We always try to reflect what our people want to say.

What is the Alutiiqs' traditional way of life?
The people had a great deal of respect for the environment and always took care of it.

In the summer, they lived in family campsites where they'd catch, dry, and store salmon for the winter when food is scarce. In the fall, they moved to large communities and collected berries and roots and hunted whales, seals, and sea lions. This food was also stored for the winter.

Different family groups from the same area would live together during the winter, and the community would have feasting ceremonies where they enjoyed mask dancing and storytelling.

Through all these seasons, however, the people mostly worked. Women preserved food and made clothing by preparing and sewing animal skins. Men repaired and made new tools and built houses and boats. The rest of the time, the men hunted or gathered food.

All this hard work meant that life was never easy. It was also difficult because the people never knew if they would have enough to eat. Those living on Kodiak Island were lucky because the ocean was teeming with fish and marine mammals. They were able to preserve food for the long winter months as long as the weather allowed them to kayak.

What happened when the Alutiiq were colonized?
The Alutiiq culture changed a great deal after the Russians arrived—and even more after Alaska was sold to the United States in 1867. People were

The Alutiiq People

The Alutiiq People are native to south central Alaska, where they have lived for more that seven thousand years. Traditionally, the Alutiiq lived off the resources that the ocean and land provided. However, in the eighteenth century, Russian explorers and the Americans colonized the area and the Alutiiq people were forced to adopt two new cultures.

This brought about changes in their traditional way of life, including their culture, language, and religion. More than ninety percent of the population died in this period. They were forced to work when they needed to be hunting and storing food for the winter. As a result of the new diseases that the Russians came with, such as smallpox, and a lack of food, the Alutiiq people were nearly exterminated.

not allowed to make their own decisions, and control of their lives was taken away from them. This meant that the Alutiiq people began to lose their culture, including their language. The past two centuries have been extremely difficult for the Alutiiq people.

How do you work to preserve the Alutiiq culture and identity?

Aside from the educational programs and displays developed by the museum, we have a traveling exhibit program that explains traditional Alutiiq culture and craft. We also exhibit materials that reflect our contemporary heritage. It's very important to make the public aware of the Alutiiq culture—and of the importance of maintaining all traditional cultures.

We've also started a program to revive the Alutiiq language. Most of my people now speak English, and saving our language is one of the museum's most important aims. We use the most up-to-date technology to preserve the language. At the museum, the Alutiiq language is kept in written, audio, and digital formats. We also house over 100,000 artifacts, which span more than 7,500 years. These convey our rich heritage in the island. We are preserving this information for future generations.

How did you get into your line of work?

I was amazed by the stories the elders told—and by the fact that they could speak several languages. The elders taught me about who I was and how important it is for anyone to understand who they are. From there, I studied archeology. I hoped this would help me learn about Alutiiq history and share it with my people.

My culture is very important to me. It links me to my heritage that is more than 7,000 years old. To know about this heritage and to be able to speak our language brings a lot of dignity into my heart.

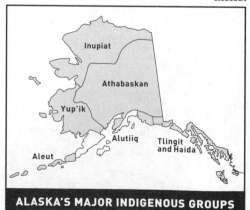

Inupiat

Athabaskan

Yup'ik

Aleut

Alutiiq

Tlingit and Haida

ALASKA'S MAJOR INDIGENOUS GROUPS

Alutiiq Nation

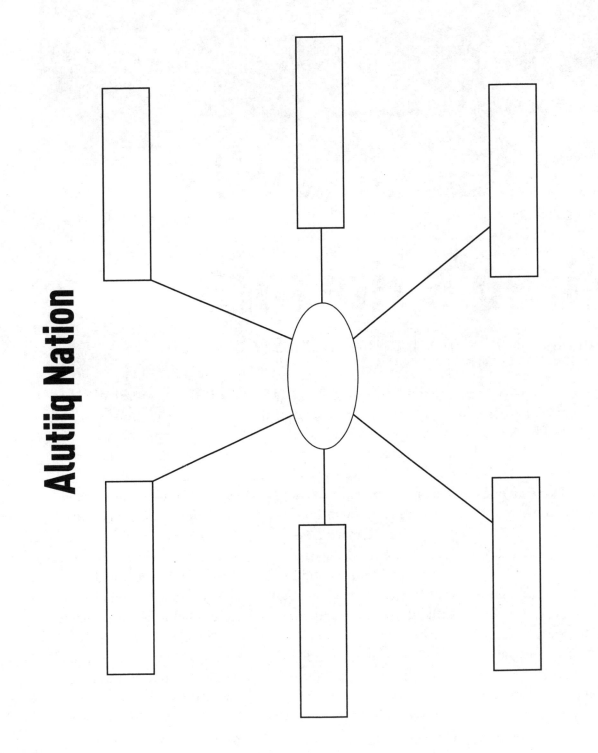

Jewish families in Poland's Warsaw Ghetto surrender to Nazi soldiers after a months-long uprising.

Hatred's Horrors

Three Holocaust Survivors Tell Their Stories

Bronia Brandman has happy memories of her early childhood in Jaworzno, Poland.

She was one of six children in a close Orthodox Jewish family. Bronia was especially close to her older sister, Mila. She followed her around like a puppy.

Her family's apartment, located in the heart of town, had a big backyard where kids would play soccer and jump rope.

"For children, it was paradise," Bronia says. "That backyard was buzzing with life."

What Bronia didn't know was that the life was about to go out of her neighborhood. Her happy, playful childhood was about to turn into a nightmare.

In 1939, Germany invaded Poland, launching World War II. Jews were the primary targets of Germany's Nazi soldiers. Adolf Hitler, the leader of Germany and its ruling Nazi Party, wanted to kill all Jews in his attempt to conquer the world.

The Nazis sent millions of Jews to concentration camps. There, Jews were killed, abused, starved, and forced to do hard labor. The systematic, government-sponsored murder of Jews and others by the Nazis during World War II is called the Holocaust.

Bronia spent a year and a half in Auschwitz, the largest of the Nazi concentration camps. This year marks the sixtieth anniversary of Auschwitz's liberation. Bronia and two other survivors of Auschwitz, Regina and Sam Spiegel, spoke to Scholastic News about their experiences.

Their memories are still painful, but they want young people to know the kind of terror that can be started by hatred and **bigotry**. They want kids to never forget what happened to them and their families.

Nazi Occupation

In Nazi-occupied towns and cities, Jews had few rights. The Nazis made them wear yellow stars or similar badges to identify them as Jewish. Their shopping was strictly limited. Jews began to starve as food became scarce.

At the age of 9, Bronia became a smuggler. She covered her yellow star so that she could walk in her neighborhood freely. She traded goods for food. If she had been caught, she would have been killed.

"Each time I went out, I was sure I would not return home," Bronia said.

In other towns and cities, the Nazis forced Jews to move into **ghettos**. When she was 14, Regina and her family were forced into a ghetto in her hometown of Radom, Poland. Regina says she is sometimes asked why they didn't try to run away.

"There was nowhere to hide," Regina answers. "And we figured if we just followed orders, we could have a chance to survive. We also thought there would be interference from the outside world. Of course, there was none."

The Nazis regularly rounded up Jews in the occupied towns and sent them to concentration camps. Both Bronia and Regina lost family members during these raids. Regina's husband, Sam, who lived in Kozienice, Poland, lost his entire family— four siblings, parents, and grandparents—all at once. "I lost them all on the same day," Sam says.

CONCENTRATION CAMPS By 1943, there were Nazi camps throughout Europe. Some were detainment camps, others were for forced-labor. Some were for extermination. Auschwitz was used for all three purposes.

word wise

- **bigotry:** (BIG-uh-tree) noun. A strong and unreasonable dislike for a certain other group of people, especially people of another race, nationality, or religion.

- **ghetto:** (GET-oh) noun. A part of a city in which Jews were made to live.

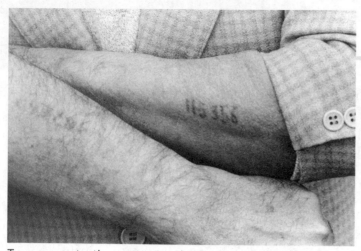

Two concentration camp survivors show their tattoos.

Life in Auschwitz

Bronia, Regina, and Sam were all eventually sent to Auschwitz, where they faced more horrors.

At the camp, Jews were separated into two lines. People in one line were sent straight into chambers where they were killed with poison gas. The others were kept alive and forced to do hard labor. They were given uniforms and a pair of wooden clogs. Their heads were shaved. Numbers were tattooed on their arms. They lived in small barracks with hundreds of other Jews. They were not allowed to bathe.

"They fed us bread made out of saw-dust and watery soup with things swimming in it," Bronia says. "The pain of hunger, you really couldn't describe it."

Many people starved to death. Others became very ill.

Bronia arrived at Auschwitz with her three sisters, including her beloved Mila. All except Bronia died in the gas chambers. Regina was eventually transferred to another camp. Sam was taken to one of Auschwitz's several subcamps.

They are three of the few who survived Auschwitz. In all, approximately 1 million Jews were killed there. Many of them were children.

All the Nazi concentration camps were liberated by May 1945, when the United States and its allies defeated Germany. By then, the Nazis had killed about two thirds of the Jews in Europe and millions of other people.

Life After the Holocaust

Regina and Sam married just after the war, settled in the U.S., and had a family. Today, they volunteer at the United States Holocaust Memorial Museum in Washington, D.C. Regina, now 78, is often asked if she ever wants revenge.

Regina says no. "My grandchildren are the revenge to Hitler," she says. "He wanted to annihilate [the Jews], but we are still alive."

"I just hope that people learn to stop hating," Regina adds.

Bronia came to the U.S. in 1946 with her brother Mendek, her only surviving family member. She became a teacher, married, and raised a family. Now 74, Bronia gives tours at the Museum of Jewish Heritage in New York City.

Bronia wants kids to see that the children of the Holocaust are not just people from a faraway time and place. They were kids who played soccer, jumped rope, and loved their families.

"Hopefully, they see that I am not different than them," Bronia says. "I want them to know—my sister Mila was just like you. She had the same dreams and the same needs. She was just like you."

Back to You

Hatred has caused suffering throughout human history. What can people do to stop hatred before it starts?

Hatred's Horrors

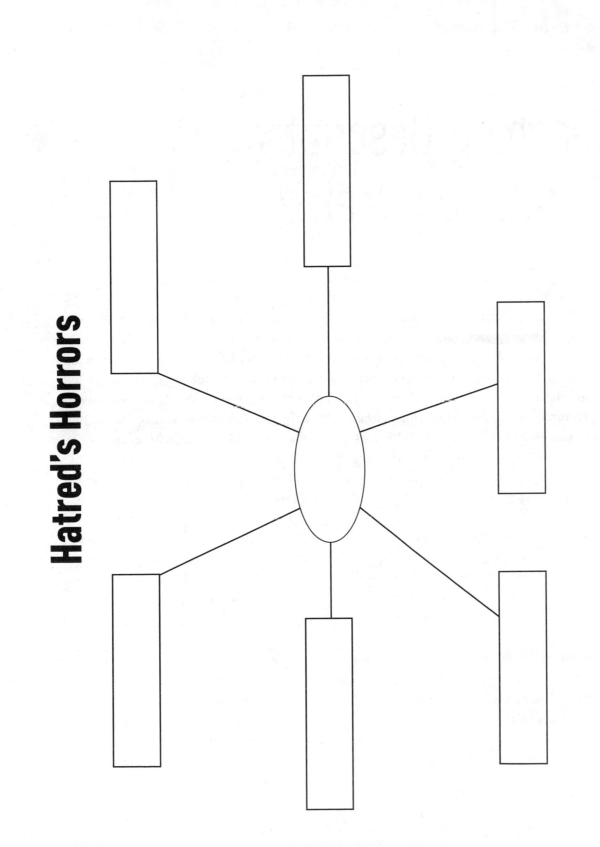

CHAPTER 4

Teaching Descriptive Structures: Matrix

Like the web structure, the matrix is descriptive, but goes a step further than the web by comparing and contrasting objects, animals, people, or places. So, for example, rather than simply describing the attributes of the polar bear the matrix text structure compares and contrasts two or more aspects. Calfee and Patrick (1995) also refer to the matrix as a weave. They explain, "Weaves are matrices, the crosshatch of cells providing opportunities for comparisons and contrasts" (1995, p. 68). The following diagram illustrates the "crosshatch of cells" Calfee and Patrick refer to, and provides a powerful image of a matrix, or compare-contrast, text structure.

The matrix diagram below is one a student might use to analyze an article comparing and contrasting information about bears. There are three subjects—polar, brown, and black bears. The matrix structure compares the characteristics of polar, brown, and black bears.

Bears	Habitat	Diet	Height	Weight	Color	Enemies
Polar						
Brown						
Black						

Other topics, such as U.S. cities, flying insects, birds, or rivers, have many subjects that can be compared and contrasted, but most matrix articles at Grades 4–6 compare and contrast three or four topics.

Calfee and Patrick (1995) explain that webs and matrix structures are particularly powerful. We agree. The web structure connects a central topic and the matrix, an extension of the web structure, enables the reader to compare and contrast topics. Lessons that teach students how to organize the content of their social studies and science material in webs and matrices bring a sense of coherence to the task when it may be incomprehensible otherwise.

An Example of How the Matrix Structure is Commonly Used in Classrooms

Sarah, a Grade 5 student, begins the first day of the week with physical education and health. She spends one class each week learning about health-related issues and three classes developing skills in ball handling, swimming, gymnastics, etc. Included in the current three-week study on food groups and diet is a section on food handling and the safe storage of food. The teacher has given Sarah's class the article "The Food Detectives" to read. It is about how foreign objects can mistakenly end up in food. After health and physical education Sarah has science. The class is commencing a study on flightless birds. Sarah's class is given the article "Birds That Cannot Fly" to read. After lunch Sarah is looking forward to her social studies class. They have been studying South America, and Sarah's family is planning a trip to Argentina, Chile, and Brazil during the next school holiday. Her older brother lived in Brazil as an exchange student the year before. The social studies lesson includes an article on Brazilian cities. Sarah's music class is studying string instruments, and in mathematics the class is studying the characteristics of polygons. What the material in the health and physical education, science, social studies, music, and mathematics classes have in common is the text structure. All followed the matrix structure. The articles compared and contrasted objects. While the content in each class was different the text structure was the same.

The question is whether Sarah recognized the descriptive structure and the matrix pattern, and that the articles focused on the similarities and differences between two or more things.

If Sarah had trouble with comprehension, she has a lot of company. The matrix text structure is more challenging than the web structure. This chapter shows how to go about teaching students to identify, diagram, and comprehend matrix structures. Because the matrix structure is an extension of the web, students should have a good understanding of how to identify and diagram web structures before learning about the matrix structure.

Matrix Articles

This chapter includes five articles that follow a matrix structure, and companion lessons. Each lesson follows the CORE model of teaching. At the end of the chapter you will find the articles and diagram templates to photocopy and distribute to students to use in small groups or in a whole-class setting. The table on the next page provides an overview of the articles included in this chapter, giving you a quick guide to the content and grade level of the articles.

When selecting additional articles to teach matrix text structure awareness it is best to begin with an easier text. Initially, the main purpose of the lesson is to teach the strategy. It is easier to learn a new strategy with simpler text. As students gain an understanding of the strategy then it is appropriate to move to more challenging texts. When introducing the matrix text structure to students in grades 4, 5, or 6, we recommend beginning with "Animal Homes."

Summary of Matrix Articles

Title	Topic	Content Area	Grade Level
Animal Homes	Homes of birds, termites, wasps, and trapdoor spider	Science	4
Survival Tactics	Different ways animals survive	Science	5
Amazing Animals	The snake caterpillar, see-through frog, and tarantula	Science	5
Animal Messages	Silent and loud messages of animals	Science	6
Swimming: Then and Now	Swimming in the 1950s and swimming today	Social Studies—Sports	6

How to Teach the Matrix Structure

The lessons in this chapter follow the CORE (Connect, Organize, Reflect, Extend) model outlined in Chapter 2:

Connect is the link between what the reader knows, and what is being learned. As readers progress through school they constantly encounter new written information. It is up to the teacher to assist students in making the link between the known and the unknown.

Organize includes both the principle of KISS (e.g., keeping the lessons simple) and a method of diagramming the text structure.

Reflect is an opportunity to look back and review content, structures, and strategies.

Extend is an opportunity to apply the lesson content to a new topic, or to expand on the existing topic. It is an opportunity for meaningful practice.

Build Knowledge Prior knowledge is an important factor in text comprehension. The pre-, during-, and after-reading discussions provide teachers with an excellent opportunity to build "prior" knowledge. Some argue (Hirsch, 2006) that teachers' lack of attention to building knowledge during the school day is one of the major reasons that students are not performing as well as they should. According to Hirsch (2006, p. 8), "I believe the neglect of knowledge is a major source of inequity, at the heart of the achievement gap between America's poor and non-poor. I also believe that if this idea about what is limiting students' comprehension isn't understood and aggressively addressed, reading scores won't move up, no matter how hard teachers try." We believe teachers must take every opportunity to build knowledge. Asking questions, answering questions, and discussing the content of the articles are all excellent ways to build knowledge.

Model How to Diagram the Text Structure

Diagramming the article using a matrix enables students to see how the text is constructed. The diagram assists students in visualizing the text and it helps them remember it better. The completed matrix becomes an excellent focus for guiding discussion.

Using Each Lesson Be sure that students have an understanding of how to go about comparing and contrasting information using a diagramming matrix. Before breaking students into groups, or requiring students to work independently, you may need to explicitly teach students or review with them how to diagram the text, and you should continue to model the strategy throughout the year (Block & Pressley, 2002; Gaskins, 2003; RAND, 2002; Sweet & Snow, 2003). In phase two, students practice the strategy with guidance, using many texts, until they have a good understanding of it (Block & Pressley, 2002). The steps below relate to the second phase.

Step 1	Introduce the article to students. Hand out copies of the article to everyone in the class.
Step 2	Make a copy of the lesson plan (and article) for yourself and use it to introduce the article to the class.
Step 3	Complete the "Connect" part of the lesson.
Step 4	Make copies of the matrix structure template and break the class into small groups. Give one copy to each group.
Step 5	Give each group 10–15 minutes to complete the matrix.
Step 6	Call the class together to "organize" as a group. Make a big copy for this activity by putting the structure template onto a transparency or the board.

Venn Diagrams

Venn structures, like matrix text structures, also compare and contrast topics. A matrix mainly shows the differences between things. The Venn diagram is used to show similarities and differences between two or more things. The two or more overlapping circles of the Venn diagram enables the reader to readily "see" the comparisons and contrasts. The similarities are found in the overlapping area of the diagram and the differences are located in the parts of the diagram that do not overlap. As with the matrix, the completed Venn diagram is an excellent focus for guiding discussion. The advantage of a Venn diagram is that you only need one diagram rather than two to sum up the information in an article. Students often prefer this overview because it does contain key information in one place.

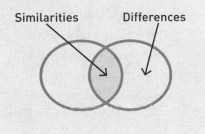

Similarities   Differences

Step 7   Ask each group to report back on one subtopic until you complete the matrix on the transparency or board.

Step 8   Follow the lesson plan for "Review."

Step 9   Follow the lesson plan for "Extend."

Lessons

Animal Homes

Rationale The article compares homes built by birds, termites, wasps, and the trapdoor spider. Each of these very different homes is built to suit the environment that the animal lives in. The text uses a matrix design because it compares each animal according to similar categories: the type of home, and each home's purpose, location, and features. Clues to the matrix design are provided by the four subheadings: bird's nest, termite tower, wasp's nest, and trapdoor spider burrow. This matrix compares four different animal homes in terms of the homes' purpose (hatch young, protection from heat and enemies), location (trees, ground), and building materials (rooms, walls, building materials, tunnels).

Animal	Home	Purpose	Location	Building materials	Shape

Summary The article's main point is set out in the title and in the first sentence, that many animals build amazing homes that are very different from each other. Birds usually build their nests in trees, using grass, leaves, and sticks. This suits their purpose, which is to give birds protection from enemies while they raise their young. The Kenyan termite builds a tower of mud and wood on the ground, providing protection against heat and predators. Wasps build nests from paper. They chew dry wood into a pulp that hardens into paper, enabling the queen wasp to build many paper cells to lay her eggs. The final home discussed in the article is the burrow of the trapdoor spider, which the spider builds by digging a hole in the ground using its front legs and mouth to dig. This home suits the trapdoor spider, which does not have a web to catch food and must hide and catch food by surprise.

There is an opportunity in this article for the teacher to discuss explicit and implicit information in texts. The article does not explicitly state the purpose of the wasp nest and the trapdoor spider burrow. This information has to be inferred from other text information and from prior knowledge.

CORE Teaching Ideas

Connect to the Content (Before reading)

TEACHER: Today we are reading a descriptive article titled, "Animal Homes." Do you think animal homes are like human homes?

STUDENTS: Yes, because everyone needs a place to protect them from the weather and to feel safe.

TEACHER: Yes, these are the main reasons for animal homes. Another reason is that they use their homes to have babies and raise their young in a place that is safe from enemies.

STUDENTS: So do most humans. They find a home so they can have children and raise them safely.

TEACHER: Where do animals build their homes?

STUDENTS: Birds build nests in trees. Beavers build homes of wood in streams.

TEACHER: Skim through the article and look at the subheadings for clues about the structure of the text. What kind of structure do you think fits this article?

STUDENTS: It can't be a web because a web is just about one thing and this article is about four things. So it must be a matrix.

TEACHER: Exactly, it's almost certainly a matrix structure since it compares more than one thing. What I'd like you to do is read the article and then we will organize the information into a matrix. As you read, think about the different animals in the article.

Organize (After reading)

Draw an empty 5 x 5 matrix structure on the whiteboard. In the first column, write Animal.

TEACHER: I've labeled one of the columns Animal. Which animals were in the article?

STUDENTS: Bird, termite, wasp, and trapdoor spider.

TEACHER: Excellent. I'll write in one animal name for each row. Now, what categories does the author use to compare the four animals? Look at the first paragraph about birds. Can you think of categories?

STUDENTS: Well, one category is the type of home. Many birds build nests. Another category is the purpose of the nest.

TEACHER: Well done. Good thinking. Can you see another possible category?

STUDENTS: Many birds make nests out of grass, leaves, and sticks. This category would be the building materials that animals use to build their homes.

TEACHER: Excellent. Now let's fill in the details about each home, using these four categories.

Reflect After finishing the matrix ask students to reflect on the structure. What were the clues in the text that indicated a matrix structure? *(there were four animals being compared)* What made you think of the categories? *(there were similar things mentioned, such as type of home, purpose of home, and so on)* What can be done about other information in the text that does not fit the matrix, such as the fact that millions of termites live in their tower, and that it can take 50 years to build. Where do you put this information? *(add another column to the matrix called "other things," where you can add extra bits of information about each animal)*

Extend

TEACHER: What could you do to follow up on this article?

STUDENTS: Well, many animals do not have homes. We could find out the reasons for that.

TEACHER: That's a good follow up to the article. I'm not sure of the answer myself. Birds need a nest because they need to lay eggs. So do termites, wasps, and spiders. That might be one reason. Perhaps you can find out more information about why it is that some animals have homes and others do not, and why this is so. I'd like you to do some reading of books on the topic and also check the Internet.

Animal Homes Answers

Animal	Home	Purpose	Location	Building materials	Shape
Bird	Nest	Hatch young, feed family, protect against enemies	Trees	Made of grass, leaves, and sticks	Round
Termite	Tower	Protection from desert heat and from enemies, can house millions of termites	On ground, in Kenya, Africa	Mud and wood	Like a tower
Wasp	Nest	(implicit) Protection from enemies, paper cells are used to lay eggs, paper gives protection from weather	Tree branch or tree trunk or in the ground	Dry wood pulp that is made into paper	Like a barrel, hanging from a tree branch or buried in the ground
Trapdoor Spider	Burrow	(implicit) Protection from enemies, can catch food by surprise	Under ground	Tunnels dug in the ground	Has secret passages lined with silk. There is an escape passage and hidden trapdoors

Survival Tactics

Rationale Since "Survival Tactics" compares and contrasts the survival tactics used by three animals it has a matrix structure. The article's subheadings provide clues for the students. One clue relates to a survival tactic used by each of the three animals. Another clue hints that the article focuses on three animals.

Summary The author has separated the article into three subsections. The first section describes the giraffe's physical characteristics, movement, enemies, unique characteristics, diet, habitat and survival tactics. The second section describes the pangolin, and the third describes the chameleon. Each subsection has a heading that highlights one of the survival tactics the animal uses.

CORE Teaching Ideas

Connect to the Structure (Introduction)

TEACHER: Today we are reading a descriptive article that follows a matrix or compare-contrast structure. Can you describe a matrix, or compare-contrast, article?

STUDENTS: A matrix article is descriptive. It gives the attributes of something. It also compares and contrasts different things.

TEACHER: Right. The article we are reading today compares and contrasts three animals. The article is titled "Survival Tactics." What do you think the article might be about?

STUDENTS: How animals survive. Like the foods they eat and how they protect themselves from enemies. If the animal cannot find food it will die. And if they can't fight off enemies they will also die.

TEACHER: That's great. The article does discuss what the animals eat and how they protect themselves from enemies.

Connect to the Structure and Content (Before and after reading)

TEACHER: The article we are reading today focuses on three animals: the giraffe, the pangolin, and the chameleon. Remember, if the article "compares and contrasts," there must be more than one subject.

As you read I want you to think about the physical characteristics of the three animals. What do they look like?

Organize (After reading)

TEACHER: I asked you to think about the physical characteristics of the giraffe, ant-eating pangolin, and the chameleon as you read. I will draw a diagram on the board so we can record the physical characteristics. First let's put the three animals down the left-hand column. The first category is "animal." The next category is "physical characteristics."

Animal	Physical characteristics		
Giraffe			
Pangolin			
Chameleon			

TEACHER: What are the physical characteristics of the giraffe?

STUDENTS: It has a long neck. It has long legs. It can grow 18 feet tall.

TEACHER: Well done. I will write this information in the column. [Repeat for the pangolin and chameleon.]

Animal	Physical characteristics		
Giraffe	Long neck Long legs Grows up to 18 ft tall		
Pangolin	Built like armored tank Body is covered in rows of overlapping scales Soft belly Huge claws Long tail Long sticky tongue		
Chameleon			

TEACHER: Reread the first page. This page describes the giraffe. Can you identify other subtopics, apart from physical characteristics?

STUDENTS: What the giraffe eats? Enemies? Where it lives? How it survives?

TEACHER: Great. I will add the subtopics to our diagram. [Refer to completed diagram, page 85.]

Together complete the diagram. After finishing the diagram of the matrix structure, the animals can be compared and contrasted in a discussion. Prompt students with questions such as those below.

TEACHER: Let's compare the survival tactics of the three animals. Do they have any tactics in common? Tactics unique to each animal? Compare and contrast their habitat?

Reflect After completing the diagram of the matrix structure, and the discussion that compares and contrasts the animals, ask students to reflect on the matrix. What were the subtopics? Ask them to close their eyes and visualize the structure.

Remind students that the matrix structure is for articles that compare and contrast different things. This article compares and contrasts three animals. Remind students that diagramming the article helps the reader to remember the information.

Extend Students could consult Web sites, books, and encyclopedias and add to the matrix. For example, the article does not identify the chameleon's enemies. Students could also research the survival tactics of another animal and add to the matrix.

Survival Tactics Answers

Animal	Physical characteristics	Movement	Enemies	Unique characteristics	Survival tactics	Diet	Habitat
Giraffe	Long neck Long legs Grows up to 18 ft Tongue: extends 18 inches	Can run 35 miles per hour	Lions Leopards	Tallest mammal in world	Height enables it to spot predators and find food Uses sticky tongue and tough upper lip to gather food. Great eyesight—can spot enemies from a distance Long legs: run 35 mph Kicks enemies—sharp hooves and strong front legs Excellent eyesight	Acacia tree's thorny leaves	African grasslands
Pangolin	Built like armored tank Body is covered in rows of overlapping scales Soft belly Huge claws Long tail Long sticky tongue	Slow moving	Humans (for meat and scales) Endangered	Can dig an 8-ft hole in less than 5 minutes	Curls into a ball Swipes attacker with tail Sprays with urine	Ants and termites	Forests Burrows Asia Africa
Chameleon	Tongue catches food (sticky) Tongue catches insects more than 3 feet away	Slow moving		Looks forward and backward at same time Moves eyes independently Tongue—secret weapon!	Eyes move independently Spots enemies without moving head.	Flies and crickets	Africa and Madagascar

Amazing Animals

Rationale This matrix article compares and contrasts three animals. It has clear-cut categories like the habitat of the animals, where to find them, their characteristics, what they eat, and how big they are. This gives five different points of comparison and contrast, which is perfect for a matrix. Students might at first think the article is a sequence because it is in diary form but you can point out that the dates don't really matter that much. What matters is that the article describes three different animals, and that gives it a matrix structure.

Summary These are notes from the diary of a nature photographer Nic Bishop, about interesting animals he has seen around the world. The three animals covered in this lesson are the caterpillar snake, the see-though frog, and the garter snake. These animals have special features. The snake-like caterpillar can make itself look like a viper. The frog is transparent and also has suction caps on its toes so it can hang upside down from leaves. The garter snake can hibernate during winter under freezing snow.

CORE Teaching Ideas

Connect to the Content (Introduction)

TEACHER:	Has anyone ever seen a snake?
STUDENTS:	Yes of course—on television
TEACHER:	Has anyone ever seen a caterpillar?
STUDENTS:	You can see them on cabbages in summer. They eat the leaves. Caterpillars live on other plants too. Caterpillars can turn themselves into butterflies.
TEACHER:	That's right. Have you ever seen a caterpillar snake?
STUDENTS:	That's impossible. A caterpillar can't be a snake.
TEACHER:	Well yes, but what if the caterpillar can make itself look like a snake?
STUDENTS:	That's a hard trick to do. Snakes are long and caterpillars are short.
TEACHER:	Yes, but some snakes are not all that long, and imagine if the caterpillar was quite long, about as long as your hand, could it look like a snake?
STUDENTS:	Well, it would look like a very tiny snake.
TEACHER:	This article is about amazing animals like a caterpillar that can change its looks so that it seems to be a snake. I want you to read it for me and then we will discuss it.

Connect to the Structure (Before reading)

TEACHER: Today we are reading a descriptive article called, "Amazing Animals." The author describes three different but amazing animals. As you read, underline words that you think are important descriptive categories for each animal, such as its location, habitat, special features, diet, and size. After you finish reading we will organize the information into a text structure that suits this article.

Organize (After reading)

TEACHER: What kind of structure do you think fits this article?

STUDENTS: It can't be a web because a web is just about one thing and this article is about three things. So it must be a matrix. The matrix structure compares and contrasts more than one thing.

TEACHER: Exactly, it's a matrix structure since it is about more than one thing.

STUDENTS: Maybe it could be a web? What if you put the three amazing animals into the web like this?

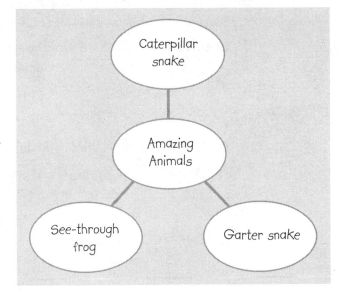

TEACHER: That would be fine, but the similarities and differences between the three animals are not as clear as in a matrix. The matrix can show at a glance how each animal differs in its special features, its diet, and so on.

STUDENTS: How would you draw a matrix then?

TEACHER: Well, we need to have columns for each point of difference among the animals. What points of difference would there be?

STUDENTS: Location, habitat, features, diet, and size.

TEACHER: Exactly. These are great ways to show how the animals are different.

Draw a matrix structure on the whiteboard. Put Amazing Animals in the first column heading. Write up the points of difference mentioned by students (location, etc.).

Reflect

TEACHER: Let's look back at this article. What is it about?

STUDENTS: It compares and contrasts three amazing animals.

TEACHER: Why are they amazing?

STUDENTS: They have special features that are not like most other animals. Caterpillars that can look like snakes, frogs that you can see through and that can hang upside down on special suction cap feet, and snakes that can survive a freezing winter.

TEACHER: Exactly. Is there anything similar about the three animals?

STUDENTS: Yes, they are all found in North and South America.

TEACHER: Why would they have these special features?

STUDENTS: It gives them an advantage over other animals. It helps them to survive better. Except for the frog—we can't figure out why you can see through it.

TEACHER: The author of the article is not sure either. Your question might be a good topic to pursue for homework, to find out why the see-though frog is like that.

Extend

TEACHER: What could you do to follow up on this article?

STUDENTS: We could look at other animals that have special features to protect them. We can look in the library to find more information, and also on the internet.

TEACHER: Excellent idea. Bring your ideas to class tomorrow.

Amazing Animals Answers

Amazing Animals	Location	Habitat	Features	Diet	Size
Caterpillar snake	Central America	Rain forest	Marks on body that look like eyes of a snake	Leaves	4.5 inches
See-through frog	Central and South America	Bushes and trees	Suction pads on toes and thin legs	Moths and flies	0.5 inches
Garter snake	Manitoba, Canada, and parts of the United States	Moist sheltered areas like marshes and streams	Hibernates in winter; slithers around in summer	Earthworms, toads, frogs, small fish	Males are 16 inches long; females are 26 inches long

Animal Messages

Rationale This article informs us about different messages that animals use to communicate. Some messages are loud and some are silent. At first, it looks like the article is a web because it is about one thing, animal messages, but a web would not capture that the article is about different kinds of messages, not just one kind of message. The article can be best summarized by treating it as a matrix structure since it compares a range of different animal messages: those that use sound, and those that are silent.

The article has subheadings that signal different categories for the matrix. The two main categories are sound and silent. In the main category of sound there are different kinds of sound: squeaks, clicks, and songs. In the main category of silent there are different kinds of silent messages: color, light, chemicals, smell, and dance. Thus the matrix has two main columns for comparison. A possible third column would be for the purposes of the messages. The text provides two charts in matrix form that compare different kinds of messages, offering important clues to the structure of this text.

Summary The article focuses on different ways in which animals communicate with other animals. While animals cannot talk, they have developed their own ways to communicate. They can use sound but they can also use non-verbal signals, such as smell, color, or even dance.

The first section of the article describes animals that use sound to communicate. Bats use high squeaks that cause an echo, which helps them to locate food and other objects around them as they fly through the air. Squeaks also help bats locate their offspring when among many other bat families. Dolphins also make squeaking noises that create echoes, which help them just as squeaks help bats. Dolphins also seem to use these sounds to communicate with each other. Birds use songs to keep other birds away, to attract a mate, to signal danger, and to identify their chicks. Young birds learn songs from older birds.

The second section describes animals that use silent signals to communicate. Poisonous snakes, frogs, and spiders use color to scare off enemies. Most lizards are not poisonous but have bright colors to scare their enemies. The octopus changes the color of its skin to scare its enemies. Fireflies and fish that live in dark places use light to attract food and mates, and to scare enemies. Ants use a strong chemical on their body to protect themselves from enemies. Skunks give off a bad smell to discourage their enemies. Worker bees do a waggle dance to tell other bees where to locate nectar.

The main point of the article is that animals have their own ways of sending messages. The messages are used to frighten predators, to attract mates, to tell other animals about food, and to find each other.

CORE Teaching Ideas

Connect to the Content (Introduction and before reading)

TEACHER: Why do we talk to other people?

STUDENTS: To ask them questions, to tell them things, to warn them about things, to make friends with them, to find out whether they are good or bad people, to be polite, to let them know that you are there. There are lots of reasons for talking to people.

TEACHER: What if we were animals? Animals can't talk like us, but do they have their own ways of talking?

STUDENTS: Dogs talk by barking or howling or growling. Cats talk by meowing. Birds seem to talk. They sing songs.

TEACHER: Are there other ways to send a message beside talking or making sounds? What do humans do?

STUDENTS: Well, one way is smell. To attract someone romantically you can smell sweet by using perfume. To make them stay away you can smell awful by eating garlic and raw onions. Another way is color. If my dad's face goes red I know he is angry! Another way is movement. If someone is far away you can use your body to signal to them, like jumping up and down and waving.

TEACHER: Excellent. Humans use sound but sometimes we use silent messages like smell or color. That's what animals do as well. This article describes the different kinds of messages that animals send to other animals to communicate with them. I'd like you to read it and think about what kind of structure it is.

Organize (After reading)

TEACHER: Well, you've read the article. What kind of structure is it?

STUDENTS: It's about several things. It's about different kinds of messages that animals send, and the ways they send those messages, and the purposes of the messages. If you wanted to summarize the article the best way would be to use a matrix.

TEACHER: That's my thinking as well. So what is the main point of difference between the kinds of message?

STUDENTS: The main difference is that some messages make sounds and some are silent.

TEACHER:	Right. We can make that the first column of the matrix. Then what do you put for the different sounds?
STUDENTS:	The sounds can be growling noises like a dog. They can be squeaks like a bat or a dolphin. They can be the songs that birds make.
TEACHER:	Excellent—good work. We'll make that the second column. That makes three different kinds of sounds: growls, squeaks, and songs. What can you remember about the silent messages that animals send?
STUDENTS:	They can be color, light, chemicals, and dancing.
TEACHER:	Nicely done. The article mentions four kinds of silent messages that animals send. So we'll list those under the category of "silent." We'll put these categories onto the whiteboard. Now I want you to work in groups to discuss the purposes of these different kinds of messages. Why do animals send these messages? Take five minutes to figure out the purposes of the messages and we will add that information to the matrix.
TEACHER:	Now, let's complete the matrix so that we have information about the kinds of messages, examples of these messages, the animals that use the messages, and the purposes of the messages. Now, for a final column, let's decide whether or not these animals are dangerous to humans.

Reflect After completing the matrix, suggest to students that they could read more about how animals communicate messages, and what happens when communication fails. For example, they could investigate whether Steve Irwin, the Australian "crocodile hunter" and television personality who died in 2006 from a stingray wound, could have been saved if the stingray had been able to send a message of "danger" to him. Students could investigate animals that have no warning signs to send, and how they manage to avoid their enemies. The stingray hides, the fly relies on speed, and so on.

Extend Students could generate a matrix of human signals that involve sound, like songs, conversation, and screams, and those that are silent, like gesture, smell, dance, and color. Then compare the signals in terms of their purpose.

Animal Messages Answers

Type of message	Example	Animals that send this message	Purposes of the messages	Are the animals dangerous to humans?
Sound	Growl	dogs	To scare enemies	Sometimes
	Squeak	Bats	To warn of danger, to locate babies, to find food	No
	Squeaks and clicks	Dolphins	To warn of danger, to find food, to communicate with other dolphins	No
	Songs	Birds	To warn off others, to find a mate, to locate their chicks	No
Silent	Color	Tree frog, octopus, spider, snake, lizard	Poisonous frogs, spiders and snakes use color to warn enemies. Lizards and the octopus use color to pretend they are dangerous.	Yes
	Light	Fireflies, fish	To attract mates, to attract food, to frighten predators	Sometimes
	Chemicals	Ants	To scare off enemies	No
	Smell	Skunks	To scare enemies	No
	Dance "figure of eight"	Worker bees	To show where nectar is located	No

Swimming: Then and Now

Rationale The article compares and contrasts competitive swimmers several decades ago to competitive swimmers today. Swim suits, training regimes, diet, drugs, and opportunities for competitive swimmers are very different today from what they were when the author, Tessa Duder, swam in the 1950s. With improved swim suits, a greater understanding of the role of diet in competitive swimming, a better understanding of effective training programs, swimmers are producing faster times. "Respectable times" for 14-year-olds today, would have been good times for a top male swimmer in the 1950s.

Summary Tessa Duder was interested to find out why swimming times have improved so much since she was a competitive swimmer in the 1950s. Tessa spoke with a coach in order to find out more about competitive swimmers today.

The article is divided into five sections: Body Gear, Training, Diet and Drugs, Opportunities, and Choices.

In the body gear section the author compares the suits swimmers wore several decades ago to those worn today. She also compares goggles. Swimmers today often shave off all their body hair and wear bathing caps whether they need one or not, practices unknown to swimmers many years ago. Today swimmers wear lycra suits that are so thin they take 10 minutes to put on. The lycra creates less drag, enabling swimmers to record faster times.

The training section also identifies significant differences between training programs today and programs in the 1950s. Today, serious swimmers train all year round, with girls and boys following the same program. Tessa trained from October to March. Coaches did not have videos, of course, so they used photographs or home movie cameras to record swimmers. Today, water or energy-replacement drinks are a staple of training, but not in the 1950s. Pullboys, cut-down flippers, and bungy cords are used today to build up swimmers' arm strength and leg strength. During the 1950s, kickboards were used. Training was lonely during the 1950s. Most swimmers had individual programs that they completed, either in pairs, or on their own. Today swimmers train as a squad.

Pools are also better designed than they were in the 1950s, which also contributes to faster times.

This article compares swimmers' diet, use of medication and other drugs, and opportunities, as well as the many water sports available to athletes today, compared to several decades ago.

CORE Teaching Ideas

Connect to the Content (Introduction)

TEACHER: What sorts of things do you do in your spare time? After school, or during weekends?

STUDENTS: I play on the computer. I watch TV and DVDs. I play football. I play PlayStation 2. I read a lot. I text my friends.

TEACHER: Some of these activities are indoor activities and some are outdoor activities. We could put these activities in a matrix. Who can tell me what a matrix is?

STUDENTS: It's a diagram. A matrix compares and contrasts different things.

TEACHER: Right you are. Let's diagram how you spend your spare time. What other activities do you do inside or outside?

	21st Century	
Inside activities	TV Computer PlayStation 2 Read Text friends	
Outside activities	Football Soccer Swim	

TEACHER: We can extend the matrix. We can compare and contrast activities children do today to what children did 50 years ago. What activities do you think your grandparents did when they were your age? Did they watch TV? Text friends? I will add another column to the matrix and record your responses.

	21st Century	1950s
Inside activities	TV Computer PlayStation 2 Read Text friends	Read Help parents do chores
Outside activities	Football Soccer Swim	Football Swim Ride bikes Build forts/tree houses Help parents do chores

TEACHER: Well done.

Continue to ask questions related to the information in the matrix. For example, What inside activities are the same? Different? What impact do the different types of activities have on children? Do you think children in the 1950s were more active than children are today? Does it matter if today's children are less active?

Connect to the Structure and the Content (Before reading)

TEACHER: Today we will be reading an article that compares and contrasts competitive swimming in the 1950s to swimming today. Do any of you swim competitively?

STUDENTS: My brother does. He swims every morning and night. He trains really hard.

TEACHER: What do you think are some of the differences between swimming in the 1950s and today?

STUDENTS: Some swimmers shave their head. I don't think they shaved their heads a long time ago. The times are also faster. Swimmers always seem to be breaking new records.

TEACHER: I agree. Swimmers are getting faster. As you read the article, "Swimming—Then and Now," I want you to think about why swim times are faster today than they were 50 years ago.

Organize (After reading)

TEACHER: What are some of the reasons why swimmers swim faster today than they did 50 years ago?

STUDENTS: There are lots of reasons. Today competitive swimmers train all year. Back in the 1950s they trained for about five months. The extra training helps them swim faster. The swim suits are better designed too. The suits swimmers wear today can take up to 10 minutes to put on. It only takes me a few seconds to put on my swim suit!

TEACHER: Great answers. Let's diagram your responses and answers. The diagram we choose depends on the article. What type of article is this?

STUDENTS: It's a matrix because it compares and contrasts swimming in the 1950s and swimming 50 years later.

TEACHER: So our topic is swimming in the 1950s and swimming today. What do you think the subtopics will be? Look at the article again and see if you can identify the subtopics.

STUDENTS: It's easy because the subtopics are larger. The subtopics are body gear, training, diet and drugs, opportunities and choices.

TEACHER: That's right. Sometimes the subtopics are easy to identify. As readers we need to keep a look out for the various signals. In this article the author has included subtopics with larger fonts. I will put a matrix on the board. Our topics are swimming in the 1950s and swimming today. I will put the topics on the left hand side of the matrix. I will put the subtopics at the top. Together, let's complete the diagram.

Reflect Reflect on the completed diagram. What were the two main topics? (*Swimming today and swimming 50 years ago.*) What were the subtopics? Discuss the advantages and disadvantages of being a competitive swimmer in the 21st century? How about 50 years ago? Have students visualize the structure. Remind students that writers follow a structure and that good readers can identify the structure the writer has followed.

Extend Students can compare and contrast other sports, like football in the 1950s compared to football today. Or they could compare any sport that was played 50 years ago, such as baseball, basketball, downhill skiing, and track and field events.

Swimming: Then and Now Answers

When	Body Gear	Training	Diet and Drugs	Opportunities
Then (1958)	Slippery nylon suits Suits not close fitting Suits create weight and drag Goggles uncomfortable	October to March Train twice a day Swim 7 Km per day Individual program Trained alone or in pairs Training was lonely No video at training Home movie cameras Photos Fewer pools Pools often unheated Choppy water Used kickboards	Pre-race: juicy steak Popped vitamin pills	Hoped for Commonwealth and Olympic Games Individual sponsorship was unheard of Travel within NZ
Present Day	Slinky lycra suits—cut to reduce drag Paper thin suits that take 10 minutes to put on Wear 2 old pairs while training Shave body hair Wear bathing caps Some boys shave their heads	Serious swimmers train all year long Girls do mostly same program as boys National-level swimmers—train 10 times a week Swim 12 Km a day Sip water, or energy replacement drinks during training Use pullboys, cut-down flippers, bungy cords Check heartbeat rates Blood tests Expert help with diet and training Psychologists advise on how to be a winner	Lots of vegetables and fruit Not much red meat No red meat before race Seldom need vitamins or extra vitamins Aware of danger of drugs/medicines Strict international rules for medicines	Compete at both national and international level Sponsorship available for training and overseas competition Can earn money

chimney

Animal Homes

by Sarah Wilson

Animals build many kinds of amazing homes, like nests, towers, and burrows. Their homes provide protection from the weather and from other animals. Animals usually make their homes from natural materials, including grass, mud, and sticks. Some animals, such as birds, termites, and wasps, live in groups while others, such as the trapdoor spider, live alone.

This tower is home to termites in Kenya, Africa.

Termite Tower

A termite tower protects the termites against the hot, dry desert air and against predators. It is built from mud and wood. Termites spend up to 50 years building a tower. A termite is as big as a matchstick and, for its size, it builds the largest home of any living creature.

Parts of a Termite Tower

Living quarters: The termites live in chambers and tunnels in the middle of the tower.

Royal chamber: The king and queen dig a chamber, where the queen lays her eggs.

Egg factory: The queen can lay thousands of eggs each day.

Nurseries: The eggs take about three weeks to hatch.

Fungus gardens: The termites grow special gardens of fungus to eat.

Ventilation: Air moves through tunnels and chimneys inside the tower. Wind blows over the chimneys, scattering the warm air inside the tower. Cool air rises to replace the warm air.

Bird's Nest

Most birds build nests, where they hatch their young and feed and protect their families. Many birds build their nests in trees and other high places. The nests are usually round and are made from grass, leaves, and sticks.

Teaching Text Structures © 2007 by Dymock & Nicholson, Scholastic. 99

Wasp's Nest

Wasps build their homes from dry wood, which they gather from trees or wooden posts. They chew the wood into a **pulp**, which hardens into paper. Then they build a nest with the paper. These layers of paper protect the living area. If holes appear in the paper walls, they are repaired with new wasp paper.

The nest hangs from a tree branch or tree trunk, or is buried in the ground. The queen wasp builds paper cells within the nest, where she lays her eggs. One egg is laid in each cell. The egg has to be glued down so that it doesn't fall out.

Trapdoor Spider Burrow

trapdoor

The trapdoor spider lives alone in a burrow that has secret passages, escape tunnels, and hidden trapdoors.

The trapdoor spider uses its front legs and mouthparts to dig a burrow. The trapdoor is built from soil, and it has silk hinges along one side, which allow the door to open and shut. A side tunnel is a handy escape route when there is danger.

The spider makes silk to line the burrow.

The female trapdoor spider digs a chamber, where she hangs her silk egg sac. The sac contains up to 300 eggs.

word wise

• **pulp:** a soft, damp material

Animal Homes

Teaching Text Structures © 2007 by Dymock & Nicholson, Scholastic, 101

Survival Tactics

by Joanne Young

To survive, animals need food, water, protection from predators, and shelter. Many have all kinds of weird and wonderful ways of surviving in the wild.

A giraffe's tongue can extend up to 18 inches!

Walk Tall

The giraffe is the tallest mammal in the world and is famous for its long legs and neck. This amazing animal can grow up to 18 feet tall. Its height allows it to spot predators and to find food on the African grasslands.

Giraffes are big eaters. They graze for up to 20 hours each day! Their favorite food is the thorny leaves of the tall acacia tree. They use their long sticky tongue and tough upper lip to gather food.

Giraffes have excellent eyesight, and they can see enemies such as lions and leopards from a great distance.

Their long legs help them to make a quick getaway, and they can reach speeds of up to 35 miles per hour. A giraffe defends itself by kicking its enemies with its powerful front legs and sharp hooves. Although it appears to be a graceful creature, a giraffe is a tough fighter when defending itself!

Teaching Text Structures © 2007 by Dymock & Nicholson. Scholastic. 102

Coat of Armor

Unlike the giraffe, the ant-eating pangolin is a shy, slow-moving creature. It doesn't need to run away from lions, leopards, and other predators because it's built like an armored tank. Its body is covered in rows of overlapping scales made from horn, which provide an excellent coat of armor.

The pangolin uses clever tactics to defend itself. To protect its soft belly and face from a predator's sharp teeth or claws, it curls into a ball. At other times, a pangolin will swipe an attacker with its long tail or spray it with urine.

The nocturnal pangolin lives on grasslands and in forests of Asia and Africa. It comes out at night when most of its predators are asleep and uses its long, sticky tongue to catch insects such as ants and termites. During the day, the pangolin sleeps in a burrow. It has been known to occupy the homes of other burrowing animals. Imagine coming home to find that a pangolin has moved into your den!

People hunt pangolins for their meat and scales, and the

A pangolin digs its burrow using its huge claws. It can dig an 8-foot hole in less than five minutes.

species is now endangered. Even though it's able to defend itself well, this weird and wonderful animal is losing its battle for survival in the wild.

Tongue Twister

Chameleons have their own cunning survival skills. Like the pangolin, a chameleon isn't very quick on its feet, but its tongue is its secret weapon for catching prey. A chameleon can shoot out its long tongue in the blink of an eye to catch flies and crickets.

A chameleon also has the amazing ability to look forward and backward at the same time! It can move its eyes independently of each other, which allows a chameleon to spot predators and prey without moving its head.

These are just a few of the weird and wonderful ways that some animals survive in the wild. Whether they live in the grasslands or a forest, physical features and skills that perfectly suit their habitat help them to survive.

Fact File

- Some chameleons use their sticky tongues to catch insects more than 3 feet away.

- Most chameleons live on the grasslands and in the forests of Africa and the island of Madagascar.

Survival Tactics

Amazing Animals

by Nic Bishop

A hungry monkey or a bird would get a big surprise if it ran into the caterpillar snake.

July 6 **The Caterpillar Snake**

I'm in the rain forest of Costa Rica in Central America looking for the snake-like caterpillar, which is very rare. They're hard to find, and when I first spotted one, I thought it was a stick covered in **lichen**.

When I touched it, the caterpillar flicked out its body and puffed up its front to look like a pit viper, which is a type of poisonous snake. Of course, the caterpillar doesn't really turn into a snake, but it easily scares its enemies. Unlike a snake, this caterpillar doesn't bite, and if you look closely, what appear to be snake eyes are actually markings on its body.

July 8 **A See-through Frog**

While I was searching for the caterpillar snake, a tiny frog jumped out of the leaves and landed on my shirt. It was about the size of a bean, and I could see right through its skin! I've since found out that it was a glass frog, but I've never discovered why it has transparent skin.

As the frog climbed over my shirt, I realized it had special suction pads on its toes for gripping on to branches and leaves. It moved very carefully on its thin matchstick legs, looking for moths and flies to eat. Sometimes, it used its suction toes to hang upside down under a leaf.

I saw the frog's lungs and stomach and its tiny heart beating inside its body!

Fact File

Caterpillar Snake

- *Distribution:* Central America
- *Habitat:* Rain forest
- *Special Features:* Disguises itself as a snake to scare off predators
- *Diet:* Leaves
- *Size:* 4.5 inches long

Glass Frog

- *Distribution:* Central and South America
- *Habitat:* Lives on bushes and trees in rain forests, often near streams
- *Special Features:* Suckers on toes for gripping branches and leaves
- *Diet:* Insects
- *Size:* About 0.5 inches long

October 23
Garter Snake

I've just returned from one of the strangest places I've ever visited—a garter snake den near Narcisse in Manitoba, Canada.

Each fall, thousands of garter snakes migrate to underground dens to hibernate. They wriggle into tiny cracks in the ground, packing together to share warmth and moisture. Their heart rates slow, and they don't eat or drink for months. The snakes stay safe underground while it's frozen and there's snow above.

I photographed the snakes wriggling back out of the ground in spring. At the entrance to the den, there were about 20,000 snakes piled two feet deep! I climbed down into the den, taking great care not to crush any of the snakes. Fortunately, garter snakes are gentle and not poisonous.

I set up my camera and lights, then I lay down and waited. At first, the snakes were a little wary, but after I'd stayed very still for about an hour, they were slithering all around me. I couldn't believe it! I was lying in the middle of a sea of snakes, but I felt quite safe, and I took some really good photographs.

Although I've photographed thousands of creatures and had some fascinating encounters with them, these three animals are the ones that I find the most weird and wonderful.

Fact File

Garter Snake

- *Distribution:* Much of Canada and the United States
- *Habitat:* Likes moist, sheltered areas: marshes, forests, meadows, and streams
- *Special Features:* Hibernates in the winter, roams free in the summer
- *Diet:* Earthworms, toads, frogs, and small fish
- *Size:* Males up to 16 inches long; females up to 26 inches long

word wise

- **lichen:** a sponge-like fungus that grows in partnership with algae.

Amazing Animals

Animal Messages

by Kevin Boon

If you own a cat, you can tell when it's happy. It purrs. When it wants a drink, it might rub against your legs. When it hisses and spits, you know it's angry.

Animals don't talk like people do, but they can still communicate with each other and with us. Some use sound. Others use smell or color to get their message across. They might even do a dance!

Sounds

Squeaks and Clicks

Bats send out high squeaks and listen for the echoes bouncing back. An echo can tell them there's a bug up ahead or to watch out for that tree!

Bats use squeaks to communicate with each other as well. When a mother bat returns from hunting, she needs to find her babies. This can be hard if there are lots of bats in a cave. Her babies know her sound and squeak back. The mother follows their squeaks and takes them to the food she has caught.

Dolphins make squeaking and clicking noises. These come from near the blowhole on top of a dolphin's head. Under water, dolphins use a high sound like bats as they hunt for food. They listen for the echoes just like bats do.

Scientists think that dolphins also use these sounds to communicate with each other. They don't know exactly what the sounds mean. They could also help a dolphin find other dolphins in its school. The sounds might also mean "Danger!" or "I've found food."

Animal	Sign	Message
Dog	Growl	Don't come near.
Bat	Squeak	Where are you? I've found food. Danger!
Tree Frog	Bright Colors	Don't eat me, I'm poisonous.
Octopus	Red Color	Keep away!
Firefly	Flashes of light	Where are you?
Bee	Dance	Follow me to find food.
Skunk	Spray	Keep away!

Red Alert

Birds often use alarm calls to warn other birds if cats or other predators are near. Here are some examples of these warning messages.

Bird	Type of Call	Message
Robin	Low whistle	Predator is somewhere near!
Redshank	Loud and shrill	Danger!
Jay	Rattling sounds	Predator is near. Please help!
Stonechat	(1) Whistle (2) Rattle	Watch out for hawks! Danger on the ground!

Songs

Birds sing for all kinds of reasons. When a male bird chooses a place for a nest, it sings to tell other males to keep away.

Male birds often sing special songs or show their colorful feathers to attract a mate. Male peacocks have very large, beautiful feathers. They can even spread them out like a fan. They might even do a special dance!

Once birds have mated and had chicks, they can tell

which chicks, are theirs in a large group. When mother penguins return from fishing, they listen for the special sounds of their chicks' voices.

Young birds learn their songs by listening to older birds. As they grow, they add their own notes.

Whales sing songs, too. They make very high sounds that travel a long way under the ocean. Scientists think that the sounds might help whales to find other whales in their school.

All the whales in a group sing the same song. If one of the whales changes the song, then all the whales start singing the new song! No one knows exactly what the whales' sounds or songs mean.

Silent Messages

Color

Some spiders have bright stripes down their backs or around their legs. These send other animals a message. "I'm poisonous. Stay away!" Many poisonous snakes and frogs have bright colors for the same reason. Some animals try to trick their enemies. They have bright colors, but they're not poisonous. The blue-tongued lizard looks very frightening when it sticks it tongue out. The frill-necked lizard has a colored flap of skin behind its head. Predators think that these lizards are poisonous, and they run away. The lizards are sending a message, but it's not true.

Some octopuses can make their skin change to a pink or red color. This sends a message to predators—"Stay away. I'm angry!"

Chemicals

Ants can make a strong chemical to tell predators to stay away. When one ant does this, it sends a message to other ants. They all make the same chemical too. This helps the whole colony of ants to protect itself.

Smell

Some animals use smell to send a quick and nasty message to animals that bother them. Skunks have a black and white coat. These colors are usually enough to tell a predator to stay away. If this doesn't work, the skunk sprays a bad smell at the predator. This gets the message across!

Light

Fireflies send out short flashes of light to find each other and to attract mates. Glowworms send out light to attract insects. When the insects come close, they catch them and eat them.

Under the ocean, many fish and animals use light to attract food and mates and to frighten predators away. The seadevil fish has a long body part, or lure, on its head that works a little like a fishing pole.

Dance

Worker bees spend a lot of time looking for food. When they find some nectar, they fly back to the hive to tell the other workers. They have a special way of telling the other workers where the nectar is. They do a kind of dance in a figure of eight. The dance was discovered by a scientist named Karl von Frisch. He called it the "waggle dance."

Animals don't communicate the way people do, but they can still find each other, frighten off predators, and tell other animals about food. They do this in lots of different ways—often without making a sound!

Animal Messages

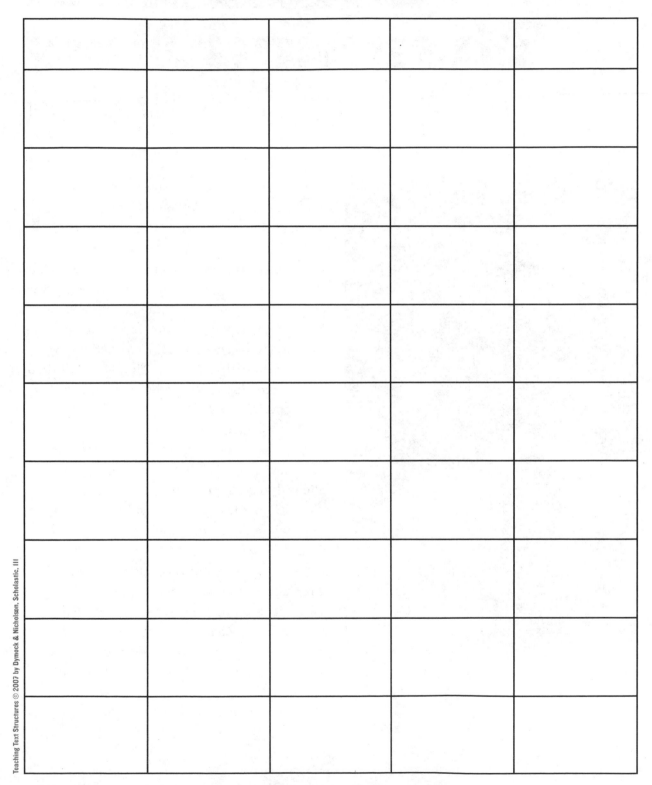

Swimming: Then and Now

by Tessa Duder

Pamela was doing her best. If she could swim a decent 200-meter time trial, she and the rest of her training squad could call it a day and go home.

So there was the squad, leaning against the land ropes, cheering her on. The air was warm and heavy: a January afternoon in Auckland. It was right at the end of their second session for the day, so she'd already clocked up over 10 kilometers in the water. They were all tired. Pamela, coming to the end of her time trial, was especially tired.

She finished. Her coach looked at his stopwatch. In a matter-of-fact voice he said, "Two thirteen. Well done." They were all allowed to go home.

Two minutes thirteen! I gulped. I know that swimming records are a lot faster now than they were 40 years ago, when I swam for New Zealand, but this was a 14-year-old girl training in a turbulent pool, dead tired. Two thirteen would have been a respectable time for a Senior Male Swimmer in my day.

To top it off, she wasn't even gasping for air. I was impressed. I was also interested to talk to the coach, and find out why times have improved so much. This is what I learned.

Tessa Duder, now an author, was once a competitive

swimmer, and in 1958, won a silver medal at the

Commonwealth Games in Cardiff, Wales.

Body Gear

Today's swimmers wear slinky lycra suits, cut to reduce drag. For competition, they wear "paper" suits—so super-thin they take about 10 minutes to put on and last only for a few races. For training, they wear two old pairs, to increase weight and resistance, and therefore make their muscle work harder.

They regularly shave off all their body hair and wear bathing caps. For really important races some boys shave their heads. Apparently it feels terrific in the water. Most people wear goggles, to protect their eyes from chlorine, and to see better underwater

Until the 1970s, swimmers raced in suits made of slippery nylon, designed more for modesty than speed. Because they were not very close fitting, they scooped up water, creating weight and drag for the swimmer. The girls often developed rashes under the arms because the suits were badly cut and they chafed. The goggles we had then were uncomfortable, so we had to put up with eyes stinging like hot coals from the chlorine.

Training

Today's serious swimmers train as a squad, all year 'round. The girls do mostly the same program as the boys. Serious swimmers at the national level do about 10 sessions a week, averaging about 12 kilometers a day.

During training, they sip water or energy replacement drinks. They use "pullboys" (placed between the thighs for arms-only training), hand paddles (to build up arm strength), and "bungy cords" attached to a waistband (to provide resistance)

Coaches use videos to check a swimmer's technique. They check heartbeat rates regularly, and occasionally take blood tests. Experts are available to help with diet, training methods, and sports medicine. Sports psychologists can teach young swimmers how to visualize themselves as champions.

Pools are better designed now, with less turbulence, heated water, and lanes set aside for training.

In the fifties, I trained twice a day, but only from October to March, clocking

up about seven kilometers a day. Training was a lonely business. We had an individual program of three to four kilometers and we just went off and did it, sometimes in pairs, sometimes alone.

No videos, of course—they hadn't been invented yet, so our coaches did what they could with photos or home movie cameras. Our coaches used stopwatches, but we didn't bother much about heartbeat rates, and I never had a blood test.

There were fewer pools, and they were often unheated, with choppy water. We used kickboards, but it never occurred to us to drink water while we were training, even though we got very hot. And we had never heard of sports psychologists.

Diet and Drugs

Today's swimmers eat healthy food: lots of vegetables and fruit, and not much red meat—none at all before the race. They seldom need vitamin pills or extra minerals.

They are very aware of the dangers of drugs and medicines. International rules are very strict. Even cough mixtures and pain relievers are banned, so athletes try not to get coughs or headaches.

For us, the best pre-race meal was a good juicy steak! We didn't know then that carbohydrates are the best pre-race food. Lots of us popped vitamin pills like jellybeans. The real problems with other performance-enhancing drugs in sports only began to be recognized later, in the sixties.

Opportunities

Today's promising swimmers get to compete all over New Zealand and internationally as well. Sponsorships are available to help them train and compete overseas for long periods. They can earn money (it has to go into their individual trust fund to be used only for swimming purposes) while still remaining amateurs.

In the fifties, before jet travel, we hoped for Commonwealth or Olympic games selection every second year. That was about it. Sponsorships for individuals was unheard of.

But we did get the chance to travel within New Zealand. In the days before television, people really enjoyed visits by stars, even junior ones! Swim meets were called carnivals, with water polo, clown divers, and water ballets as well as races.

Choices

If you enjoy the water, there are many choices now besides competitive swimming: water polo, triathlons, life saving, synchronized swimming, diving, distance swimming, canoeing, rowing, and yachting.

So competitive swimming has become more specialized. If you choose to go for it, you have to be very disciplined. You learn to manage your time. You have to get used to travel, to talking to the media, and to getting up at 4:45 A.M.!

In the fifties, boys had many more choices than girls. Girls can now do triathlons, play water polo, compete in overseas canoeing, rowing, or sailing, or become professional lifeguards. None of these were likely then.

But we all needed the same dedication to our sport to succeed. I traveled and made lifelong friends from my sport.

Swimming: Then and Now

CHAPTER 5

Teaching Descriptive Structures: List

The list structure is the most basic descriptive text pattern. What makes the list pattern "basic" is that there is no real structure to the pattern, unlike the web (see Chapter 3) and matrix (see Chapter 4). The list structure is like a grocery list, or the list of ingredients needed to bake chocolate chip cookies, or a list of materials and tools required to make a bookcase. With the list structure it does not matter what goes first. For example, when listing the ingredients needed for baking chocolate chip cookies it does not matter if flour is listed before or after sugar, or if eggs are listed before the chocolate chips. Order is not a characteristic of the list structure.

The list structure is common in social studies (e.g., a list of countries where Spanish is the dominant language) and science (e.g., the physical characteristics of the polar bear). Though the list structure is basic, it is also considered the most difficult to remember as there are few, if any, links between the elements. An author may consider the reader when organizing list patterns. For example, the countries where Spanish is the dominant language may be listed in alphabetical order. Ingredients may be listed in the order they are assembled. Dry ingredients (e.g., flour, baking powder, baking soda, and salt) are usually grouped together. But this is not the case for all list patterns. In this chapter, for example, you'll find the items found in the sparrow's nest are randomly listed, as are the toys children play with in the Solomon Islands.

While the three articles in this chapter present a list structure, students can analyze them in a variety of ways. "Toys From the Solomon Islands" has three different lists: the things Solomon Island children use to make their toys, the toys children make, and the things needed to make a push truck.

"Making Ice Cream" has two different text patterns, list and linear string (sequence). There are two separate lists of items required to make ice cream: equipment and ingredients. The article also outlines the sequence involved in making ice cream. For an explanation of linear string text refer to Chapter 6.

"Picking Up Rubbish," which describes a sparrow's nest, contains two descriptive text patterns: list and web.

List Articles

Each lesson follows the CORE model of teaching. At the end of the chapter, you will find the articles and diagram templates to photocopy and distribute to students to use in small groups or in a whole-class setting. The table below provides an overview of the articles included in this chapter, giving you a quick guide to their content and grade level.

Summary of List Articles

Title	Topic	Content Area	Grade Level
Making Ice Cream	A homemade recipe for making ice cream	Science—Health	4
Picking Up Rubbish	A sparrow's nest is made from rubbish (or garbage) people have dropped.	Science	5
Toys From the Solomon Islands	Children in the Solomon Islands make their own toys	Social Studies	5/6

How to Teach the List Structure

Following the CORE model of instruction enhances students' learning (refer to Chapters 2 and 3 for a detailed description of the CORE model). First "connect" to students' background knowledge. Then "organize," at which time students diagram the text and ask questions about the text design. It is important to encourage them to "reflect" on what they have read, and to "extend," or transfer, what they have learned to new text.

Build Knowledge Before they begin reading list patterns, it is important to help students make meaningful connections to the text. Many students will have little background knowledge about the Solomon Islands, for example, so it is very important to connect students to the content. You can do this by making links between what they do know (e.g., Hawaiian Islands, Caribbean Islands, or isolated indigenous groups) and what is being learned. Jumping straight into the article, without making links to prior knowledge, makes it much harder for students to make sense of what they're reading. It is also helpful to guide them to the article's Fact File where they will find more information about the Solomon Islands that will also put the article in context.

Model How to Diagram the Text Structure Model how to go about diagramming the text (refer to Chapter 2). Use a whiteboard, smart board, overhead projector, or large sheets of paper. It is important that students can see both the text and the diagram. The demonstration phase may continue for several days or until students are able to proceed with guided practice. The progress will vary from student to student, group to group, or class to class.

Our experience is that students do not take long to gain an understanding of how to identify the text structure and diagram the text. The following diagram represents the list structure:

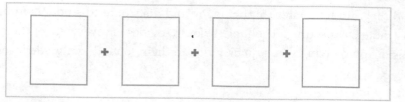

Lessons

Making Ice Cream

Rationale This article has a list structure and a sequential structure. It lists the equipment needed to make ice cream and it also lists the ingredients. With list structures, the order of the items in the list does not matter. The article also describes the sequence involved in making ice cream. Time is a critical element in sequential texts. The steps must happen in a particular order. There is a first-to-last pattern.

Summary An elementary school teacher found a recipe for making ice cream that does not require a freezer. The teacher knew that the students in her class liked ice cream and that they would enjoy making it. She told the class that if they brought the necessary equipment for making ice cream, she would bring the ingredients. The article lists the equipment needed for making ice cream as well as the ingredients. This section of the article has a list structure.

The second half of the article is sequential in structure. It explains the sequence involved in making ice cream. Cream, sugar, and vanilla are put in the small jar. The students put ice in the bottom of the large jar. The small jar is placed on the ice, more ice is added, salt is sprinkled over the ice, and then the lid is screwed on tight. Jars are rolled back and forth for four minutes, then the jar is rested for a minute. This process is repeated five times. Eventually the lids come off and the ice cream is ready to be eaten.

CORE Teaching Ideas

Connect to the Content (Introduction)

TEACHER: Who likes to eat ice cream?

STUDENTS: I love ice cream. My favorite is Baskin-Robbins. Me too but we don't have it very often. I like Ben and Jerry's. Chocolate is my favorite flavor. I like cookies and cream. There are so many flavors I have a hard time choosing.

TEACHER:	I agree. There are so many flavors to choose from. Did you know that there are many ways to make ice cream? Today we are going to be reading about one way of making homemade ice cream. After we read the article we may also want to make ice cream. If you are going to prepare food, what is one of the first things you do?
STUDENTS:	Wash your hands.
TEACHER:	Yes, it is important to wash your hands before preparing food. What do you do next?
STUDENTS:	If you are going to make something you have to have the ingredients. Mom always tells me to check the cupboard to make sure we have the ingredients before I start to cook something.
TEACHER:	Yes, it is helpful to make sure you have all the ingredients you need. A recipe usually begins with a list of ingredients. The order of the ingredients does not matter. What is important is that all the ingredients are listed so you know which ones to gather.

Connect to the Structure (Before reading)

TEACHER:	Today we will be reading an article on how to make ice cream. The beginning of the article has two lists. The first list is the equipment needed to make the ice cream and the second list is the ingredients that we need. Both lists have bullet points next to the items. This tells the reader that part of the article follows a list structure.
	Read the first page of the article. As you read I want you to think about the equipment that is needed to make ice cream. What ingredients are needed to make ice cream?

Organize (After reading)

TEACHER:	I have put two list structures on the board. Why have I put two lists?
STUDENTS:	Because the article has two lists. One list is for the equipment and one is for the ingredients.
TEACHER:	Let's record the information in the diagrams. Diagramming the information in the text helps us to remember it better. Keep in mind that it does not matter which items go first. We can change the order and it won't affect the outcome.

TEACHER:	The rest of the article describes the sequence the students followed in making ice cream. The sequence follows a particular order. Unlike the list structure, the steps cannot be changed around. Most recipes begin with a list of the ingredients followed by the sequence to follow in making the recipe. It is important to follow the correct sequence otherwise the cookies or cake or ice cream may be a disaster.
	As you read the rest of the article, think about the sequence the students follow to make ice cream.

Organize (After reading)

TEACHER:	I have put a sequential diagram on the board so we can record the sequence. What is the difference between the list diagram and the sequential diagram?
STUDENTS:	They are very similar. The boxes are the same. The list diagram has a plus sign between the boxes and the sequence has arrows between the boxes.
TEACHER:	You are right.
STUDENTS:	With the list structure the order does not matter but in the sequential structure the order is very important.
TEACHER:	Let's diagram the sequence for making ice cream. What is the first step? The second?

Diagram the sequence together.

Reflect

TEACHER:	What can you tell me about the article we read today?
STUDENTS:	The article is really a recipe for making ice cream. It has two structures. First the article lists the equipment and the ingredients for making ice cream. The second part of the article is sequential. The steps for making ice cream are set out in a first-to-last order.

Extend Students can research different ways of making ice cream. The ingredients can be compared and contrasted, and the sequences can be compared. Students can also carry out a small research project. They could survey students' favorite ice cream brands and flavors. The results from Grade 4 students could be compared to those of Grade 5 students. Boys' preferences could be compared to those of girls. Students could carry out a taste test of different brands of vanilla ice cream (e.g., homemade, store brands from chain grocery stores, ice cream shops).

Making Ice Cream Answers (List)

Equipment needed:

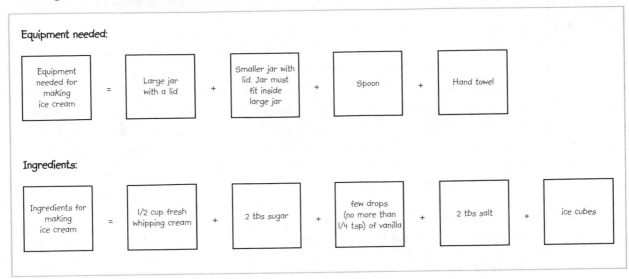

| Equipment needed for making ice cream | = | Large jar with a lid | + | Smaller jar with lid. Jar must fit inside large jar | + | Spoon | + | Hand towel |

Ingredients:

| Ingredients for making ice cream | = | 1/2 cup fresh whipping cream | + | 2 tbs sugar | + | few drops (no more than 1/4 tsp) of vanilla | + | 2 tbs salt | + | ice cubes |

Making Ice Cream Answers (Sequence)

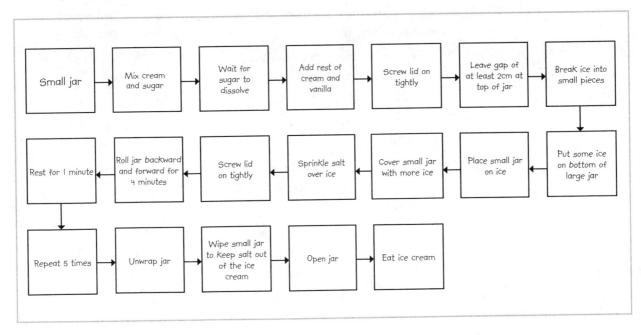

Small jar → Mix cream and sugar → Wait for sugar to dissolve → Add rest of cream and vanilla → Screw lid on tightly → Leave gap of at least 2cm at top of jar → Break ice into small pieces → Put some ice on bottom of large jar → Place small jar on ice → Cover small jar with more ice → Sprinkle salt over ice → Screw lid on tightly → Roll jar backward and forward for 4 minutes → Rest for 1 minute → Repeat 5 times → Unwrap jar → Wipe small jar to keep salt out of the ice cream → Open jar → Eat ice cream

Picking Up Rubbish

Rationale "Picking Up Rubbish" describes a sparrow's nest. The article has two descriptive structures, a web and a list structure. The first two paragraphs follow a web structure. The main topic is the sparrow's nest that was found lying on the grass. The three subtopics—which indicate a web structure—include the nest's purpose, what the nest looks like, and a brief overview of what the nest is made from. The author then takes the nest apart. He discovers that the sparrow used a lot of rubbish, or trash, dropped by people to make its nest. The author then lists the rubbish and other items the sparrow used to make its nest, using bullet points. The bullet points are a good signal for students that this section of the article follows a list structure.

Summary The author of the article was visiting a friend when he spotted a sparrow's nest lying on the grass. He explains briefly the purpose of the nest, what it looks like, and what it is made from. Then he takes the nest apart. He lists the items found inside the nest.

CORE Teaching Ideas

Connect to the Structure and Content (Introduction)

TEACHER: I have put some words on the board. What do you think the words relate to?

- Lunch
- PE gear
- Homework
- Drink bottle
- School bag
- Money for school trip to museum

STUDENTS: It looks like a reminder list. A list of things you need to take to school the next day.

TEACHER: Yes, it is list of things to remember to take to school. Would it matter if I moved "lunch" to the end of the list and "school bag" to the beginning?

- School bag
- PE gear
- Homework
- Drink bottle
- Money for school trip to museum
- Lunch

STUDENTS: No it does not matter. With a list it does not matter what goes first. The important thing is that you remember everything on the list. It would not be good to forget your lunch or homework.

TEACHER: You are right. It does not matter what goes first, second, or third. Some articles we read follow a list structure. The article may be listing the items you need to make a necklace. Or a list of words that describe the features of whales or New York City.

Connect to the Structure (Before reading)

TEACHER: The article you are reading today, "Picking Up Rubbish," is not about garbage collectors. It is about a sparrow. The sparrow has used people's rubbish to build its nest. I wonder what the sparrow has used—you are about to find out. As you read I want you to think about what the sparrow has used to make its nest.

Organize (After reading)

TEACHER: What did the sparrow use to make its nest?

STUDENTS: Feathers . . .

TEACHER: We can put this information into a list diagram. I have put a blank diagram on the board. Remember that with a list text structure it does not matter what goes first, second, or third.

TEACHER: Let's return to the first two paragraphs. The two paragraphs describe the nest. They follow a web structure. Some articles have more than one text structure. This article has two text structures, a web and list. What is the main topic of the two paragraphs?

STUDENTS: The sparrow's nest.

TEACHER: Good. What are the subtopics?

STUDENTS: What the nest looks like. The article says the nest looks large and that it looks like a messy ball of string!

TEACHER: Excellent. I will put this information on the board. The nest is the main subject so this goes in the middle of the web. What is another word for "looks like"?

STUDENTS: Appearance?

TEACHER: Yes, that's a good word. What would another subtopic be?

STUDENTS:	The purpose of the nest. The nest keeps the eggs warm. It insulates. Another subtopic is what the nest is made from. The items in the list could be put here.
TEACHER:	Very true. Now continue to complete the web on your own.

(Web diagram with ovals labeled "Purpose," "Sparrow's nest," "Made from," and "Looks like")

Reflect

TEACHER:	Today we read a descriptive article with two text structures. Tell me about the two structures.
STUDENTS:	Part of the article is a list structure. It is like a grocery list where the items found in the sparrow's nest are listed. It does not matter what goes first or second. The other structure is a web. The topic is the sparrow's nest and the subtopics are what the nest looks like, its purpose, and what was found in the nest.
TEACHER:	Well done. Next time you find a bird's nest that you are sure is no longer being used, take it apart and see what the bird used to make the nest. Be sure to wash your hands afterward! Some readers may think it is good to drop their garbage so birds have something to build their nests with. What do you think?
STUDENTS:	We should not drop our garbage. Birds can use sticks and leaves to build their nests. They don't need trash. Birds do not pick up all the garbage people drop. There is a lot of garbage lying around the roadside. And birds only build their nests in the spring. They do not build nests in the fall or during winter!
TEACHER:	I agree. We should not drop our garbage. Instead we should put it in the garbage can. Birds can use sticks, leaves, moss and other "natural items" to build their nests.

Extend Students could compare and contrast different types of bird nests. Subtopics could be size of nest, location of nest, and what different birds use to make their nests. Students could also create a web structure from the list of items found in the sparrow nest. Subtopics could include hair, paper, cellophane, and feathers.

Picking Up Rubbish Answers

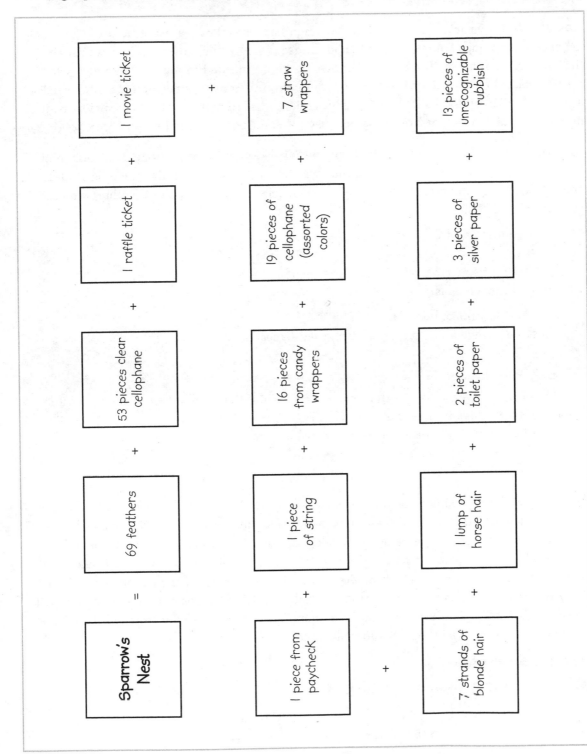

1 movie ticket + 7 straw wrappers + 13 pieces of unrecognizable rubbish

+   +   +

1 raffle ticket + 19 pieces of cellophane (assorted colors) + 3 pieces of silver paper

+   +   +

53 pieces clear cellophane + 16 pieces from candy wrappers + 2 pieces of toilet paper

+   +   +

69 feathers + 1 piece of string + 1 lump of horse hair

=   +   +

Sparrow's Nest + 1 piece from paycheck + 7 strands of blonde hair

Toys From the Solomon Islands

Rationale The article "Toys From the Solomon Islands" follows a list structure. The first list shows the things Solomon Island children use to make their toys. The second list shows the toys children make. The third list shows the things needed to make a Solomon Islands Push Truck. The list structure is the most difficult to remember since no associations exist among the items in the list. A list of things children use to make toys—sticks, nails, fishing line, old metal cans, palm fronds—is not easy for children to remember.

Summary This article contains a fact file with background information on the Solomon Islands, but its main purpose is to list the toys children play with in the Solomon Islands. It does not compare and contrast toys, nor is the article in a web structure. Rather, the article consists of three lists.

To make toys children use:
- sticks
- fishing line
- old metal cans
- palm fronds
- nails

The toys they make include:
- carved wooden motorboat
- fancy hats
- dolls
- airplanes
- huts

One of their favorite toys is the "push truck." The article concludes with a list of items needed to make this toy. The items needed are:
- two metal lids for wheels
- three sticks
- eight nails
- fishing line
- a hammer or rock

Background The Solomon Islands is near Papua New Guinea, which is not too far from Australia. The islands have been inhabited by Melanesians for about 30,000 years. The Solomon Islands is considered a lesser-developed country. A large portion of its labor force is engaged in subsistence farming or fishing. It is also very hot in the Solomon Islands. The mean annual temperature is about 80 degrees Fahrenheit. Many of the people live in villages. They fish and grow vegetables and fruit. The Solomon Islands does not have shopping malls like in the United States and other modern countries. There are no toy stores in the villages. So if children want toys, they have to make them.

CORE Teaching Ideas

Connect to the Content (Introduction)

TEACHER: What are some of the toys you have at home? I will list them on the whiteboard.

STUDENTS: *(brainstorming)* PlayStation 2, mountain bike, Legos, skateboard, Barbie, doll house, model airplane.

STUDENT: My baby brother has lots of toys. He has a toy lawn mower, hammer, and tons of puzzles. My little sister has lots of toys too. She has about 10 dolls and loads of stuffed toys. She also has a toy kitchen.

TEACHER: Where do all these toys come from?

STUDENTS: The toy stores. Sometimes the grocery store has toys. Malls have toy stores too.

TEACHER: Yes, there are lots of places to buy toys in America. Today we are going to be reading about a country thousands of miles away from the United States. The country is called the Solomon Islands. It consists of many islands. Let's find it on the map.

Many of the people live in small villages. To earn money many of the islanders fish or farm. They have very little money. Children have to make, rather than buy, their own toys. Even if they had a lot of money, they would not be able to buy toys because there are no toy stores in the villages.

Connect to the Structure (Before reading)

TEACHER: The article you will be reading follows a list structure showing the toys Solomon Island children play with—like the list of toys here on the board. It also lists the things they use to make their toys. The third list is the list of things children need to make a push truck.

As you read this article, I want you to think of the toys Solomon Island children play with and what they use to make their toys.

Organize (After reading)

TEACHER: Tell me about the toys that Solomon Island children play with.

STUDENTS: They are quite different from the toys we play with. They don't seem to play with toys that use electricity like PlayStation 2 or computer games. The children make their toys. I think that would be fun. They play outside too. I live in an apartment and there is really no place outside that I can play—unless my mom takes me to a playground. It must be hard making your own toys.

TEACHER: What are some of the toys children play with in the Solomon Islands? I will list them on the board.

STUDENTS: Carved wooden boats. They make hats, dolls, pretend watches, airplanes from palm fronds. They make huts and the push truck.

TEACHER: They sure do. What do the children use to make the toys? I will list the things on the board. This is the second list in this article.

- sticks
- fishing line
- old metal cans
- palm fronds
- nails

The third list in this article is the list of things that children use to make a push truck.

Reflect

TEACHER: What type of article did we read today?

STUDENTS: An article that has a list structure. The article lists the toys the children make and the things they need to make the toys, like balsa wood and palm leaves.

TEACHER: Excellent.

Extend Have students research the types of toys their parents or grandparents played with. Are they different from the types of toys children play with today? Students can create a matrix to compare and contrast their findings:

	Inside Toys (no electricity needed)	Inside Toys (electricity needed)	Inside Toys (from toy shop)	Outside Toys (handmade)
Toys American children play with today				
Toys Solomon Island children play with	dolls airplanes			push truck huts
Toys my parents played with				
Toys my Grandparents played with				

Toys From the Solomon Islands Answers

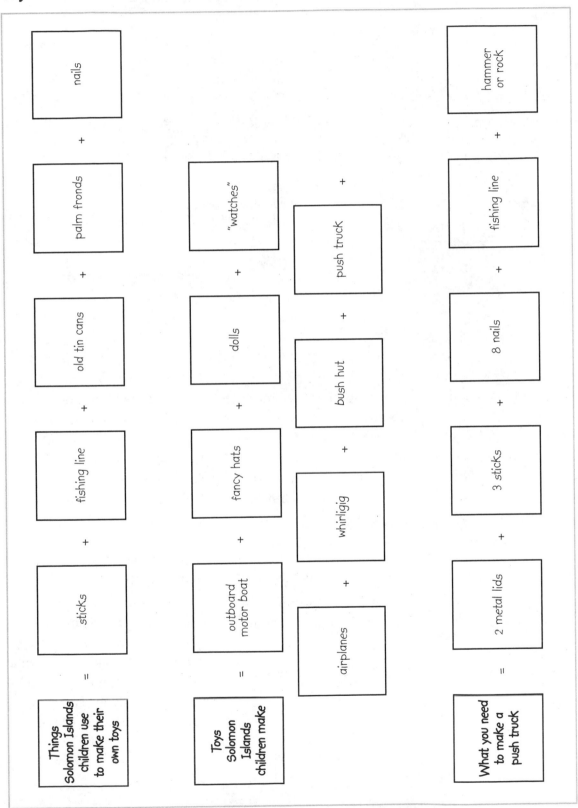

Things Solomon Islands children use to make their own toys
= sticks + fishing line + old tin cans + palm fronds + nails

Toys Solomon Islands children make
= outboard motor boat + fancy hats + dolls + "watches"

airplanes + whirligig + bush hut + push truck +

What you need to make a push truck
= 2 metal lids + 3 sticks + 8 nails + fishing line + hammer or rock

Making Ice Cream

by Jill MacGregor

Everyone in our class likes ice cream.

Our teacher found a recipe for making ice cream without a freezer. She said that if we brought the equipment, she'd bring the ingredients. Next morning, everyone arrived at school with:

- a large jar with a lid
- a smaller jar (with a tight-fitting lid) that would fit inside the larger one
- a spoon
- a hand towel

The teacher brought fresh whipping cream, sugar, vanilla essence, ice cubes, and rock salt.

First, we measured the ingredients. We each needed:

- 1/2 cup of fresh whipping cream
- 2 tablespoons of sugar
- a few drops (no more than 1/4 teaspoon) of vanilla extract
- 2 tablespoons of salt
- ice cubes

In the smaller jars, we mixed a small amount of the cream with the sugar until the sugar dissolved. Then we added the rest of the cream and the vanilla, leaving a tiny gap at the top of the jars.

We screwed the lids on tightly. Now it was time to make our "freezers." We broke up the ice into small pieces and put some of it into the bottom of the large jars. Then we placed the smaller jars into the bed of ice and added more ice to cover them. Lastly, we sprinkled the salt over the ice and screwed the lids on tightly. Our ice cream makers were ready.

To turn our cream into ice cream, we had to roll our jars backward and forward for four minutes, then rest for one minute. We had to repeat this five times altogether.

The ice cubes clinked against the glass. The jars clattered on the desks. The classroom was so noisy that our teacher told us to roll the jars on the carpet instead of the desks.

The jars grew colder and colder. The ice inside them began to melt. It turned slushy and sloshed around in the jars. On the outside, the glass frosted over, and we scratched our names in the ice. Our hands started to freeze, so we wrapped the jars in towels. When our arms started to ache, we rolled the jars with our feet.

We kept out eyes on the clock. We wanted to open the jars and check the ice cream, but the teacher said we had to be patient. When the time was up, we unwrapped our "freezers."

It was hard to get the lids off. "Remember to wipe the jars," said the teacher. "Otherwise you might get salt in your ice cream."

When we opened our ice cream makers, all our hard work was worthwhile. The ice cream was really ice cream. It was smooth and creamy. "It's delicious," said Juliana.

"This is better than store-bought," said Shannan.

We learned that it was important to follow the recipe carefully. Emma and Daniel had used too much cream, so they had to drink their ice cream. It was more like a frothy milk shake. Robert had used too little cream, and his ice cream was so solid that he needed a sturdy spoon to get it out of the jar. But by the end of the day, everyone's ice cream had disappeared.

Next time, we decided we'd add our favorite flavors— chocolate chip, marshmallow, strawberry, or . . .?

Variation

If this recipe is too rich, you could try using half yogurt and half cream.

Making Ice Cream

Equipment needed =

[ ] + [ ] + [ ]

Ingredients =

[ ] + [ ] + [ ] + [ ]

Making Ice Cream

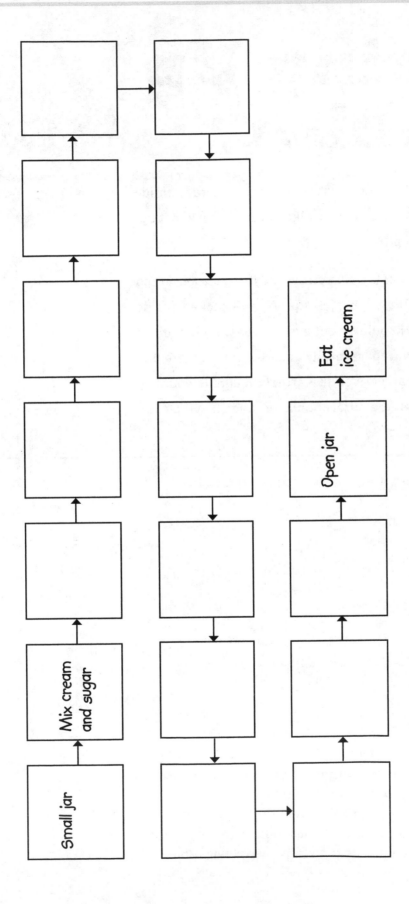

Small jar → Mix cream and sugar → □ → □ → □ → □

□ → □ → □ → □ → □

□ → □ → Open jar → Eat ice cream

Picking Up Rubbish

One day when I was visiting a friend, I noticed a large, untidy ball of straw lying on the grass. I walked over and picked it up. It was a sparrow's nest.

by Gerry Brackenbury

Sparrows build their nests using straw and dried leaves, along with anything else they can pick up. When I looked inside this particular nest, I couldn't believe my eyes. It was full of rubbish, or trash, woven carefully together to insulate the nest and keep the sparrow's eggs warm. I thought it would be interesting to count all the different bits of rubbish in the nest. And this is what I found.

- 69 feathers, mainly from chickens, but also, 2 magpie feathers, 1 fantail feather, and 1 pretty rosella feather
- 53 pieces of clear cellophane
- 7 straw wrappers
- 2 pieces of toilet paper
- 1 raffle ticket (number 99 with green diamonds)
- 1 movie ticket
- 1 piece torn from someone's paycheck

- 1 piece of string (with a knot in it)
- 16 pieces of candy wrappers
- 19 pieces of cellophane, paper, and plastic in assorted colors
- 3 pieces of silver paper
- 1 lump of horse hair
- 7 strands of human hair (blond)
- 13 assorted pieces of unrecognizable rubbish

Fact File

- The scientific term for the sparrow is Passer Domesticus meaning a "flutterer around the house." It is a small bird about 5 inches in length. The male has a gray crown and black face and bib. The female has a buff stripe over the eye.

All this was carefully woven into the nest with grass, leaves, seeds, and weeds. Next time you feed crumbs from your lunch to the sparrows, or shoo them away from the strawberry plants, perhaps you could think about how useful they are, picking up some of the litter which people carelessly leave lying around.

Teaching Text Structures © 2007 by Dymock & Nicholson, Scholastic, 134

Picking Up Rubbish

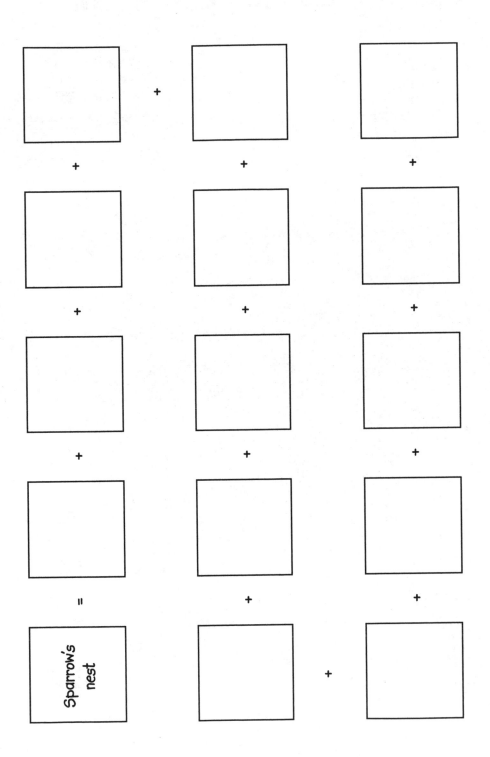

+

+   +   +

+   +   +

+   +   +

=   +   +

Sparrow's nest   +

Picking Up Rubbish

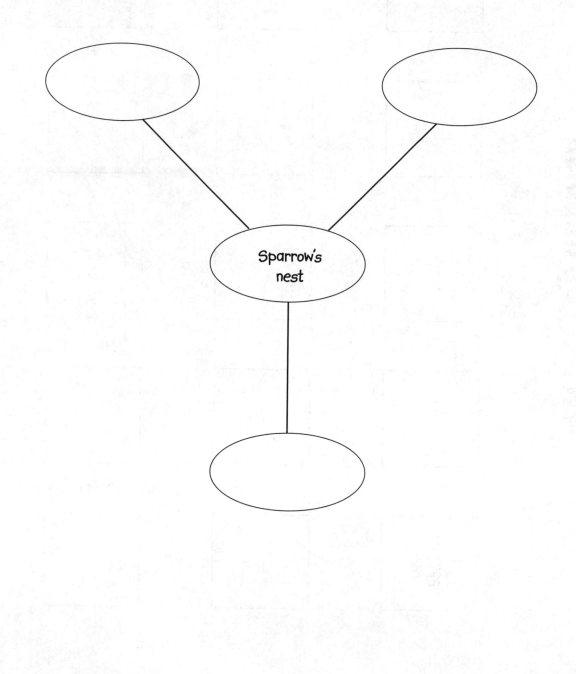

Sparrow's nest

Toys From the Solomon Islands

by Dean Schneider and Adele Vernon

If Solomon Islands children want toys, they can't go to the toy store to buy them. There are no toy stores in the villages, and usually there is no spare money to spend on toys anyway. So Solomon Islands children make their own toys with things they find, such as sticks, fishing line, old tin cans, palm fronds, and nails. These are some of the toys that children on the island of Kolombangara make.

An outboard motorboat can be carved from the branch of a balsa tree. Palm fronds can be used to make fancy hats, dolls, make-believe watches, airplanes, or a whirligig that will spin in the wind. With vines, palm leaves, and sticks, children can make a bush hut.

A "push truck" is one of their favorite toys. Children race their trucks, take them on to the beach or into the bush, and even carry things on them.

Fact File

- The Solomon Islands is a nation of nearly 1,000 islands in Melanesia.

- The capital city is Honiara. It is located on the island of Guadalcanal where fierce battles were fought in World War II between the allied forces and the Japanese imperial army.

- *Main industries*: farming, fishing, palm oil, and copra (dried coconut meat used for making coconut oil).

A Solomon Islands Push Truck

To make this truck, you will need:

- two metal lids for wheels
- three sticks
- eight nails
- fishing line
- a hammer or rock

The truck can be steered by moving the handle as you push the truck along.

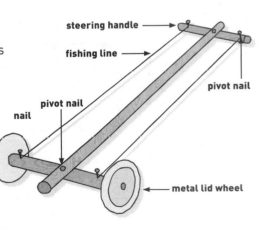

steering handle

fishing line

pivot nail

pivot nail

nail

metal lid wheel

Toys From the Solomon Islands

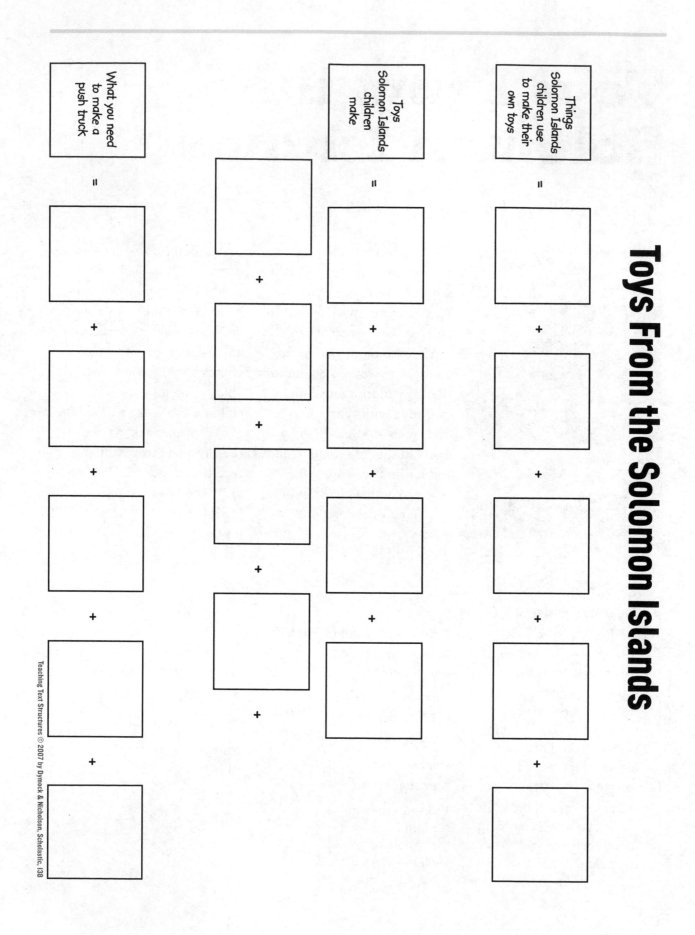

Things Solomon Islands children use to make their own toys = □ + □ + □ + □ + □ + □

Toys Solomon Islands children make = □ + □ + □ + □ + □ + □

What you need to make a push truck = □ + □ + □ + □ + □

CHAPTER 6

Teaching Sequential Structures: Linear String

The sequence structure presents information in a different way than the other patterns we've covered so far. Let's look at some text excerpts and review some of the structures.

1. Once upon a time on a shelf in a junk shop there was a dusty green bottle. Inside it lived a genie named George. George was scrawny, all skin and bones. He was like this because he was a worrier. *(This is a narrative text, a fictional story. It has a main character, which is a genie called George.)*

2. Come on legs! Why won't you stand when I tell you to? Yes, I heard you rattling the spoon in that half-empty can of sludge called dog food. Straight out of the fridge too. And I'm supposed to be grateful. No wonder I'm getting skinny. *(This is a narrative text, a fictional story. The main character is a dog. The dog has a "Garfield"-type personality, a bit lazy and sarcastic.)*

3. What is a door for? Doors are for keeping in or out. There are French doors, folding doors, and oven doors. There are revolving doors, sliding doors, and roller doors. Early doors were hung on pivots. Later came hinged doors. In China, doors had a solid lower half and a top half of lattice panel to let air through. Some doors are to keep things safe and secure . . . *(This is an expository text, or nonfiction. It conveys information. It has a web structure. The key to the web is that it focuses on one thing. This text is about doors, their features and their uses.)*

4. Monday. 4 p.m. I'm flying above the central Kalahari Desert Game reserve in Botswana. 5 p.m. Our tour guide Kaisa meets us at the airstrip and introduces Seeli, our cook. Tuesday. 4 a.m. There's a lot of rustling in the tents as everyone struggles to get dressed and out to the four wheel drive. 6 a.m. When we stop for coffee and biscuits I see my first giraffe.

(This is a sequence structure. It is nonfiction. It is different from a web in its structure. It is a diary of events on a special trip to see wild animals. It describes a systematic process, what happens one day after the next. It has a step-by-step design.)

A sequence structure is systematic. If you want to capture the information in a sequence text, you need to construct a flowchart that shows each step in the sequence of information. The sequence might be a diary, how to bake a cake, someone's life story, or the history of a country. The important thing is that one thing comes after the other in a logical order. It is not just a jumble of facts or a list of things to do. A list is not a sequence; its elements are unrelated in time or place. For example, a list of friends coming to your house for dinner is not necessarily linked in any way. In a list, there is no order. But if you provide order, such as listing the names in alphabetical order, then the list becomes a sequence. The difference between list and sequence is order. In a sequence, you do this, then that, then this, then that, in a certain order. In a sequence the elements are linked in some way, like in time or location (Calfee & Chambliss, 1987; Calfee & Patrick, 1995; Dymock & Nicholson, 1999, 2002). You cannot mix up the order of time or location and still make sense in a sequence design. There are three main sequence structures: linear string, cause-effect, and problem-solution.

The difference between using the term *sequence* and using other terms such as *biography*, *report*, or *procedure* is that these other terms can overlap with each other. The term *recount* sometimes refers to a single topic, such as "Life in Ancient Rome," which is really a web design. *Recount* should only refer to a sequence of events. We have seen the terms *recount* or *biography* to describe someone's life history, and we would agree that this is a sequence pattern though in this chapter we refer to a biography as a "continuum" pattern. A continuum is a special type of sequential text design where one thing follows the other in chronological order. The term *procedure* describes how to make something, such as baking a cake. Our term is "linear string." A linear string can be a procedure such as baking a cake, but it can also be a series of events, such as the civil rights protests of the 1960s, where one event followed another and led to law reform.

Linear String

A very common sequence structure is linear string. It is a step-by-step structure where one unit of information leads to the next, in a particular order. You cannot jumble up the units in the sequence and still have it make sense. Time is a key element in the linear string.

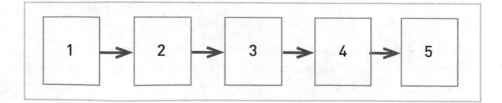

There are often trigger words in the text that signal a linear string. For example, in "Hunting the Horned Lizard," there are trigger words such as "to start with" and "then" that suggest one thing happening after the next.

Students will also encounter other sequential structures in expository text.

Cyclical String

Instead of showing a process that has a beginning and an end, a cyclical string diagram shows a process that continues without end. Some other examples of cycles students might find in their science or social studies reading include the water cycle, the life cycle of a bird, and so on.

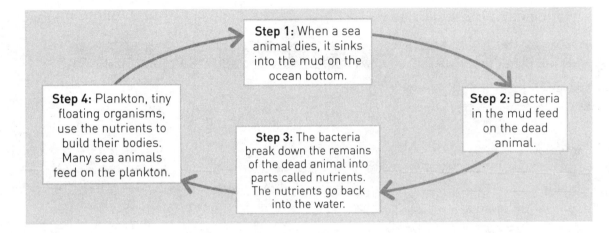

Continuum

The continuum sequence pattern is more common in a biography or a historical text where certain dates and events that happened on those dates are linked together. The continuum pattern best suits an article where there is a series of dates in chronological order, such as a biography of a famous person, or a history, such as the history of the U.S., England, India, or China. The continuum template (a timeline) is shown below:

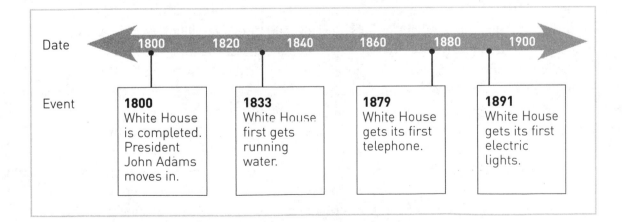

Linear String Articles

This chapter includes four articles that follow a linear string sequence structure, and companion lessons. Each lesson follows the CORE model of teaching. At the end of the chapter you will find the articles and diagram templates to photocopy and distribute to students to use in small groups or in a whole-class setting. The table below provides an overview of the articles included in this chapter, giving you a quick guide to the content and grade level of the articles. A special note about "Heart of a Champion": students will first encounter the linear string, but they will also work with the continuum pattern and have an opportunity to use a web structure to analyze part of the article.

Summary of Linear String Articles

Title	Topic	Content Area	Grade Level
From Grower to Seller—9,000 Miles	Growing and sending peony flowers from New Zealand to New York	Social Studies	4
The Fight to Have a Voice	History of a civil rights march in 1965 and how the Voting Rights Act came about—with a special section on how laws are made	Social Studies	5
Heart of a Champion	The life story of boxer Muhammad Ali	Social Studies	5/6
Hunting the Horned Lizard	Searching for the Horned lizard in Arizona	Science	6

How to Teach the Linear String Structure

When you introduce the passages to students, we suggest using the CORE model explained in Chapter 3 to tap into students' prior knowledge, discuss unfamiliar concepts, and pronounce words that are hard to decode before students start reading for themselves.

Before you start the lesson be sure to check the readability of the passages. If the passage is above the assigned grade level in reading difficulty, spend time going over possible sticking points in the text. Show how to pronounce difficult words. Check concepts in the text to see if students have prior knowledge about them. Check if students are interested in the topic—find a way to relate the topic to their own experiences.

For example in the article "Heart of a Champion," there are some words that might be hard to decode, such as: newsreel (a compound word), determination and competition (that have the Latin ending –tion where the –ti can be pronounced as "sh"), and amateur (from a

French word, with the e and u in an unusual order). You may need to explain certain words such as "segregated," "convert," or "drafted."

It might spark your students' interest to relate concepts in the article to current events in the news.

Lessons

From Grower to Seller—9,000 Miles

Rationale It seems incredible that a New Yorker can go into a flower shop and buy flowers that were picked two days previously in a country 9,000 miles away. The article uses a sequence structure to show in step-by-step fashion how the process works, from the time the flowers are picked in a New Zealand field to the moment they end up in a New York City flower shop.

Summary People in the United States like to buy peony flowers at all times of the year but peonies only flower in springtime. How can a flower seller locate peonies at other times of the year? The solution is to import peonies from other countries. This article explains how peonies are exported from New Zealand to the United States from September to November, when it is springtime in New Zealand and fall in the United States. Using a daily diary format, the article describes the 48-hour period which flowers are cut and packed in New Zealand and then flown to the United States and on to New York City.

The article's events that take place are shown as a time sequence that spans 48 hours:

1. Locate and cut the flowers in Nelson, New Zealand.

2. Store them in ice water in a chiller.

3. Pack the chilled flowers into boxes.

4. Transport the boxes to the local airport.

5. Fly the boxes to Auckland International Airport.

6. An exporter checks the flowers for bugs and damage.

7. The boxes are flown to Los Angeles.

8. The boxes are flown on to New York City.

9. A refrigerated truck takes the peonies from JFK Airport to the flower seller in New York City.

CORE Teaching Ideas

Connect to the Structure (Introduction)

TEACHER: This article is called "From Grower to Seller—9,000 Miles." Today we'll read the article and then figure out how the writer designed it. The main design structures we have discussed are the web (about one thing), the matrix (about two or more things), and the linear string (showing the step-by-step process of making or doing something). Looking at the title of this article, what do you think the design will be?

STUDENTS: The words "from grower to seller" seem like a journey, going from one place to another, like in a sequence.

TEACHER: That's great! Now look at the key headings in the article. Are there any clues to support the idea that this is a sequence?

STUDENTS: There are some good clues like "Day 1, 8:00 a.m., Day 2," and so on. It's like a diary.

TEACHER: Yes, the headings are good indicators that the writer is going to state a step-by-step process. Are there any other clues to suggest that it is a sequence?

STUDENTS: The photos. The first one shows someone cutting the flowers. The next one shows someone packing the flowers.

TEACHER: Yes, these indicate a definite sequence: cut, pack, take to airport, and fly to location. Let's see if this is the case. I want you to read the article for yourself. Then we will construct a diagram of the structure.

Connect to the Content (Before reading)

TEACHER: Before you start reading, check the first sentence and tell me what kind of flowers the article is about.

STUDENTS: What are "peonies"?

TEACHER: Well, what do you think they are? Do the photographs help?

STUDENTS: Not really. The dictionary says that peonies have beautiful showy flowers. They can be white, pink, or red. The word comes from the Greek language, meaning to heal.

TEACHER: It's great that you are using the dictionary to help with difficult words. Now read the article and tell me what you think.

Organize (After reading)

TEACHER: Do you still think it is a sequence structure?

STUDENTS: Definitely.

TEACHER: Here is a template of a sequence structure. Work in pairs and write down the sequence of events in getting the peonies from grower to seller.

Reflect

TEACHER: Any questions about the time sequence?

STUDENTS: It doesn't make sense that the peonies are put on a plane on Day 3 in New Zealand and then flown for 12 hours to Los Angeles, and then flown another 5 hours to New York and it is still only Day 3! What a rip-off. The article says that the flowers take 48 hours to get to New York. Instead of two days it really takes three days! The author got it wrong.

TEACHER: Not really. There is a clue in the text that can help you with that question. Look for the asterisk near Day 3, when the boxes arrive at Los Angeles Airport.

STUDENTS: Oh yes, it says that L.A. is 20 hours behind New Zealand time. How can that be?

TEACHER: There is an international date line. New Zealand is on one side of it and the United States on the other. If you cross the date line then there can be up to a one-day difference.

STUDENTS: So New Zealand is one day ahead of the U.S. and the U.S. is one day behind New Zealand in time.

TEACHER: Yes, almost, that's the secret of the article.

STUDENTS: So it's not really 48 hours is it? It's really 72 hours but because the United States is behind New Zealand in time the three days turns into two days.

TEACHER: Exactly.

Extend

TEACHER: Is there another text structure that you could have used for this article?

STUDENTS: Not really. It was about one thing, peonies, so it could not be a matrix. It could have been a web but the information was more about how the peonies got from one country to another. It did not actually give much information about the peony flower itself. It did not say anything about its size, color, or anything like that.

TEACHER: Perhaps the article could have said a bit more about the
                peony flower?

STUDENTS: Yes, then we would not have to go look in the dictionary.

TEACHER: For homework, find out more about the peony flower, its
                habitat, size and color, its enemies, and so on.

From Grower to Seller—9,000 Miles Answers

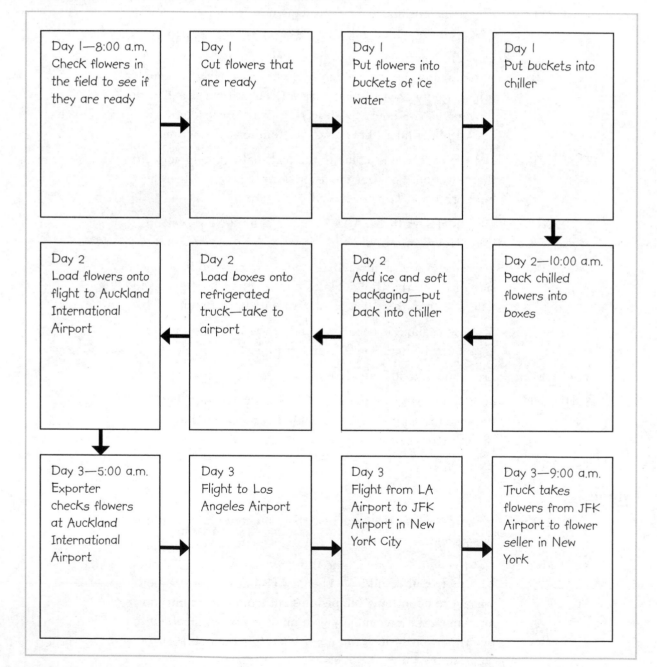

Day 1—8:00 a.m.
Check flowers in
the field to see if
they are ready

Day 1
Cut flowers that
are ready

Day 1
Put flowers into
buckets of ice
water

Day 1
Put buckets into
chiller

Day 2
Load flowers onto
flight to Auckland
International
Airport

Day 2
Load boxes onto
refrigerated
truck—take to
airport

Day 2
Add ice and soft
packaging—put
back into chiller

Day 2—10:00 a.m.
Pack chilled
flowers into
boxes

Day 3—5:00 a.m.
Exporter
checks flowers
at Auckland
International
Airport

Day 3
Flight to Los
Angeles Airport

Day 3
Flight from LA
Airport to JFK
Airport in New
York City

Day 3—9:00 a.m.
Truck takes
flowers from JFK
Airport to flower
seller in New
York

The Fight to Have a Voice

Rationale The structure of this article is linear string and it contains two sequences. The first part of the article is a sequential description of a protest march in Selma, Alabama, which helped the passage of the Voting Rights Act of 1965. The events have to follow the sequence; they can't be mixed up, making it a linear sequence. The second part of the article describes the process of making a law like the Voting Rights Act. It is also a linear string sequence.

Summary In Alabama in 1965, African-American voters faced formidable obstacles to prevent them from voting. In March of that year, 600 people tried to march across a bridge to the state capital, Montgomery. First, people lined up on the bridge to begin the march. Second, Alabama state troopers blocked their way. Third, when the marchers refused to turn back, the troopers attacked them. Fourth, the events of that day attracted public attention, and this helped to bring about a law passed by the federal government called the Voting Rights Act. The Act guaranteed a person's right to vote. Fifth, this law led to an increase in the number of African Americans who vote.

The second part of the article contains a description of the steps involved in making a law. There is a sequence of steps that have to be followed in a fixed order:

1. Congressperson introduces a bill to Congress.

2. The bill is voted on by Congress.

3. The bill is sent to the Senate.

4. The bill is voted on by the Senate.

5. If the Senate and Congress disagree, they meet to find a compromise. The compromise goes back to Congress and the Senate.

6. If the bill is approved by Congress and the Senate it goes to the president.

7. The president can sign the bill or veto it.

CORE Teaching Ideas

Connect to the Content (Introduction)

TEACHER: Is there anything about school that bothers you and that you would like to be changed?

STUDENTS: Yes! We should not have to go to school. It's a waste of our precious lives.

TEACHER: How would you bring about this change?

STUDENTS: We could write letters to the government and to newspapers. You shouldn't have to go to school. It's an infringement of our right to live in freedom.

TEACHER: Yes, you could write letters. Is there anything else you could do?

STUDENTS: We could go on strike. We might not win our cause but we might get a shorter school week.

TEACHER: Yes, you could do that. What would happen if you went on strike?

STUDENTS: Well, our parents would probably force us to go to school against our will.

TEACHER: Do you think they would do that?

STUDENTS: Yes, because they might get into trouble if they did not send us to school.

TEACHER: There is a law that makes it compulsory for you to attend school. One way to make the change you want would be to change the law. How would you do that?

STUDENTS: No idea.

Connect to the Structure (Before reading)

TEACHER: Well, this article is about how, in 1965, 600 African Americans tried to bring attention to the problems they had in voting so that they could get some change. The article is also about how to bring about a new law. As you read the article, think about what kind of design structure it has. Is it a web, a matrix, or a sequence design?

Organize (After reading)

TEACHER: What structure does the first part of the article have?

STUDENTS: It is a linear sequence. It shows what happened when African Americans tried to march in protest.

TEACHER: Yes, it is a sequence. Let's write down the details of the sequence.

Continue the lesson using the article's sidebar.

TEACHER: Why is the sequence linear?

STUDENTS: Well, the sequence follows a set order. You can't reverse the sequence or mix up the events.

TEACHER: Yes, that's it. Now look at the second part of the article on how a bill becomes law. What kind of structure is it?

STUDENTS: It has to be a linear sequence.

TEACHER: Why is that?

STUDENTS: Each step in the process has a number. You have to follow the sequence in a set order. That's why it is a linear sequence.

TEACHER: Exactly. It is always a good idea when studying a sequence structure to put numbers next to each step in the sequence. Now we can put together a sequence diagram to show the steps in turning a bill into a law.

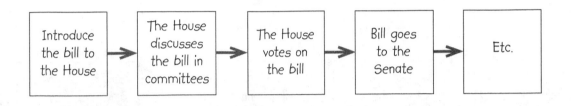

Reflect After completing the two sequence structures for the text, ask students to reflect on the structure. What kind of article is it? Possible responses: sequence, linear string, flowchart, a description of events that happen in a certain order.

Extend

TEACHER: Sequence articles have a set order but sometimes you can alter the order to suit a particular purpose. This is what journalists do when writing an article for a newspaper or magazine. They might start with the sentence, "In Alabama today a large group of protest marchers were brutally beaten by police." Why would they start the article like that?

STUDENTS: Probably to attract attention. More people will read the newspaper.

TEACHER: Yes, this is a strategy, to start with one part of the sequence that will attract attention. Then the journalist can write the rest of the article in the correct sequence.

I'd like you to look at some sequence writing in the newspaper tonight to see if you can find some other sequence structures. Bring them to class tomorrow and we can discuss them.

The Fight to Have a Voice Answers

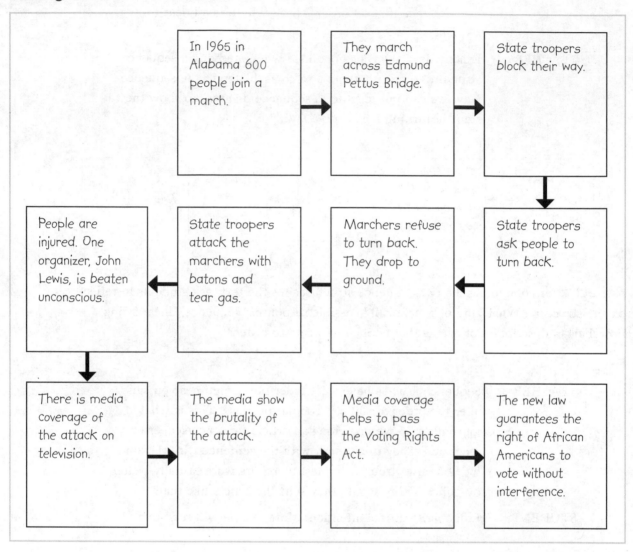

Heart of a Champion

Rationale The article uses a sequence structure to describe the life of Muhammad Ali, from the time he was born to recent times. The first section describes the new museum named after the boxer, but it also employs a sequence structure when describing the major events in Ali's life so the best way to conceptualize this article is by using a linear string. Because the other section is a timeline charting Ali's career, students may also analyze this article using a continuum pattern. This pattern is described on page 141.

The article also describes Ali's motivation to succeed against the odds, his strong personal beliefs, and other information, but since this does not fit a sequence structure, it could be presented separately as a web structure.

Summary Muhammad Ali was born in 1942 in Louisville, Kentucky. He grew up in the segregated South, where life was very hard for African Americans. Ali had dyslexia, which made school especially difficult, so he turned to boxing. He felt this would be his path to greatness. Ali joined a youth boxing program at a local gym and trained very hard. In his teenage years he won four national boxing titles and six state titles. In 1964, when he was 18 he competed in the Olympic Games in Rome, Italy, and won a gold medal for boxing. In 1967 he won the world heavyweight championship, converted to Islam, changed his name to Muhammad Ali, and refused, on religious grounds, to join the army to fight in Vietnam. For this he lost his world boxing title, and was sentenced to jail. His conviction was overturned in 1970. In 1974 he regained his world boxing title in Zaire. He fought for seven more years, finally retiring in 1981. In later years he contracted Parkinson's disease, which causes trembling and shaking, and slow speech. In 2005 the Ali Center opened in Louisville, Kentucky. It is a museum about his career, built in his honor. Its aim is to inspire young and old to fulfill their dreams. Muhammad Ali continues to inspire people all over the world not only because he was a great boxing champion but because he was not afraid to take an unpopular stand when he truly believed in it.

CORE Teaching Ideas

Connect to the Content (Introduction)

TEACHER: What would you think of someone who refused to fight for his country because of his religious beliefs?

STUDENTS: Maybe he was afraid. Or maybe the war was wrong and he did not believe in it.

TEACHER: Well, the person in this article is Muhammad Ali, a world champion boxer who also refused to fight in the Vietnam War in the 1960s. This was a very unpopular war. Many Americans protested against it.

STUDENTS: In that case he might not have been a coward. Sometimes you have to take a stand when you think something is wrong or unfair.

TEACHER: Yes, maybe he did not believe the war was right, or maybe his religious beliefs stopped him from going to war. The important thing about this article is that this person took a stand. He did not let others tell him what to do. He wanted to be "the greatest" and he achieved that goal. Was it a good thing to do? Or was boxing too violent a way to achieve his goal? You will need to think about these things as you read the article.

Connect to the Structure (Before reading)

TEACHER: As you read the article I want you to think about its message but also about the structure of the article. Is it a web, a matrix, or a sequence structure? After reading the article we will draw the structure on the whiteboard and fit relevant information from the article into the structure.

Organize (After reading)

TEACHER: What kind of structure would you give to this article?

STUDENTS: It might be a web because it's about one thing, Muhammad Ali. On the other hand, it follows a timeline. There is a timeline in the article, from 1942 to 2005. The rest of the article also follows Ali's career from childhood to the end of his career. This would make the structure a sequence.

TEACHER: Good thinking. I also think it's mostly a sequence structure. So let's see if we can summarize the information in the article using a sequence structure.

Reflect

TEACHER: Let's review what we have done today. Why did we read the article?

STUDENTS: To learn about Muhammad Ali.

TEACHER: Yes, absolutely. But we also learned about the structure of this article. This structure would have been in the writer's mind when putting together the information about Muhammad Ali.

STUDENTS: We thought it was a sequence structure. It was a good way to summarize the main points of the article.

TEACHER: Yes, it was.

Extend

TEACHER: There are still some missing points, though. The article has a message about Ali's motivation to succeed, his belief that he could be "the greatest," and the way he stuck to his beliefs even when they were unpopular. How do you summarize that?

STUDENTS: We could draw up a web as well. It would include some points about Ali's motivation to succeed and his personal beliefs.

TEACHER: Yes, great idea. Why not do that for homework? Look up books about Muhammad Ali and search the Internet. There may be other interesting facts that we can add to the web. Let's draw a draft web now, and you can complete it for homework.

Heart of a Champion Answers

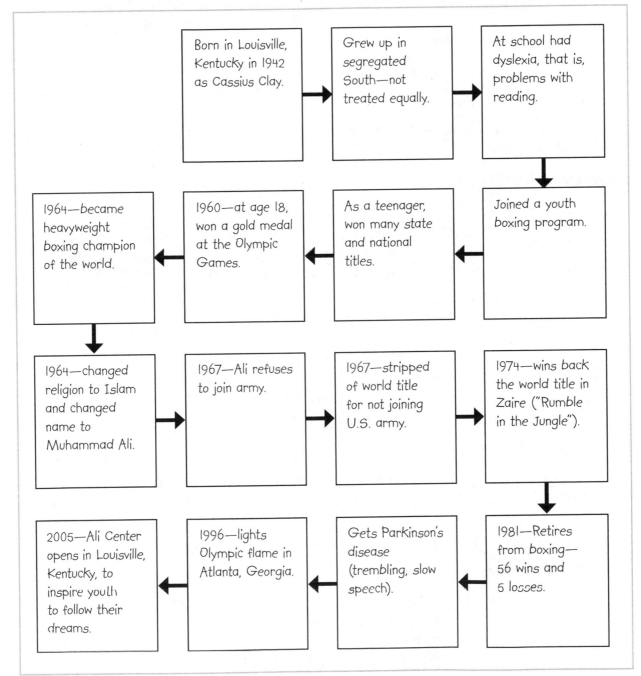

Hunting the Horned Lizard

Rationale The focus of this lesson is the section "Day 2: The First 'Hunt'" in "Hunting the Horned Lizard." It has a sequential text structure because it tracks a day in the life of some biologists as they attempt to locate the somewhat elusive North American horned lizard.

The article also briefly describes the Southwestern Research Station, which is owned and operated by the American Museum of Natural History, and different kinds of lizards. This information can be diagrammed using webs. For more information on the web structure, refer to Chapter 3.

Summary Biologists visiting the Southwestern Research Station in Arizona want to find out more about the horned lizard. The first part of the field study involves locating and catching horned lizards. Scientists then attach a radio transmitter to the lizards, enabling the scientists to locate the lizards during the field study. After attaching the radio transmitters, the scientists will return the lizards to their home environment.

CORE Teaching Ideas

Connect to the Structure (Introduction)

TEACHER: Tell me about the main parts of your school day, from the time you get up to the time you go to bed. What are some of the things you do on a school day. [record on board]

STUDENTS: Well we go to school. We eat breakfast, lunch, and dinner. I play soccer after school. On Tuesdays I have piano lessons. I take a shower before I go to bed. I am learning the guitar. Sometimes I do my homework. As soon as I get home I check to see if I have any emails. Then I play computer games. The first thing I do after I get up is have breakfast!

TEACHER: Great. We can put these activities in order from the time you get up to the time you go to bed. We call this a sequence. A sequence is affected by time. Let's put the activities into order according to time. What would be first? Second? Third?

Get up ➜ Have breakfast ➜ Go to school ➜ Eat lunch ➜ After school activities ➜ Homework ➜ Shower ➜ Bed

Organize (Before reading)

TEACHER: Today we are reading an article that is based at the Southwestern Research Station in Arizona. This research station is run by the American Museum of Natural History. What do you know about the state of Arizona?

STUDENTS: It is very hot in Arizona. There are lots of deserts and desert animals like the roadrunner and rattlesnakes. Phoenix is one of the major cities in Arizona. My grandparents go there each winter because it is warm in the winter. Yes—it's too hot to visit Arizona in the summer. I heard that the runway at the Phoenix Airport "melts" in the summer. My grandparents live in Chicago. Chicago is very cold in the winter so most winters they spend January in Arizona—where it is a lot warmer.

TEACHER: Yes, Arizona is a very warm state. And there are many interesting desert animals. The article we are going to read focuses on one animal—the horned lizard. Biologists who are visiting the Southwestern Research Station want to find out more about the lizard. The article, however, begins with a brief description of the Southwestern Research Station in Arizona. As you read, think about the animals they study there, the researchers, and the purpose of the research station. [Use the diagram at right to get students started with this activity.]

TEACHER: The main part of this article is sequential in structure. Biologists want to find out more about the horned lizard. To find out more about the horned lizard they must locate some. So one day they go on a lizard hunt. As you read "Day 2: The First 'Hunt,'" I want you to think about the sequence involved in finding horned lizards. What happens first? Second?

Organize (After reading)

TEACHER: I have drawn a blank sequential diagram on the board. Diagramming the article helps us to "see" the text structure the writer has followed. This article is primarily sequential. It is affected by time. That is, the day happened in a particular order. You don't have dinner and then go to school. And you don't go to school and then get out of bed. What happened first on Day 2?

STUDENTS: Well the scientists got in a van and drove to the site. And then they got out of the van. It would be hard to find lizards sitting in a van!

TEACHER: I agree. I will put these steps in the diagram. Where does the day start?

STUDENTS:	At the research station.
TEACHER:	Great. I will put "Southwestern Research Station" in the first box. What should I put in the in the second box? What happened next? Great, I will record the first three steps in the diagram.

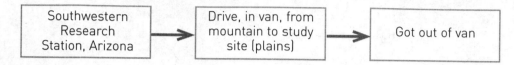

TEACHER:	OK. What happened next?

Continue diagramming the sequence with the class.

Reflect

TEACHER:	Today we read a sequential article on the horned lizard. What is a sequential text?
STUDENTS:	Sequential text is affected by time. Sequential text follows a first-to-last pattern. The events happen in a particular order. You can't change the events around.
TEACHER:	Excellent answers. Why did we diagram the text?
STUDENTS:	So we can "see" the text.

Extend The core of the article follows a sequential structure. The lesson also includes a short web description of the Southwestern Research Station. The article also describes lizards. As an extension activity, ask students to create a web diagram for lizards.

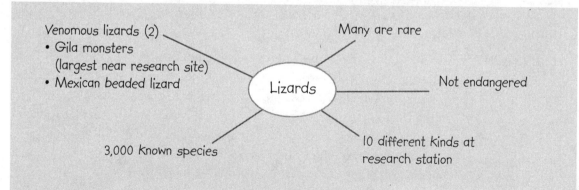

Hunting the Horned Lizard Answers

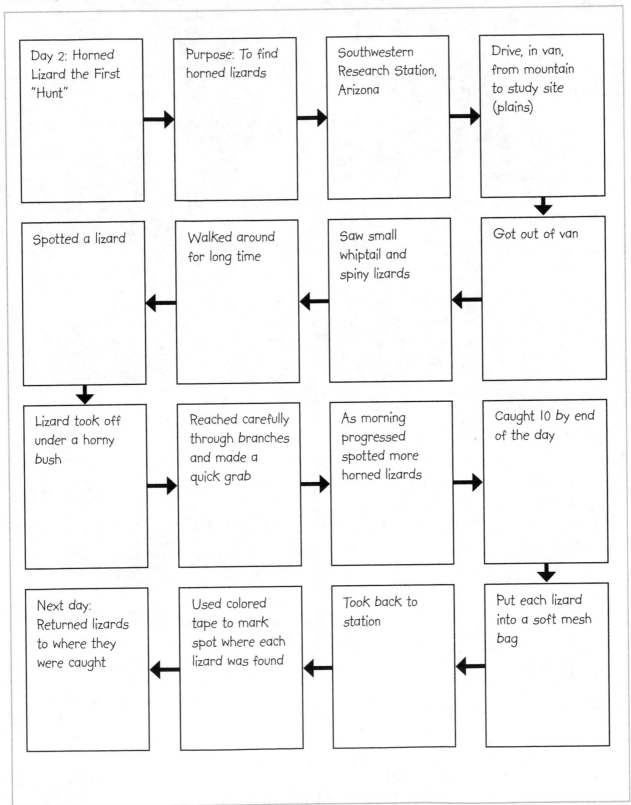

Day 2: Horned Lizard the First "Hunt" → Purpose: To find horned lizards → Southwestern Research Station, Arizona → Drive, in van, from mountain to study site (plains) ↓

Got out of van ← Saw small whiptail and spiny lizards ← Walked around for long time ← Spotted a lizard ↓

Lizard took off under a horny bush → Reached carefully through branches and made a quick grab → As morning progressed spotted more horned lizards → Caught 10 by end of the day ↓

Put each lizard into a soft mesh bag ← Took back to station ← Used colored tape to mark spot where each lizard was found ← Next day: Returned lizards to where they were caught

From Grower to Seller— 9,000 Miles

by Pat Quinn

People in the United States like to buy peony flowers all year 'round. But peonies are only available in spring, when the flowers come out. So, at other times of the year, peonies are transported to the United States by air from countries where it is spring.

Joy-Anne grows peonies in New Zealand. In spring (which is from September to November in New Zealand), Joy-Anne **exports** them to New York— 9,000 miles away. The flowers must arrive in the United States in perfect condition, so they have to be kept cool and arrive within two days of being transported.

word wise

> **export:** to send goods to another country for sale
>
> **exporter:** a person who arranges for goods to go to another country for sale

Preparation

After peonies are planted, they take up to three years to grow into large plants.

Day 1
8:00 A.M.—Nelson, New Zealand
- Go into the field and feel each flower bud to test whether it's ready for picking.
- Cut the flowers that are ready.
- Put the flowers into buckets of ice water and then put the buckets into the chiller (about 35°F).

Teaching Text Structures © 2007 by Dymock & Nicholson, Scholastic, 158

Day 2
10:00 A.M.
- Pack the chilled flowers into boxes.
- Add ice to keep the flowers cool and soft packaging to protect the buds and stems. Put the flowers back into the chiller.

Day 2
2:30 P.M.
- Load the boxes onto the refrigerated truck, which transports the flowers to the local airport.
- Travel time to the local airport is 30 minutes.
- Distance: 25 miles

Day 2
5:00 P.M.—Nelson Airport
- Load the flowers onto a flight to Auckland.
- The flight to Auckland International Airport takes 1 hour, 20 minutes.
- Distance: 310 miles

Day 3
5:00 A.M.—Auckland International Airport
- The **exporter** collects the flowers at Auckland International Airport. She checks each flower for quality*, repacks each box with new ice, and stores the boxes in the chiller at the airport.

This means that the bud and stem of each flower are the correct size and length, there are no bugs, and there is no damage to the flower.

Day 3
12:00 P.M.—Auckland International Airport
- Load the boxes into another chiller and put them on a flight to Los Angeles.
- The flight from Auckland to Los Angeles takes 12 hours.
- Distance: 6,508 miles.

Day 3
5:00 P.M. (L.A. time*)—Los Angeles International Airport
- The boxes of flowers arrive and are then put on a flight to New York City.
- The flight from Los Angeles to New York City takes 5 hours.
- Distance: 2,462 miles

L.A. is 20 hours behind New Zealand time.

Day 3
5:00 A.M. (NYC time*)—John F. Kennedy International Airport
- The flowers that arrived overnight at JFK are loaded onto a refrigerated truck.
- The flowers are transported to a flower seller.

NYC is 17 hours behind New Zealand time.

Day 3
9:00 A.M. (NYC time)
- Joy-Anne's flowers arrive at the store, ready for you to buy. It has taken less than 48 hours to transport the flowers from the grower in New Zealand to the seller in New York!

From Grower to Seller—
9,000 Miles

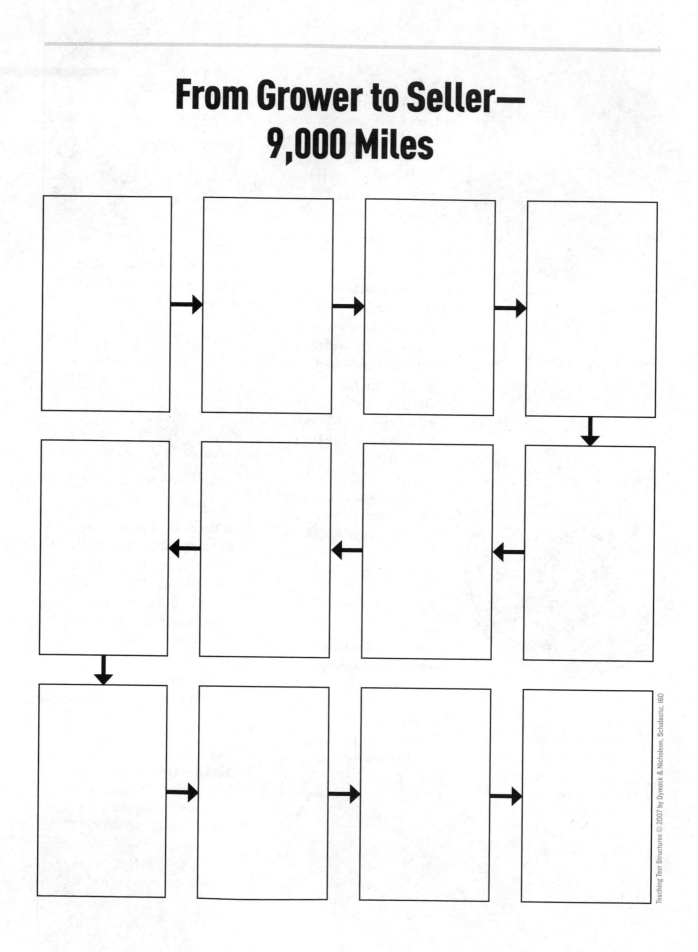

by David Hill

The Fight to Have a Voice

2005 marked the 40th anniversary of a move that secured voting rights for all Americans

One Sunday afternoon, about 600 people lined up to march across the Edmund Pettus Bridge in Selma, Alabama.

This was no parade. The date was March 7, 1965, and the marchers were taking a stand to protect the right of African Americans to vote. At the time, African Americans often faced racially biased obstacles meant to discourage them from voting. The people gathered on the bridge hoped that a peaceful march from Selma to the state capital, Montgomery, would bring attention to the problem.

Alabama state troopers and other law enforcement agencies blocked the marchers' way and demanded that they turn back. When the marchers refused, and kneeled on the ground instead, the troopers attacked them with clubs and tear gas. The day came to be known as "Bloody Sunday."

John Lewis, then a member of the Student Nonviolent Coordinating Committee (also known as SNCC, pronounced "snick"), was one of the organizers. Standing at the front of the line, he was beaten unconscious.

"We never thought anything would happen like it did," Lewis recalled in an interview years later. "We thought we would just be arrested."

Their sacrifice paid off. TV images of the brutality the marchers suffered helped speed passage of the Voting Rights Act of 1965 (*see* How a Bill Becomes a Law). The Voting Rights Act guarantees federal law enforcement of voter rights. The act is credited with increasing the number of African-American voters, as well as the number of elected African-American officials.

Lewis is now a U.S. Congressman from Georgia. Both he and the nation as a whole have come a long way since that Sunday in 1965.

"Before 1965, millions of African Americans had been denied the right to vote simply because of the color of their skin," Lewis said.

"We must not ever forget that the vote is the most powerful nonviolent tool we have in a democratic society."

word wise

obstacle: (AHB-stah-kuhl) noun. A challenge or difficulty.

How a Bill Becomes a Law

Laws like the Voting Rights Act begin life as a proposal in the U.S. Senate or House of Representatives. This proposal is known as a bill.

Do you know how a bill becomes a law? In this example, the bill is started in the House:

1. A congressperson introduces the bill to the House.

2. The bill is discussed and voted on by House committees.

3. Once the committees okay the bill, the full House votes on it.

4. If the House approves it, the bill is introduced in the Senate.

5. The bill is discussed and voted on by Senate committees.

6. Once the committees okay the bill, the full Senate votes on it.

7. If the House and Senate versions differ, the bill goes to a House-Senate conference committee for a compromise. The compromise bill goes to the full House and Senate for a vote.

8. If the bill is approved, it then goes to the president.

9. The president can sign the bill and make it a law, or veto it.

10. If the president vetoes the bill, the House and Senate can still make the bill a law if two thirds of the members agree to override the veto.

The Fight to Have a Voice

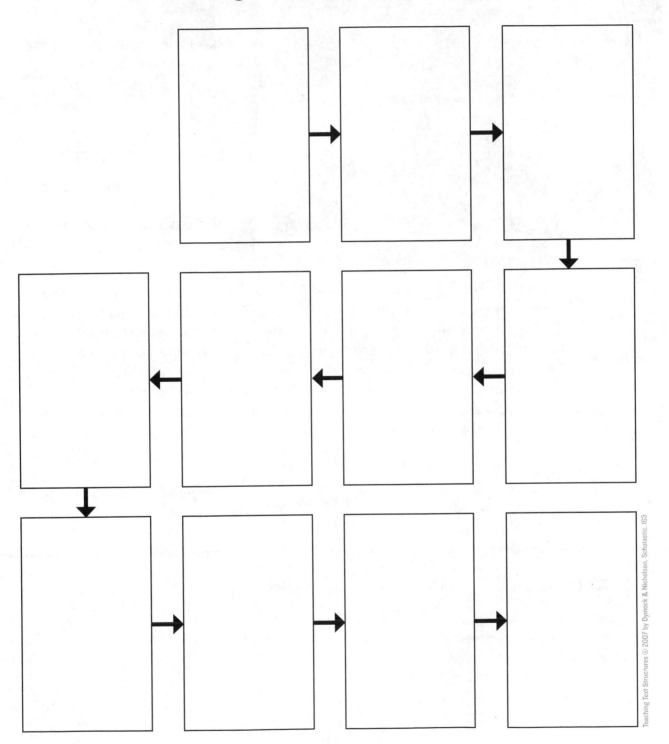

Heart

by F. Romall Smalls

MUHAMMAD ALI'S MUSEUM HOPES TO INSPIRE KIDS TO FOLLOW THEIR DREAMS

When he was a boy, Muhammad Ali, the international **icon** and former boxing champ, always believed in himself—even when others did not.

With the opening of the Ali Center in his hometown of Louisville, Kentucky, Ali hopes to inspire people, both young and old, to believe in themselves and follow their dreams, too.

"No one should allow others to determine who they are or their potential for greatness," Ali says. "All of us are born with the potential for greatness."

Early Challenges

Born Cassius Marcellus Clay, Jr., in Louisville on January 17,1942, Ali grew up in the segregated South. This meant that there were separate rules for blacks and for whites. Blacks and whites attended separate schools, drank from separate water fountains, and used separate bathrooms.

"I can't say that where I grew up was as bad as other places," Ali told *Scholastic*

ALI TIMELINE
People are shaped by the times in which they live. Muhammad Ali grew up in a segregated nation and became an adult during the civil rights era. This timeline lists key events in Ali's life.

January 17, 1942—Born Cassius Marcellus Clay, Jr., in Louisville, Kentucky.

1960—Cassius Clay wins the light-heavyweight gold medal at the Summer Olympics in Rome, Italy.

1964—Clay wins his first world heavy-weight championship. He becomes friends with Malcolm X, joins the Nation of Islam, and announces that he has changed his name to Muhammad Ali.

Teaching Text Structures © 2007 by Dymock & Nicholson. Scholastic. 164

# of a Champion

News, "but segregation still had a chilling effect on me as a young black boy. I found out at an early age that not all people were treated equally in America."

The young Ali also struggled at school. He suffered from dyslexia, a condition that makes it difficult to read. "No one knew about dyslexia then," Ali says. "I didn't enjoy school because I could never seem to do well in my classes. So I chose boxing as my vehicle for greatness."

Entering the Ring

As an adult in the boxing ring, Ali was a 6-foot-3-inch powerhouse, but as a kid, he was awkward and skinny.

When he was 12, Ali's bike was stolen. Devastated, he told police about his stolen bike and said that he wanted to beat up the thief. A police officer suggested that Ali redirect his anger at a boxing bag at the local gym, which had a youth boxing program. Ali took up the offer. Back then, other boys often outmatched Ali in the ring. But there was one thing about Ali that made him noticeably different from the other boys. Ali was extremely **dedicated**. He pursued his dream of becoming

a great boxer with great determination and eventually started training in the gym six days a week.

Becoming a Champion

Ali's talents as a boxer developed quickly. As a teenager, he won two national Amateur Athletic Union titles, six Kentucky Golden Gloves, and two national Golden Gloves championships. At the age of 18, Ali represented the U.S. at the Olympic Games in Rome, Italy. There, he had to compete against some of the best amateur fighters from around the world.

1967—Protests over the Vietnam War occur throughout the U.S. Ali refuses to join the U.S. Army due to his religious beliefs. He is stripped of his title, fined $10,000, and sentenced to five years in jail.

He remains free on appeal. The conviction is overturned in 1970.

1974—Ali regains the heavyweight title in the "Rumble in the Jungle" boxing match in Zaire.

1981—Ali retires from boxing with an overall record of 56 wins and 5 losses.

1996—Ali lights the Olympic flames at the Summer Games in Atlanta, Georgia.

2005—The Ali Center opens in his hometown of Louisville, Kentucky.

Getting to Rome was not easy—not only because of the tough competition, but because Ali was afraid to fly in an airplane. He overcame his fear and brought home a gold medal in the 178-pound light-heavyweight division in 1960. Within a few months of winning the gold, Ali decided to become a professional boxer. He went on to become the heavyweight boxing champion of the world, a title he would hold for more than 10 years.

Believing in Yourself

As a fighter, Ali was as well known for his quick wit outside the ring as he was for his quick moves in the ring. He often referred to himself as "The Greatest," a nickname he gave himself when he was just a kid because he believed in his heart that he could become the best at anything he wanted to do, even if others thought little of him.

Ali also believed in doing what he thought was right, even if it was not popular with others.

When he was a young man, he decided to convert to Islam and change his name from Cassius Clay to Muhammad Ali. This decision caused a major controversy. Ali was even sentenced to jail and stripped of his world championship boxing title when he refused to be drafted to fight in the Vietnam War because of his religious beliefs.

"Taking the stands I took as a young man made me famous all over the world because there were national consequences to my decisions, but it was a price I was willing to pay to do what I knew to be right," Ali explains.

A New Day

Today, Ali is not as fast as he used to be when he was a world-class boxer. The champ suffers from Parkinson's disease, which causes people to tremble uncontrollably and slows their speech. But he remains dedicated to helping others.

The Ali Center, which opened November 21, 2005, features videos, newsreel footage, and photos of Ali and historical events. Ali hopes to inspire kids today to be willing to stand up for what they believe in, and to make good choices that will bring them success in their own lives.

Back to You

Have you ever stood up for your beliefs, no matter the cost? If so, which beliefs, and why?

word wise

icon: (EYE-kon) noun. An idol; a person or object of uncritical devotion.

dedicate: (DED-uh-kate) verb. To give a lot of time and energy to something.

Heart of a Champion

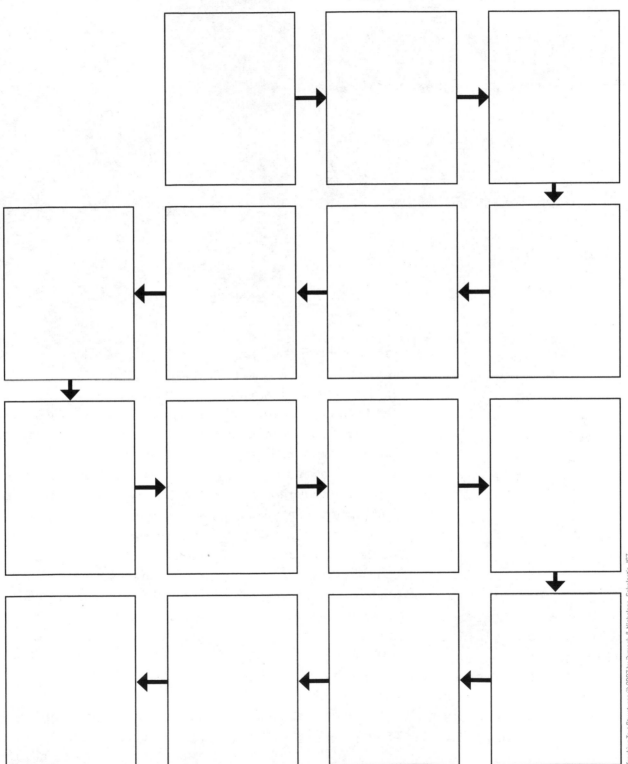

Hunting the Horned Lizard

by Nic Bishop

I'm looking forward to meeting my first horned lizard, but I hear they're hard to find. One of the ways they survive in this environment is by being very good at hiding from predators. I guess I'll find out tomorrow when we go on our first "hunt." But for today, I'm happy just to be here.

Day 2
The First "Hunt"

Today we went on a horned lizard hunt, which is the first part of the field study. We wanted to catch some lizards and attach small radio transmitters to them. This means that we can track the radio signal with a radio receiver and know where our lizards are. This will make it much easier to carry out the study.

But first, Doug talked about how a good biologist collects a lot of information and puts it together to build a bigger picture of an animal's life. Biologists know so little about horned lizards that even the smallest piece of information that we record might be an important part of that picture.

We want to know more about which ants are important in a horned lizard's diet and the kinds of plants that grow in places that horned lizards need in order to survive.

The horned lizards don't live near the station. We had to take a van and drive from the mountains down to a study site on the plains. It's a hot and dry area with small scrubby bushes and dead-looking grass. I thought that nothing could live there, but I was wrong. As soon as we got out of the van, we saw small lizards zipping everywhere—mostly whiptails and spiny lizards.

To start with, we couldn't see any horned lizards. We walked around for a long time, looking here and there. Then, suddenly, when I nearly

The Research Station

The Southwestern Research Station is run by the American Museum of Natural History. It provides biologists with a place where they can study the animals of the American southwest. The area is very rich in reptile and ant life, and most of the people who come to work here study ants, lizards, snakes, and spadefoot toads. Researchers come from all over the world, and at any one time, there may be between 20 and 60 people working at the station.

Arizona

Southwestern Research Station

tramped on what I thought was rock, it sprouted legs and scuttled off under a bush. It looked so much like a piece of the desert that I didn't even notice it until it moved.

We took a while to catch that lizard. It ducked under a really thorny bush and stayed there, right in the middle. I had to reach through the branches very carefully so that I wouldn't get pricked, then make a quick grab.

As the morning went on, we got better at spotting horned lizards. The next one was easier to catch, and by the end of the day, we had 10. We put each lizard into a soft, mesh bag so that we could take them safely back to the station. We used colored tape to mark the spot where each lizard was found. That way, we could return each of the lizards to its proper home tomorrow.

Lizard Varieties

There are at least 3,000 known species of lizard living today. There are about 10 different kinds in the horned lizard research site, including the whiptail lizard, and a further 16 kinds have been found on other sites nearby. None of these lizards is endangered, but many are rare. The largest kind of lizard likely to be found near the research site is the Gila monster—one of only two venomous lizard species in the world. The other is the Mexican beaded lizard, also found in the American southwest and parts of Mexico.

whiptail lizard

Hunting the Horned Lizard

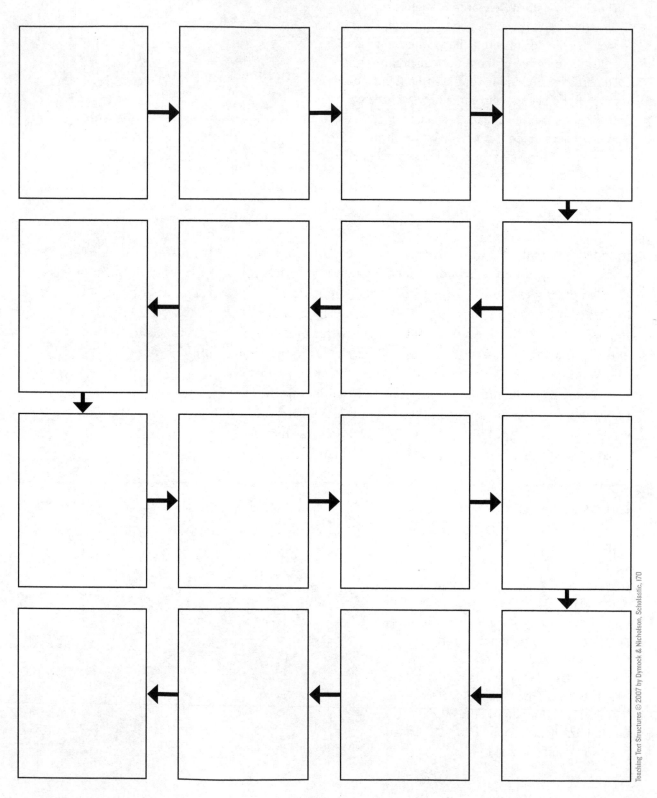

CHAPTER 7

Teaching Sequential Structures: Cause-Effect

A cause-effect article proceeds in a step-by-step fashion but it is different from the linear string in that each step in the process directly causes the next step to happen. The causes in such a structure are not always easy to see, such as the causes of the American Civil War, for example, or the causes of global warming. In this type of sequence text, causes are necessary and sufficient for the next events to occur (Calfee & Chambliss, 1987; Dymock & Nicholson, 1999).

We identify two types of cause-effect designs: "falling dominoes" and "branching tree." In this chapter, all of the articles can be analyzed using the falling dominoes structure. Using the branching tree, where one event might cause several events to occur—or one event might have more than one cause—is also an effective way to take the analysis of these articles a bit deeper.

Falling Dominoes

The following template is for a "falling dominoes" cause-effect structure:

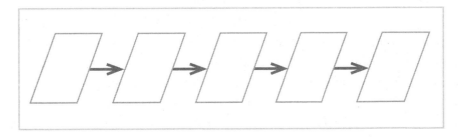

"Volcanoes: Indonesia's Deadly 3" talks about the effects of eruptions from three different volcanoes. The first volcano caused an ice age; the second killed 60,000 people; the third caused a tsunami. This article lends itself to the falling dominoes diagram because each volcanic eruption caused an event, which then caused the next event to happen.

Branching Tree

In this type of sequence design, an event can have several consequences rather than just one. The template for a branching tree design is shown below:

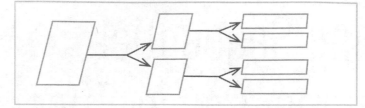

An everyday example of a branching tree structure might be an article or discussion about the consequences of making a certain decision. For example, if a student bullies or attacks another student, this will have consequences. Other students will avoid that student, the student may end up in the principal's office, or the student may be expelled from school. Another discussion topic with a branching tree structure might be the effects of moving to a new place. It might lead to several consequences, such as having to find a new job that is closer to where you live, having to buy a vehicle because there is no public transportation, having to make new friends, having to find a new school for your children, a sense of loneliness in having to live in an unfamiliar neighborhood, and so on. The one event can have several effects. This is the branching tree structure. While these are good examples of actions with several immediate consequences, sometimes effects can take time to materialize.

Cause-Effect Articles

Every classroom will have a range of reading levels. It's important to ensure that students are reading articles with an appropriate difficulty level: not too easy and not too hard. Research suggests that students are better behaved and happier when the texts are not too hard to read (Jorgenson, 1977). We suggest that more difficult texts be used for discussion. You can read these texts aloud to the class while they read along, then you can discuss the text structure. In this way students improve their oral language, and learn new words, ideas, and concepts.

This chapter includes three articles that follow a cause-effect sequence structure, and companion lessons. Each lesson follows the CORE models of teaching. At the end of the chapter you will find the articles and diagram templates to photocopy and distribute to students to use in small groups or in a whole-class setting. The table on the next page provides an overview of the articles included in this chapter, giving you a quick guide to the content and grade level of the articles.

Summary of Cause-Effect Articles

Title	Topic	Content Area	Grade Level
Warming Up	How an event like global warming can threaten the lives of many animals and cause land to be flooded	Science	4
Why Do I Blush?	What happens when we are embarrassed or if we tell lies. The heart beats faster, we overheat, and then the body tries to cool itself down	Science	5
Volcanoes: Indonesia's Deadly 3	The devastating effects of three major volcanic eruptions in Indonesia	Social Studies	6

How to Teach the Cause-Effect Structure

When you introduce the passages to students, we suggest using the CORE model (explained in Chapter 3) to tap into students' prior knowledge, discuss unfamiliar concepts, and pronounce words that are hard to decode—before students start reading for themselves.

Before you start the lesson, be sure to check the readability of the passages. If the passage is above the assigned grade level in reading difficulty, spend time going over possible sticking points in the text.

For example, the articles in this chapter contain long words that may be hard to decode, such as "devastating" and "detonation," or unfamiliar words, such as "Richter scale." You may also need to explain concepts, such as "extinction" or "ice age."

It's also a good idea to make links between the topic and students' lives. This will help pique students' interest and keep them focused on the material.

Lessons

Rationale This article follows a cause-effect structure. Cause-effect is a kind of sequence. First one event happens and the next event occurs as a result. The article contains a diagram showing the greenhouse effect. This is also a sequence, represented by the linear string structure discussed in Chapter 6.

Summary Global warming is controversial. Not all scientists agree as to why parts of Earth are getting warmer. Recent studies show that temperatures are rising in the world's coldest places: the Arctic and the Antarctic. This article explains why ice is important. It shows what will happen if too much ice melts. It discusses what might be causing the warming effect apart from natural causes. It states that some of the warming could be due to human activity, especially the use of fossil fuel for heat and power.

CORE Teaching Ideas

Connect to the Content (Introduction & before reading)

TEACHER:	Is global warming a problem?
STUDENTS:	What exactly is global warming?
TEACHER:	It's when temperatures start to rise in places in the world that are usually very cold. What happens when the temperatures rise?
STUDENTS:	The ice will melt . . .
TEACHER:	Yes, and what will happen next?
STUDENTS:	It's hard to say. Maybe when the ice melts the sea levels will rise and we will all drown!
TEACHER:	Perhaps but perhaps not. When you put a cube of ice in a glass of water, what happens?
STUDENTS:	The ice melts.
TEACHER:	What happens to the level of the water? Does the glass overflow?
STUDENTS:	Not really. If that happened, people would put ice in their drinks and then their drinks would spill all over the floor.
TEACHER:	Yes, exactly. The melting ice is not going to cause a flood.
STUDENTS:	But what about glaciers? If they melt, that would be like pouring extra water into the glass and it will overflow.

TEACHER: Yes, that could be a problem. That's what this article is about. It is about the possible effects of global warming, and what is causing the warming to happen. I'd like you to read the article and then we will discuss what kind of structure the author has used to write the article.

Organize (After reading)

TEACHER: What structure do you think this article has?

STUDENTS: It could be a problem-solution. One of the subheadings says "Global problem." But the article doesn't give a solution so it can't be that kind of structure. It might be a cause-effect structure. The article talks about causes and effects.

TEACHER: Here is a template of a cause-effect structure. We can work together to put in details from the text that will fit the structure.

Information from the article that can be put into the cause-effect structure:

1. Natural causes and possibly the use of fossil fuels for energy are causing temperatures to rise in the North and South poles.

2. Burning fossil fuels such as oil, coal, and natural gas releases carbon dioxide into the atmosphere and this traps heat in Earth's atmosphere, which causes the warming.

3. The warming can have bad side effects.

4. At the North Pole, in the Arctic region, a huge amount of ice has melted. The Ward Hunt ice shelf has already broken apart.

5. Some animals that live in the Arctic may not survive. Polar bears live on the ice. Seals like to rest on the ice and they have babies on the ice.

6. At the South Pole, one fifth of the ice has melted in the last 20 years. The Larsen B ice shelf is breaking apart.

7. Penguins may not survive in the Antarctic because they now have to live closer to the South Pole, where it is colder.

8. If glaciers, which are on the land, start to melt, this will add a huge amount of water to the oceans and sea levels could rise. This would flood areas where people now live.

Reflect

TEACHER: Any questions about the article?

STUDENTS: Global warming is very slow. Maybe it is due to natural causes and it will reverse itself in the future. We don't know if it will be a big problem or not.

TEACHER:	Yes, that's right. It is a problem that scientists still argue about. No one is exactly sure what is causing it or what can be done about it.
STUDENTS:	So is it really a cause-effect structure if we do not know the real causes?
TEACHER:	I think it is a cause-effect structure because the writer is suggesting that the use of fossil fuel by people might be creating problems that will have bad side effects in the future.
STUDENTS:	Could we call it linear string structure and not cause-effect?
TEACHER:	We could do that. What do you think?
STUDENTS:	A linear string is step by step. So maybe this is a cause-effect article after all. One thing causes another thing to happen. It might be fossil fuels or it might not, but something is causing temperatures to rise in the Arctic and Antarctic.

Extend Have students go onto the Internet to find more information on global warming and to make a list of other possible causes of warming. Students could get a range of different points of view about the global warming debate. They could view documentaries that try to explain what is happening, such as "An Inconvenient Truth." The film's Web site is http://www.climatecrisis.net/ (Note: Please keep in mind that Internet locations and content can change over time. Always check Web sites in advance to make certain the intended information is still available to students.)

Warming Up Answers

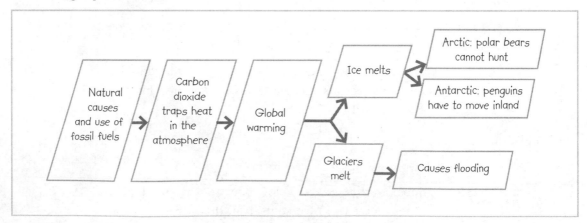

Why Do I Blush?

Rationale This article has a cause-effect structure. It gives possible causes for why we blush, which is, itself, an effect. The article details 10 steps in the process happening in the body.

Summary When we feel awkward, our faces turn red. Your feelings have an effect on your body and in the case of certain feelings, the effect is that you blush. When this happens, everyone can see how you feel. If you have told a lie or are uncomfortable or nervous, then others will be able to tell how you feel by the color of your face. This article explains what happens to make your face turn red.

CORE Teaching Ideas

Connect to the Content (Before reading)

TEACHER:	Sometimes our faces turn red. Why is that?
STUDENTS:	Running around too much. You got hot and your face turns red.
TEACHER:	Yes, but are there any other times when this happens?
STUDENTS:	If you tell a lie. My parents always catch me when I don't tell them the truth.
TEACHER:	Yes, and are there any other situations?
STUDENTS:	Sometimes if you are embarrassed. Or when my sister teases me.
TEACHER:	You are right. Your face goes red when you are feeling a bit uncomfortable or worried about what others will think. It is called blushing. Do you know why this happens?
STUDENTS:	Not really.
TEACHER:	This article explains what happens to make you blush.

Organize (After reading)

TEACHER:	What structure do you think this article has?
STUDENTS:	It seems like a cause-effect structure. It is not problem-solution because there is no solution.
TEACHER:	Yes, I agree. Here is a template of a cause-effect structure. Work in small groups to write down the causes of blushing and the effects. Let's brainstorm some ideas now: 1. Causes of blushing are being in a group, feeling embarrassed, not telling the truth, running around too much.

2. Effects of the embarrassment or worry are that you start to feel all hot and anxious and your face turns red.

Now you can read the article again and find out more details about blushing.

Reflect

TEACHER: What did you think of the writing style of this article?

STUDENTS: It started well. The author picked up on the fact that when our face turns red we usually feel awkward. This happens to just about everybody so it draws in the reader.

TEACHER: And how about the ending of the article?

STUDENTS: It had a good ending. You realize that what happens is normal.

TEACHER: And were there any clues in the article that it was cause-effect?

STUDENTS: There were a few clues, not many. There is the sentence, "Sometimes embarrassment causes the blushing." The word "cause" was a sign that it was cause-effect.

Extend As an extension, ask students to find out more about how the blood lets out the heat into the capillaries. Perhaps students can learn more about how the cooling-off effect works. They can write some definitions of key words, such as artery, vein, and capillaries, and explain the differences among them.

Why Do I Blush? Answers

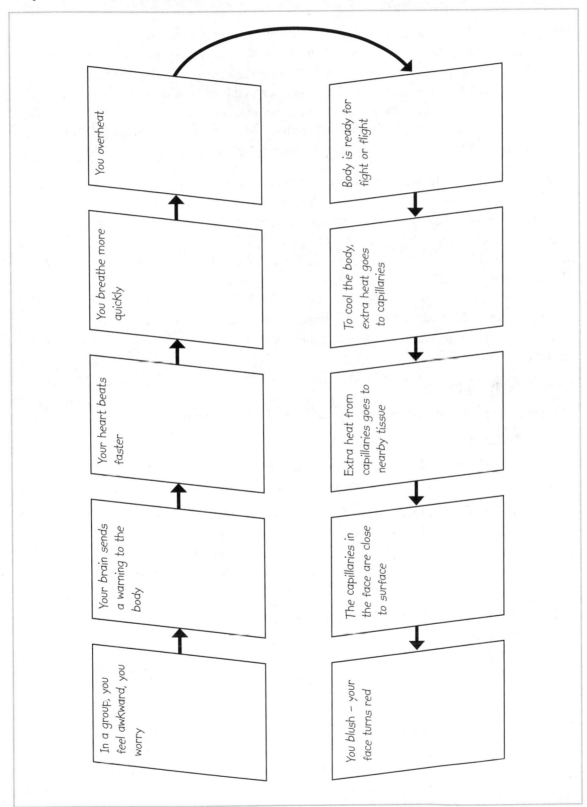

The flowchart reads:

In a group, you feel awkward, you worry → Your brain sends a warning to the body → Your heart beats faster → You breathe more quickly → You overheat → Body is ready for fight or flight → To cool the body, extra heat goes to capillaries → Extra heat from capillaries goes to nearby tissue → The capillaries in the face are close to surface → You blush – your face turns red

Volcanoes: Indonesia's Deadly 3

Rationale This article presents a good example of cause and effect. A volcanic eruption (the cause) can have many devastating effects. One effect is that volcanic ash and sulfur gas can stop the rays of the sun and reduce the temperature of the surrounding area and sometimes the whole planet. This can kill almost everything. Another effect is that many thousands of people in the area around the volcano, and sometimes far away, can be killed from the impact. Depending on their level, students can analyze the structure of this volcano article by using the falling dominoes or the branching tree diagram.

Summary Three of the world's worst volcanic explosions have been in Indonesia. There have been other major explosions, such as Mount Vesuvius in Italy and Mount St. Helens in the United States, but these three explosions were particularly violent. The eruption of Mount Toba took place 73,000 years ago. It was so violent it caused an ice age. The Tambora volcano erupted in April 1815. It was not as bad as Toba but the ash and sulfurous gases spread around the world and dropped temperatures. What is left of Toba today is a beautiful lake that attracts many tourists. The most famous explosion was on Krakatau Island in 1883, which blew the whole island apart. The explosion was heard several thousands of miles away. It caused a huge tsunami that killed many thousands of people. (Note: Krakatau is also known as Krakatoa.)

CORE Teaching Ideas

Connect to the Content and the Structure (Before reading)

TEACHER: What is a volcano?

STUDENTS: The dictionary says it is a hole in the Earth that can erupt. It comes from the Latin word Vulcan, the god of fire.

TEACHER: Yes, there are many volcanoes around the world but most of them are dormant, meaning they are unlikely ever to erupt again. But sometimes a volcano does erupt. There are usually warning signs, but often the size of the eruption takes people by surprise.

STUDENTS: Is it like an earthquake?

TEACHER: No, an earthquake is different.

STUDENTS: Is it like when someone gets really angry and suddenly bursts out shouting and throwing things. Everyone has to watch out!

TEACHER: Yes, but much worse. A person can have a temper that is a bit like a volcano. But a real volcano can cause huge destruction and kill thousands of people. So, what kind of structure does this article have?

| STUDENTS: | There aren't any clues in the headings in the article. There are only three headings: Toba, Tambora, and Krakatau. But it is probably cause-effect because if a volcano goes off there have to be a lot of bad effects. |
| TEACHER: | That's a good guess. Now I'd like you to read the article. As you read, think about the structure the writer has used to write the article. When you have finished reading we will discuss your ideas. |

Organize (After reading)

TEACHER:	What structure do you think this article has?
STUDENTS:	Definitely cause-effect. There were some horrible effects when the volcanoes erupted.
TEACHER:	Yes, I agree. I'm not sure how best to put the information together. There were three eruptions in the article so maybe you need to have three cause-effect structures. Here is a template of a cause-effect structure that you can use.

Together as a class, diagram Toba Mountain. Then divide students into small groups to diagram the Tambora and Krakatau sections.

Reflect

TEACHER:	What was the aim of the lesson today?
STUDENTS:	The aim was to read about volcanoes.
TEACHER:	Yes, but why did we put together a cause-effect structure?
STUDENTS:	Not sure . . . so that we could write a short summary?
TEACHER:	Not really. What I wanted was for you to see how the writer organized the information. The writer wrote not just about the volcanoes but the effects of the volcanoes.
STUDENTS:	Oh yes, the author showed how much damage they could cause.

Extend

STUDENTS:	This article has a branching tree structure. Each explosion had multiple effects. Why didn't we use a branching tree?
TEACHER:	Good thinking, why don't you try that as an extension activity but on a different volcano?
STUDENTS:	Which volcano?
TEACHER:	You could try Mount Vesuvius—that was a famous explosion in Italy thousands of years ago. Or you could write about Mount St. Helens in Washington State.

Volcanoes: Indonesia's Deadly 3 Answers

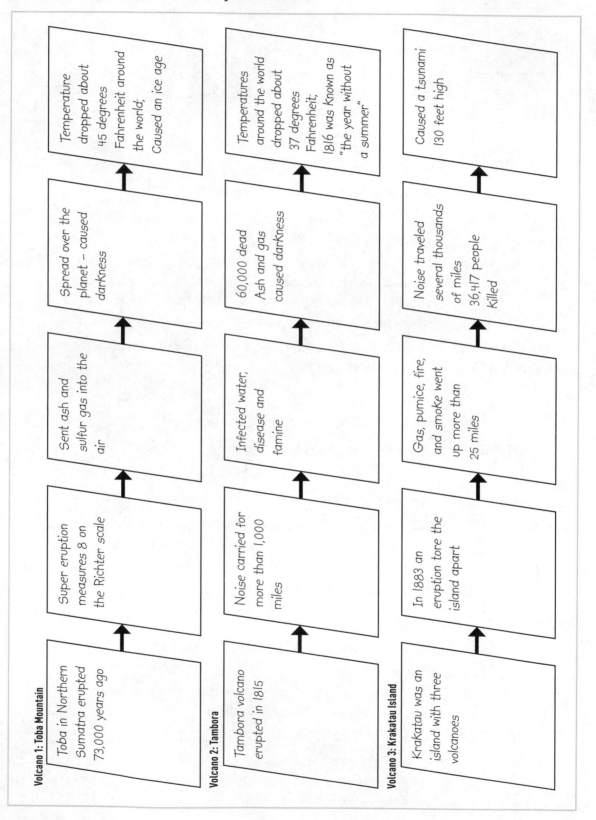

Volcano 1: Toba Mountain

Toba in Northern Sumatra erupted 73,000 years ago → Super eruption measures 8 on the Richter scale → Sent ash and sulfur gas into the air → Spread over the planet – caused darkness → Temperature dropped about 45 degrees Fahrenheit around the world; Caused an ice age

Volcano 2: Tambora

Tambora volcano erupted in 1815 → Noise carried for more than 1,000 miles → Infected water, disease and famine → 60,000 dead Ash and gas caused darkness → Temperatures around the world dropped about 37 degrees Fahrenheit; 1816 was known as "the year without a summer"

Volcano 3: Krakatau Island

Krakatau was an island with three volcanoes → In 1883 an eruption tore the island apart → Gas, pumice, fire, and smoke went up more than 25 miles → Noise traveled several thousands of miles 36,417 people killed → Caused a tsunami 130 feet high

Warming Up

by Paul Coco

BREAKING UP
Part of Antarctica's Larsen B ice shelf collapsed in 2002 and sent thousands of icebergs floating out to sea.

Melting ice in the world's coldest regions is causing trouble for humans and animals

Many animals like penguins and polar bears need to live where it's cold and icy all year. But what will happen if those places get too warm?

It's impossible to predict the future, but recent studies show that temperatures are rising in two of the world's coldest regions—the Arctic and Antarctica. The Arctic is the area around the North Pole *(see map)*, and Antarctica surrounds the South Pole. Warmer weather is causing ice to melt more rapidly than before. That's bad news for the animals that live there.

Although not everyone agrees, some scientists blame the problem on global warming—a gradual rise in the Earth's temperature.

Keeping Cool

Ice is important to the animals and people who live in the polar regions. Polar bears walk on the ice to hunt for food, like seals and fish. Seals come from the water to rest on the ice and to give birth. The Arctic's **indigenous** people hunt and live on the ice.

Now life in the Arctic is getting more difficult. According to a new report called the Arctic Climate Impact Assessment (ACIA), Arctic temperatures have risen by up to seven degrees over the past 50 years. The warm-up has melted an area of ice about the size of Texas and Arizona combined. Some scientists believe the Arctic, which has ice year-round, could be ice free during the summers in about 100 years.

Arctic

Arctic Circle
RUSSIA
FINLAND
SWEDEN
Oslo
NORWAY
North Pole 90° N
Arctic Ocean
ICELAND
Reykjavik
GREENLAND
(Kalaallit nunaat)
(Denmark)
Alaska (U.S.)
Nuuk
Juneau
CANADA

KEY
☆ Country Capital
★ U.S. State Capital
● Area where Ward Hunt Ice Shelf broke apart

POLAR REGION This map shows the Arctic, the area around the North Pole. In 2002, the Ward Hunt Ice Shelf, the largest in the Arctic, broke in two.

Teaching Text Structures © 2007 by Dymock & Nicholson, Scholastic, 183

CHILLING OUT A polar bear takes a rest in Manitoba, Canada.

The report says that polar bears are unlikely to survive as a species if most of the summer sea ice is lost. If the ice disappears, the number of seals will decrease and the bears will have no place to hunt. As a result, many polar bears will starve.

The melting Arctic ice could also affect areas far away. If enough glaciers, which rest on land, melt into the water, global sea levels could rise by about four inches in less than 100 years. Rising sea levels could cover areas of land.

On the opposite side of the world, sea ice in Antarctica is also vanishing: 20 percent of it has melted over the last 50 years. On the Antarctic Peninsula, glaciers are thinning and ice shelves, like the Larsen B, are breaking apart.

Warmer weather is forcing penguins to waddle closer to the South Pole, where it is colder. Penguins need sheets of ice to survive. They raise their young on the ice and that is where they find the sea life that they eat.

Global Problem

Although natural causes can affect Earth's temperatures, some scientists say human activity may be to blame for global warming. Humans use fossil fuels such as oil, coal, and natural gas for heat and power. Burning those fuels releases carbon dioxide, a natural gas, into the air. Too much carbon dioxide traps heat in the Earth's atmosphere, causing temperatures to rise *(see diagram, below)*.

According to geologist Richie Williams, the amount of carbon dioxide released into the atmosphere is rising every year. "No scientist can say for sure what's going to happen next," says Williams, "[but] human activity is accelerating the melt sooner than it would occur naturally."

Although not everyone agrees about global warming and its causes, it's important to find out what can be done to keep the polar bears, penguins, and other creatures happy and healthy on the ice.

Back to You

You can help reduce greenhouse gases in the air. Follow the tips below.

- Turn off lights, computers, televisions when they're not in use.

- In warm weather, ride your bike or walk if you're not going a far distance.

word wise

indigenous: (in-DIJ-uh-nuhss) adjective. Native to a particular environment or region.

atmosphere: (AT-muhss-fihr) noun. The mixture of gases that surrounds a planet.

GREENHOUSE EFFECT
The Earth's atmosphere, or the gases surrounding the planet, holds heat in naturally. Too many gases, like carbon dioxide, can cause it to trap too much heat.

The Greenhouse Effect

ATMOSPHERE

EARTH

1 Sunlight hits Earth.

2 Most heat is trapped in Earth's atmosphere.

3 Some heat escapes to space.

4 Carbon dioxide from cars and factories adds extra heat to Earth's atmosphere.

5 Earth's temperature rises.

SPACE

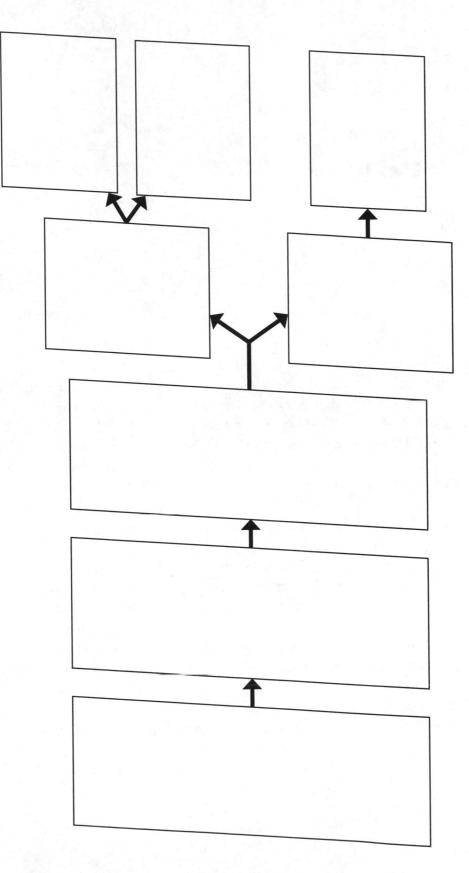

Why Do I Blush?

by Julia Wall

Don't you just hate it when you feel awkward and your face turns red? It's as though the whole world knows exactly how you're feeling—without you telling them!

Blushing usually happens when you are around other people because a group situation makes you more sensitive to what's being said or done. Sometimes embarrassment causes the blushing. Sometimes not telling the truth can make you blush—which can be very awkward because the person you are talking to will have a pretty good idea that you're not telling things the way they really are!

Blushing is connected to feelings, but what's actually happening to you, physically, when your face does the horrible "red" thing? For a start, your brain signals to your body that something is wrong. In response, your heart beats faster, you breathe more quickly, and you start to overheat.

These reactions are signs that your body is preparing itself to either fight or run away from a situation. (This is how our ancestors often reacted a long time ago, for example, when they came face to face with a large woolly mammoth!)

To help cool you down from your "fight or flight" reaction, your blood carries your body's extra heat into tiny vessels called capillaries. The capillaries release the heat into nearby tissue. Because blood is red and the capillaries in your face are very near the surface of your skin, this heat-release makes your face appear red, too.

The situations you experience are much less extreme than those our ancestors faced, so while you deal with the "something wrong" feeling and the fact that you're blushing, you usually just keep behaving normally. Eventually, your face returns to its normal color.

Sounds simple, doesn't it? If only it were as simple not to blush! Next time you feel hot and bothered because of something that embarrasses you, think about all the capillaries in your face that are working to cool you down. This might help take your mind off whatever it is you're blushing about!

Teaching Text Structures © 2007 by Dymock & Nicholson. Scholastic. 186

Why Do I Blush?

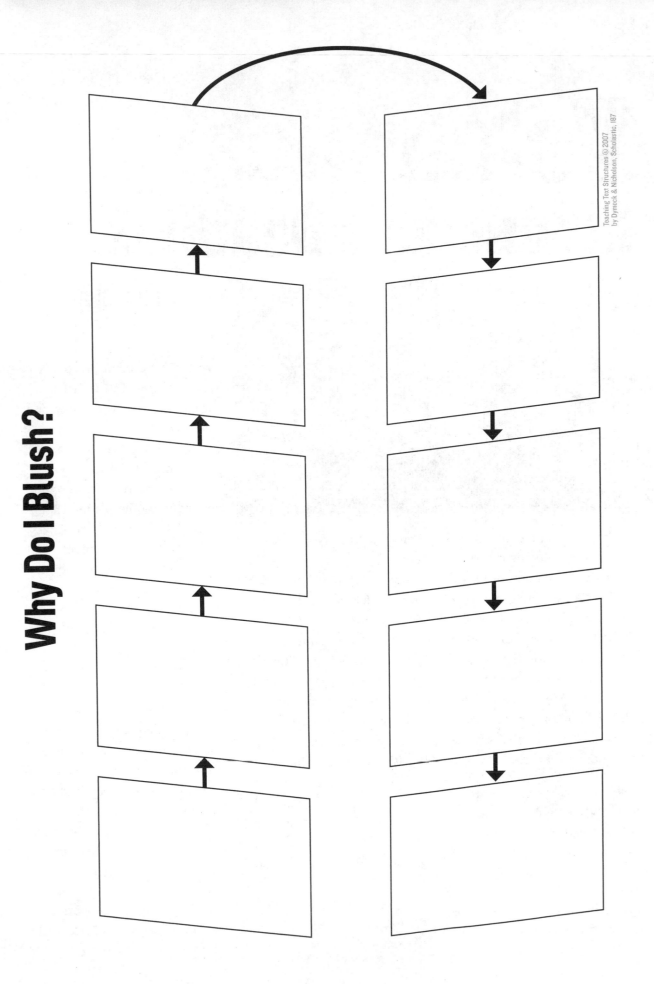

Volcanoes: Indonesia's Deadly 3

by John Malone

Three of the Earth's most violent volcanic explosions have occurred in Indonesia. Krakatau is the most famous of the three—perhaps the most famous of all volcanoes. Most people have never heard of the other two, Mount Toba and Mount Tambora, but in some ways each of them was more destructive than Krakatau.

Toba

The most violent of these three volcanic eruptions happened longest ago, at Toba in northern Sumatra. Today, Lake Toba—62 miles long and around 1,400 feet deep—is a thriving tourist paradise, its waters surrounded by restaurants, resorts, and traditional villages. Evidence of its violent past is well hidden.

But about 73,000 years ago, there was not a lake but a mountain—Mount Toba, a caldera volcano—and it exploded in a *super eruption*, causing earth tremors that would have measured 8 on the Richter scale. That's a very serious earthquake.

The amount of material hurled into the air was massive, enough to bury the whole of Australia under at least 3 feet of ash!

Needless to say, anyone anywhere near the blast would have been killed immediately. But its effects were far more wide ranging than that.

The Toba blast sent so much ash and sulphurous gas into the air, spreading over the whole planet, that scientists believe it must have blocked 90 percent of Earth's usual supply of sunlight! The results were devastating. Darkness covered the Earth's surface and temperatures plummeted, perhaps by as much as 47 degrees Fahrenheit, and even more in the tropics. Such a gigantic cold snap would have caused many plants to die and brought extreme misery to the inhabitants—both animal and human—of our planet.

It was like global warming in reverse, except the temperature change happened over six years instead of over centuries. And instead of warming up after the skies cleared, the

Earth went into a thousand-year-long winter followed by an ice age. Some scientists believe that for 20,000 years after that blast, the human population of our planet did not exceed a few thousand people. When the numbers get this low, some species just "give up" and die out. That was probably as close as humankind has ever come to extinction.

Tambora

The next super eruption took place more recently—April 1815. While the armies of Napoleon (France) and Wellington (England) were fighting over the future of Europe at the Battle of Waterloo, the little-known volcano of Tambora on the island of Sumbawa was preparing to blow up.

Tambora (a stratovolcano, or composite volcano) had been quiet for more than 5,000 years. Then, possibly as early as 1812 it had started giving off big puffs of steam. People living on nearby islands kept hearing small detonations. A large explosion occurred on April 5, 1815 and ash fell on east Java—thunder-like sounds were heard up to many hundreds of miles away.

Six days later the big one occurred. Tambora ripped itself apart.

The explosion was heard more than 1,000 miles away. Like the Battle of Waterloo the eruption had significant consequences. The casualties from both events were similar: some 60,000 dead in Europe from war injuries, and about the same number in Asia

from the explosion and from disease and famine caused by contaminated water and damage to crop lands.

However, Tambora's effect was not just local. Ash and sulphurous gases spewed into the air by the volcano were carried around the planet by the winds, smothering the sunlight. The results were not as severe as when Mount Toba erupted, but they were serious. Global temperatures dropped as much as 37 degrees Fahrenheit. In Europe and North America, 1816 was known as "the year without a summer." That was the year that Mary Shelley wrote her spooky novel, *Frankenstein*. Who knows, without the gloomy atmosphere created by Tambora, she might not have written it.

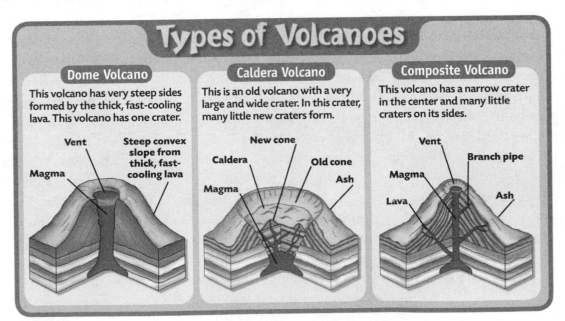

Types of Volcanoes

Dome Volcano
This volcano has very steep sides formed by the thick, fast-cooling lava. This volcano has one crater.

Vent
Steep convex slope from thick, fast-cooling lava
Magma

Caldera Volcano
This is an old volcano with a very large and wide crater. In this crater, many little new craters form.

New cone
Caldera
Old cone
Ash
Magma

Composite Volcano
This volcano has a narrow crater in the center and many little craters on its sides.

Vent
Branch pipe
Magma
Lava
Ash

Krakatau

Krakatau is one of the most famous of all volcanoes—right up there with Mount Vesuvius, which buried the ancient city of Pompeii. Krakatau is the *Titanic* of volcanoes. Though in the long run it had much less impact on our planet than Toba or Tambora, it earned its fame by the *way* it created damage.

Krakatau was actually a small island with not one but three volcanoes, named Rakata, Danan, and Perboewatan. The island lay in the Sundra Strait between the large islands of Java and Sumatra. (It is no longer there, as you will see.)

The destruction of Krakatau—which happened in August 1883—did not happen overnight: there were many warning signs. Several earthquakes occurred in the area up to seven years before the explosion. In 1880 a strong earthquake shook the west end of Java and there was another one only two months before the catastrophe.

Ash and steam eruptions began happening in late May 1883. Within a few months, there were 11 separate volcanic vents spewing out ash and steam. Krakatau was gearing up for something big.

On August 24 the small eruptions grew much stronger—and more frequent. Three days later there were four massive explosions in just under four hours, the first just before dawn. The fourth explosion, at exactly 10:02 A.M., tore Krakatau apart. It is said to be the most violent explosion recorded and experienced in modern times—more violent even than a nuclear bomb. The cloud of gas, white-hot pumice stone, fire and smoke was hurled almost 25 miles into the air. The explosion was heard several thousands of miles away.

One hundred sixty-five villages were destroyed by Krakatau, and 36,417 people were killed. But only about a thousand of those people died from the suffocating gases and scalding heat of the eruption. The rest were killed by the deadly sea waves or *tsunamis* (incorrectly called "tidal waves"—they have nothing to do with tides) that swept villages of Java and Sumatra on either side of the Sunda Strait.

How big were those waves? The tsunami that destroyed one of the villages in Sumatra was more than 130 feet high! Look at a 10-story building and imagine what it would be like to have

An illustrated view of Krakatau, August 26–28, 1883, from the front page of the *Illustrated London News*, September 8, 1883

that height of water come crashing down on you. There is no way you or anyone could survive. You can't run from such a massive wall of water. Not when it's traveling more than 18 miles per hour.

By the time the tsunami reached Surabaya at the eastern end of Java nearly 12 hours after the final explosion, the reported wave was only 8 inches high. Yet a woman in Ceylon (now Sri Lanka), about 3,000 miles away from Krakatau in the other direction, was swept off a harbor jetty by a huge wave and died of her injuries—the most distant death caused by the eruption.

Volcanoes: Indonesia's Deadly 3

Volcano 1: Toba Mountain

Volcano 2: Tambora

Volcano 3: Krakatau Island

CHAPTER 8

Teaching Sequential Structures: Problem-Solution

Problem-solution texts describe a problem and suggest one or more solutions. The author may also offer possible outcomes to the "solved" problem. Time is an element in problem-solution texts. First the problem is explained, solutions to the problem are considered, and over time, the problem is either solved, partially solved, or is not solved. The time it takes to solve a problem can be a matter of minutes, hours, days, or even years. And it is possible that the problem may never be fully solved.

Problems are part of everyday life. From an early age, we encounter problems, and we continue to on a day-to-day basis. The toddler, for example, will need to find a solution to the "square block in a round hole" problem. The toddler might attempt to put the square block into the triangle or the hexagon-shaped holes, but these "solutions" will not solve the problem. It is not until he or she puts the square block into the square hole that the toddler will solve the problem.

Primary-age children encounter many problems at school: social, physical, and educational. These problems can be solved. Because we experience problems, and attempt to solve problems, on a day-to-day basis, the concept of problem-solution is not foreign to students. However, problem-solution texts will most likely be unfamiliar to grades 4 and 5 students because they have not often encountered this text type. Students need to be explicitly shown how problem-solution text is structured. According to Richard Vacca (1998, p. 608), "Often they [students] have trouble learning with texts because, in many cases, they were never shown how." Vacca (1998, p. 608) also suggests that many good decoders don't "know what to do with texts beyond just saying the words." Teaching students how to identify and diagram problem-solution text structures is a research-based strategy that students can learn to enhance their understanding of this text type.

Even though problem-solution structures are not as common in grades 4 to 6 reading material as the web, matrix, and linear string text structures, these readers do, however, encounter problem-solution text structures from time to time—enough that it is important that they learn about this text type. We recommend introducing problem-solution texts when students have a good understanding of the web, matrix, and linear string text structures.

There are several ways of diagramming problem-solution text structures, depending on the way the author has structured the content. Diagram 1 represents a text that begins by identifying a problem. Next the author explains the sequence involved in solving the problem. Diagram 1 shows just two steps, but there will often be more than two steps in the sequence. Finally the solution to the problem is given. This problem-solution text structure explores one solution to the problem.

Diagram 1

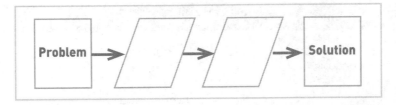

The following two diagrams enable the reader to represent articles that have multiple problems and solutions.

Diagram 2

Problem	Solution

Diagram 3

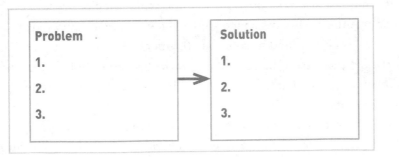

Problem-Solution Articles

This chapter includes three articles that follow a problem-solution structure, and companion lessons. Each lesson follows the CORE model of teaching. At the end of the chapter you will find the articles and diagram templates to photocopy and distribute to students to use in small groups or in a whole-class setting. The table below provides an overview of the articles included in this chapter, giving you a quick guide to the content and grade level of the articles. Keep in mind that sometimes articles also have a secondary structure you can use to enhance the lesson. Refer to the chart on page 7 to cross reference the structures found in the articles.

Summary of Problem-Solution Articles

Title	Topic	Content Area	Grade Level
Going for Green	Busy intersection near school	Social Studies	4
Get Fit	Overweight	Science—Health	4
Koala Chaos	Koala "pests"	Science	5/6+

How to Teach the Problem-Solution Structure

The lessons in the chapter follow the CORE (Connect, Organize, Reflect, Extend) model. When you introduce the passages to students, we suggest using the CORE model (explained in Chapter 3) to tap into students' prior knowledge, discuss unfamiliar concepts, and pronounce words that are hard to decode—before students start reading for themselves.

Prior knowledge is an important factor in text comprehension. The pre- and during-reading discussions provide opportunities to help students connect to the text, by bringing their own knowledge to the "problem" in the article. Remember to encourage students to think about what might be the possible solution while they are reading the article. Comprehension is enhanced if you make students aware beforehand that they will be looking for both a "problem" and a "solution" (Dymock, 1998).

Before you start the lesson, be sure to check the readability of the passages. If the passage is above the assigned grade level in reading difficulty, spend time going over possible sticking points in the text.

For example, the articles in this chapter contain words that may be hard to decode, such as "diabetes" and "ecosystem," "Surgeon General," or "eucalyptus." You may also need to explain concepts, such as "culling," or even places outside of students' experience, such as "City Hall" or "Australia."

Lessons

Going for Green

Rationale "Going for Green" has a problem-solution text structure. The first heading—A Problem—provides an important clue for the reader. The first paragraph then discusses a problem facing a group of school children. The article then explains the steps they take to solve the problem.

Summary Some students at Jefferson Elementary School face a dangerous problem getting to and from school each day. They must cross a busy intersection to get to school. The intersection has a yield sign and during peak traffic times cars back up at the sign. Children going to and from school have to wait for a gap to appear and hurry across the street. Sometimes they walk between cars. Residents at the nearby retirement home also experience difficulties getting to the grocery store across the street. The students decided to collect evidence, write a report, and send the report to City Hall, showing that the problem could be solved by installing traffic lights. After reading the report the mayor agreed that traffic lights were needed. Several weeks later traffic lights were installed. The problem was solved.

To convince City Hall that traffic lights were necessary the students required evidence that there was, in fact, a problem. They decided to conduct a survey to show how busy the intersection was. The survey would:

- Count vehicle numbers

- Show the direction vehicles were traveling

- Count number of pedestrians

- Conduct survey between 8.30 a.m. - 9.00 a.m.; 12 noon - 12.30 p.m.; 3.00 p.m. – 3.30 p.m.

- Videotape cars waiting on 14th street (to enter Main Street)

- Talk to people living at the retirement home who were also affected

The survey, which took place over 10 days, showed that many cars traveled along Main Street—one every four seconds. Many cars also turned into, or out of, 14th Street. The survey also found that between 8.30 a.m. and 9.00 a.m., 55 children crossed 14th Street.

The students felt that traffic lights would solve the problem. They presented their evidence to the mayor and she agreed with their solution. Traffic lights were soon installed at the intersection.

CORE Teaching Ideas

Connect to the Content (Introduction)

TEACHER:	How do you get to and from school each day?
STUDENTS:	I ride my bike. My mom takes me on her way to work. I take the bus.
TEACHER:	Is the bus stop far from your home?
STUDENTS:	I have to walk about three blocks to the bus stop. I have to cross two or three streets. There is not a lot of traffic in the morning but in the afternoon there is a lot of traffic. Once a car nearly hit me. My mom takes me to school on her way to work. I have to cross several busy streets to get to school. Once my friends and I were so busy talking we forgot to check if any cars were coming before we crossed the road. The car driver honked his horn at us. Intersections can be really dangerous.
TEACHER:	I agree. Intersections can be very dangerous. There are different ways of controlling intersections. What are the different ways?
STUDENTS:	Stop signs. Traffic lights.
TEACHER:	Yes, stop signs and traffic lights are two ways of controlling an intersection. How does the city decide whether to use a stop sign or a set of traffic lights at an intersection?
STUDENTS:	We have stop signs near my home but when we go downtown there are mostly traffic lights. Maybe stop signs are used when there is not a lot of traffic. But if there are a lot of cars they use traffic lights.
TEACHER:	Today we are reading an article about children who walk to and from school each day. Many of the children cross a busy intersection to get to school. The intersection has a yield sign. What does yield mean?
STUDENTS:	It means to give way but you don't have to stop. I think you are supposed to slow down and check to see if any cars are coming but you don't have to stop. We have a yield sign near my house. Dad slows down but there are hardly ever any cars.
TEACHER:	Good point. Yield signs are great when there is not a lot of traffic.

Connect to the Structure (Before reading)

TEACHER: This is not the case in the article we are going to read. The children in the article "Going for Green" must cross a busy intersection to get to school. The intersection has a yield sign. The children think the yield sign is causing a problem. The cars back up behind the yield sign and when there is a gap the cars move fast to get through the intersection. The children think the intersection is dangerous.

        As you read the article I want you to think about how the children go about solving their problem.

Organize (After reading)

TEACHER: What did you think of the article?

STUDENTS: I think it is great to see that children can make a difference! I can see why the children wanted to solve the problem.

TEACHER: I can too. I have drawn a problem-solution structure on the board. What was the problem in this article?

- Children had to cross a busy intersection to get to and from school
- The intersection had a yield sign so cars back up
- Some cars drove fast when a gap in the traffic appeared
- People in the retirement village also had difficulties crossing the road

How was the problem solved?

- Children needed evidence that there was a problem.
- Children conducted a survey. The survey
  - Counted vehicle numbers
  - Showed the direction vehicles were traveling
  - Counted the number of pedestrians
  - Survey conducted between 8.30 a.m.-9.00 a.m.; 12 noon-12.30 p.m.; 3.00 p.m.-3.30 p.m.
  - Videotaped cars waiting on 14th street (to enter Main Street)
  - Talked to people living at the retirement home
- Survey results showed that there was a high number of cars traveling along Main Street and turning into, and out of, Main Street.
- The children presented their evidence to the mayor showing that traffic lights were needed.
- The mayor agreed and traffic lights were installed.

Problem	Solution
Children cross a busy intersection to get to and from school. At times it is very dangerous.	Traffic lights.
The intersection is controlled by a yield sign. Cars back up.	Traffic lights.
Some cars drive fast when a gap in the traffic appears.	Traffic lights.
Elderly people living in a nearby retirement home also have difficulties crossing the road.	Traffic lights.

Reflect

TEACHER: What text structure does "Going for Green" have?

STUDENTS: A problem-solution structure.

TEACHER: Yes. This article has clues that it is a problem-solution structure. What are the clues?

STUDENTS: The first heading is "A Problem." This is a good clue that the article will be a problem-solution structure. Toward the end of the article there is a heading "Solution." Between these two headings the author explains how the children went about solving the problem.

TEACHER: An excellent answer. However, not all problem-solution articles begin with this kind of heading. Readers must know how to identify the structure when there are no headings. Why is it important to identify the text structure the writer has used?

STUDENTS: So we know what to look for when we read. If it is a matrix structure we will be looking for different information than a problem-solution text structure.

Extend Students could consider alternative solutions to the problem in "Going for Green"—exploring the advantages and disadvantages of each solution. For example, school patrols could monitor the crossing before and after school. This solves the problem for the school children but not the people in the retirement home who cross the road to get to the grocery store. The retirement home might consider having a small grocery store at the home for its residents to use.

Students could investigate problems that their fellow students have getting to and from school. Are there safety issues that need to be addressed?

Going for Green Answers

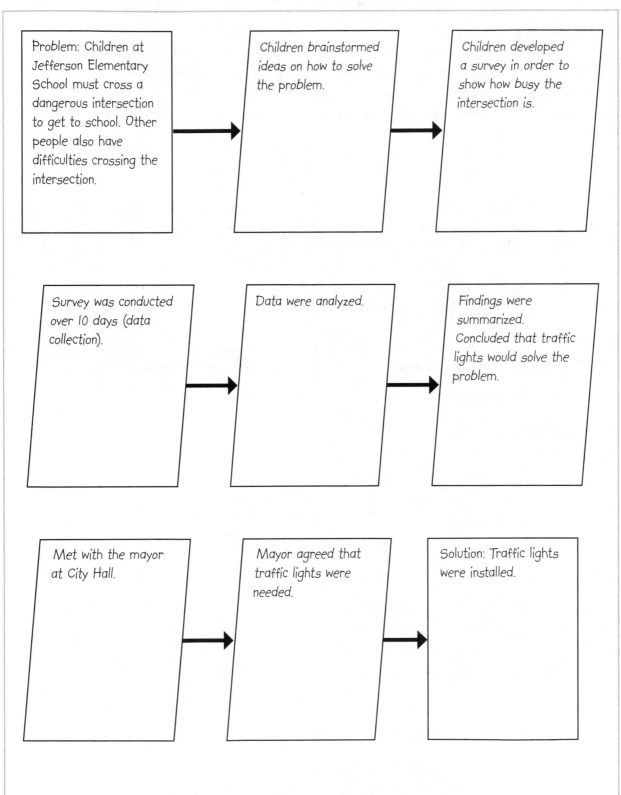

Problem: Children at Jefferson Elementary School must cross a dangerous intersection to get to school. Other people also have difficulties crossing the intersection.

Children brainstormed ideas on how to solve the problem.

Children developed a survey in order to show how busy the intersection is.

Survey was conducted over 10 days (data collection).

Data were analyzed.

Findings were summarized. Concluded that traffic lights would solve the problem.

Met with the mayor at City Hall.

Mayor agreed that traffic lights were needed.

Solution: Traffic lights were installed.

Get Fit

Rationale The structure of "Get Fit" is problem-solution. This article illustrates the structure well because it states a problem—many American kids are overweight. Then it gives several reasons for the problem, followed by some solutions. Reading the article is a great lead in to a discussion on what schools might do to combat obesity. For example, schools in New Zealand now provide fruit to their pupils every day and have banned fatty foods altogether. Students could discuss whether that is a good solution. Will it solve the problem? Should schools even be involved? Exploring questions like these will help prepare them for the lessons in Chapter 9 on the persuasion/argument text structure.

Summary "Get Fit" discusses why we need to exercise often and eat the right foods. It explains that about 9 million young Americans are overweight, about one in every six children. Research suggests that the percentage of children between 6 and 11 years who are overweight has tripled since the 1970s. It seems that children are eating too many sugary foods and they are not exercising. Instead they are watching TV or playing video games on computers. This is a real problem. Weight gain is due to a poor diet and lack of exercise. Children need to eat the right foods and get more active. Some schools are introducing exercise programs that include jumping jacks, sit-ups, and yoga. Other good exercises are riding a bike, jogging, jumping rope, dancing, walking, and swimming.

CORE Teaching Ideas

Connect to the Content (Introduction)

TEACHER:	How did you get to school today?
STUDENTS:	My dad drove me. I caught the bus.
TEACHER:	Did anyone ride a bike or walk?
STUDENTS:	It's too dangerous. The roads are busy. If we walk we might get mugged.
TEACHER:	Yes, but how else will you get exercise?
STUDENTS:	Watching TV? Working on our computers?
TEACHER:	Not really. If you work on your computer you will use 30 calories an hour. If you watch TV for an hour you will use 20 calories but if you go jogging for an hour you will lose 500 calories. Even if you walk fast for an hour you will lose 200 calories. The problem is, if you do not get enough exercise you will put on weight because you will be eating more calories than you are losing.

Connect to the Structure (Before reading)

TEACHER: This article is called "Get Fit" and it explains that we are taking in more calories than we are using up. The article suggests a solution to the problem. So, before you start reading, what kind of text structure do you think this article will be?

STUDENTS: Problem-solution, that's easy.

TEACHER: Is there anything in the key headings in the article that would support the idea that it is a problem-solution text?

STUDENTS: There are some key words. There is a subheading called "a big problem." In one paragraph it states "To fight the problem,..." When you see words like "problem" it makes you think that this is a problem-solution type of article.

TEACHER: Exactly. I want you to read the article, and then use the problem-solution worksheet to fill in the main points. Work in small groups to do this activity.

Organize (After reading)

TEACHER: What did you think of the article?

STUDENTS: It is quite scary that so many children are overweight. It says in the article that children should exercise every day for an hour.

TEACHER: Now that you have read the article what ideas do you have to improve your diet?

STUDENTS: Instead of eating chips for lunch I can eat fruit. I can eat a sandwich instead of cake, and drink water instead of soda.

TEACHER: What about exercise?

STUDENTS: I can ask my dad if he will walk me to school. It will take a bit longer but it will be good exercise.

TEACHER: I've heard that in some schools parents take turns walking a whole lot of children to school. It's called a "walking bus." I'll see if your parents might be interested.

Draw a problem-solution structure on the whiteboard. Ask students for a statement of the problem.

- Children aren't eating enough healthy foods
- Children aren't getting enough exercise
- 9 million children in America are overweight
- Children are spending too much time using computers, playing video games, and watching TV.
- Children are eating too many sugary foods like chocolate and drinking too much soda

Ask students for a statement of the solution.

- Health experts recommend an hour of exercise every day
- Exercise can mean jogging, riding a bike, jumping rope, dancing, swimming, and many other fun activities.
- Some schools have started exercise programs like Power 90, which include jumping jacks, sit-ups, and yoga.
- Health experts recommend eating the right combination of fruits, dairy, meats, and whole grains.

Reflect

TEACHER:	What was the purpose of the lesson today?
STUDENTS:	To find out how heavy we are!
TEACHER:	Not really. The article is not suggesting that everyone should be skinny. It is suggesting that we will be a lot healthier if we exercise and eat the right foods.
STUDENTS:	We learned that the article had a problem-solution structure. These structures seem easy to figure out because they often have key words like "Problem" and "Solution."
TEACHER:	Good point. But not all articles have such clues. You still need to be able to think for yourself about how the article is structured.

Extend Students could do a small project. Suggest to them that they might keep a food and exercise diary that describes the foods they eat and the exercise they are doing each day. They could keep the diary for two weeks to see if it helps them to eat better foods and engage in more exercise. In addition, they could write an article about their progress over the two weeks. They could state the problem: what they are eating and doing now. At the end of the two weeks, they could write in their solution: eating better foods and getting more exercise.

Get Fit Answers

Problem	Solution
1. Children are eating more calories than they are losing	1. Eat healthier foods. Eating smart means more vegetables, meats, dairy products, and whole grains.
2. 9 million American children are overweight	2. Schools can ban fattening food like ice cream.
3. Children are eating too much junk food and sugary food	3. Schools can have fitness programs that include going to the gym and doing yoga
4. Children are not getting enough exercise	4. Experts recommend that children exercise for an hour every day: biking, jogging, swimming, dancing, jumping, or some other games that involve moving your body.
5. Children are watching TV, using computers, playing video games	5. Keep a fitness plan. Write down what things you do each day so you can see your progress.

Koala Chaos

Rationale "Koala Chaos" has a problem-solution text structure. The article discusses how what is once believed to be a solution can actually become another problem. It also shows that one problem can have several different solutions.

Summary "Koala Chaos" discusses the problem facing the koala population living on Kangaroo Island, located off the southern coast of Australia. During the 1920s many Australians were concerned that koalas would become extinct so scientists took 18 koalas to Kangaroo Island. The koalas liked their new home and today there are over 27,000 koalas living on Kangaroo Island. The problem is that their only food source, the eucalyptus tree, is dying. When koalas eat the leaves of the eucalyptus tree, the branch dies, and if too many branches die, the tree dies. The farming industry is also affected by dying eucalyptus trees. The roots keep the soil in place, and soil can be washed away by rain if it is not held in place by the roots of trees. Controlled killing of koalas, relocating some of the koalas, and using surgery that prevents koalas from reproducing are all possible solutions to the problem. Scientists believe that if the problem is not solved soon, the "koalas may eat their way out of a home."

CORE Teaching Ideas

Connect to the Content (Introduction)

Show students a picture of a koala. Find out what students know about the koala.

TEACHER: What is the name of this animal? Where does it live? What can you tell me about the animal? How do you think it spends its day?

If students are unable to answer these questions, explain that koalas are a native animal of Australia. Locate Australia on a map. The koalas' diet consists only of eucalyptus leaves. Eucalyptus leaves are not very nutritious so koalas sleep for about 20 hours a day.

TEACHER: "Koala Chaos" is the title of the article you are reading today. Why do you think the article has the word "chaos" in it?

STUDENTS: Maybe the koalas are causing problems in Australia. They might be bothering tourists or the people living in Australia. They don't look like they would cause chaos. They sleep most of the day and night —so how could they cause chaos?

TEACHER: Good question. How could a cuddly animal that sleeps for about 20 hours each day cause chaos?

Connect to the Structure (Before reading)

TEACHER: Let's read the article and find out. The article we are going to read today has a problem-solution text structure. The article talks about the koala problem on Kangaroo Island and offers several solutions. One problem is that the people cannot agree on how to solve the problem. As you read "Koala Chaos" think about the problem and the various solutions that are suggested.

Organize (After reading)

TEACHER: What is the problem in the article?

STUDENTS: There are too many koalas living on Kangaroo Island and soon there will not be enough food for them all. Another problem is the people cannot agree how to solve the problem.

TEACHER: Excellent point. What are some of the solutions discussed in the article? *(Controlled killing, relocate some of the koalas, surgery to prevent koalas from having babies)*

STUDENTS: But some people think the koalas are not the problem. They think the problem is because the land has not been managed well. It seems they think that if the land on the island was better managed then there would be enough food for the koalas. Eventually there will not be enough food. The last sentence of the article says that "koalas may eat their way out of a home." It would be awful if they starved to death.

TEACHER: I agree. It would not be good if the koalas starved. But I'm sure that the scientists and others will find a good solution. In the meantime, let's focus on diagramming the article. If we do this, the diagram will help to show the problem and the solutions more clearly.

Reflect

TEACHER: What have we learned from this article?

STUDENTS: People do not always agree on the same solution. There are the people who live on Kangaroo Island, the scientists, the Australian government and the Australian Koala Foundation all trying to solve the problem. Hopefully everyone will be happy with the final solution. Perhaps there will be several solutions. In the meantime the koalas keep having babies and so there are even more koalas. The problem just gets worse.

TEACHER: I agree. This is not an easy problem to solve. But it can be solved.

Extend Students can explore additional possible solutions to the koala problem. See if they can reach a consensus.

This article also has a list structure because the characteristics of the koala are found throughout the article. Students could list the characteristics that are stated in the article and then carry out further research on koalas, adding to their list. Students could also develop a web that describes the characteristics of koalas from information in the article and from their own research.

Koala Chaos Answers (Problem-Solution)

Problem	Solution
Residents of Kangaroo Island say the 27,000 koalas have become a giant pest	Residents & Scientists: Controlled Kill Government: Relocate Koalas Government: Surgery to prevent Koalas from having babies.
Koalas eat eucalyptus leaves. When a branch is stripped of its leaves the branch dies. When branches die eventually the tree dies. Koalas are killing the trees.	Residents & Scientists: Controlled Kill Government: Relocate Koalas Government: Surgery to prevent Koalas from having babies.
Kangaroo Island's ecosystem is in danger. Why? - One group blame koalas - One group blames industries that have cut down eucalyptus trees.	Residents & Scientists: Cull Koalas AKF: Manage land better.
Farming industry has been affected.	Manage land better.

Koala Chaos Answers (List)

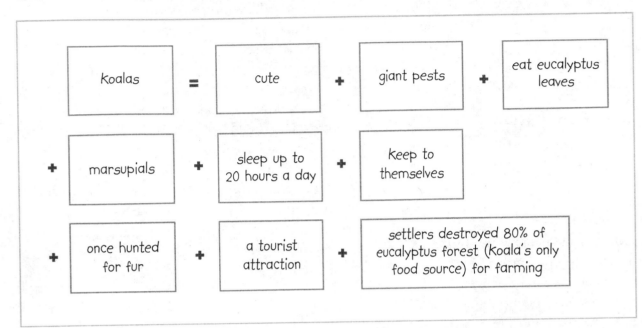

Going for Green

by Bill O'Brien

A Problem

Jefferson Elementary used to have a big problem. Getting there could be very dangerous. The school is near the busy intersection of Main and 14th streets. The traffic on 14th Street would often back up at the yield sign. Sometimes there would be a long wait for a break in the traffic on Main Street. When a gap came, drivers on 14th Street would drive fast to get through the intersection. Often, children crossing 14th Street had to walk between the cars that were waiting at the yield sign. This was dangerous.

A group of fourth grade students had been thinking about this problem. It wasn't just their friends that they were worried about. People from the nearby retirement home had trouble getting to the grocery store on the corner. Maybe the traffic lights would solve the problem.

Ideas

After a brainstorming session, the students decided to do a survey to show how busy the intersection was. Their teacher, Mrs. Sanchez, agreed. She said that the people of City Hall would need **evidence** to be convinced that something needed to be done.

The students wrote some survey forms. They needed to count the number of vehicles using the roads and show which way those vehicles were traveling. They also needed to count the number of **pedestrians**. The best times to do the survey were just before school began, lunchtimes, and when school had finished.

The Survey

The class separated into five groups. Three groups did the **tallies** on the corner of Main and 14th streets. One group

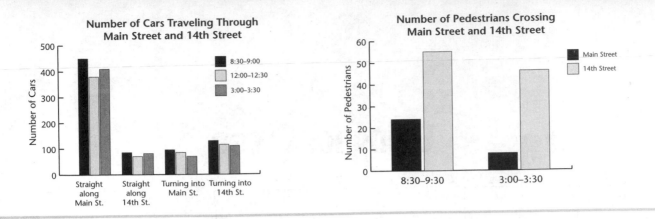

Number of Cars Traveling Through Main Street and 14th Street

Number of Cars / 500 / 400 / 300 / 200 / 100 / 0

8:30–9:00 / 12:00–12:30 / 3:00–3:30

Straight along Main St. / Straight along 14th St. / Turning into Main St. / Turning into 14th St.

Number of Pedestrians Crossing Main Street and 14th Street

Number of Pedestrians / 60 / 50 / 40 / 30 / 20 / 10 / 0

Main Street / 14th Street

8:30–9:30 / 3:00–3:30

was there from 8:30 A.M. to 9:00 A.M., another group from 12 noon to 12:30 P.M., and another from 3:00 P.M. to 3:30 P.M. The fourth group made a video of the cars that were waiting on 14th Street. While they were filming, a car went through the intersection and crashed into a van that hadn't yielded at the sign.

The fifth group talked to the people at the retirement home, some of whom were in wheelchairs. They asked about how difficult it was to get to the grocery store. Most answered that it was almost impossible to cross the road.

Results

To get a good **sample**, the students carried out the survey over 10 days. When they had their tallies, the students made bar graphs. The graphs showed that the busiest times were before and after school.

Between 8:30 A.M. and 9:00 A.M. each day, an average of 450 cars traveled along Main Street. That's one car every four seconds. At the same time, 130 cars turned into, or out of, 14th Street.

Because the cars on 14th Street backed up, the children had to walk between them to cross the road. In the 30 minutes before school, an average of 55 children crossed 14th Street.

Summary

The students wrote statements to summarize their findings.

1. The intersection of Main and 14th streets is close to Jefferson Elementary, and lots of children cross there.

2. There is a lot of traffic at certain times of the day.

3. The intersection is close to a retirement home, and it's often hard for the people to get to the grocery store.

4. Children often follow adults and cross between waiting cars, which is dangerous.

Solution

The students agreed that the intersection needed traffic lights. They went with their principal to City Hall. They showed the mayor the evidence that they'd collected. She promised to look into the problem. A couple of weeks later, the students got a letter from the mayor. City Hall had

decided the students were right. Traffic lights would be installed at the intersection.

Conclusion

It didn't take long for this to happen. In a few weeks, traffic lights were put in. Now the children at Jefferson Elementary and the people at the retirement home can get to where they're going safely. The solution to the problem was a good one.

word wise

evidence: proof of something

pedestrian: a person who travels by foot

sample: an example of a whole thing

tally: a number that is recorded

Going for Green

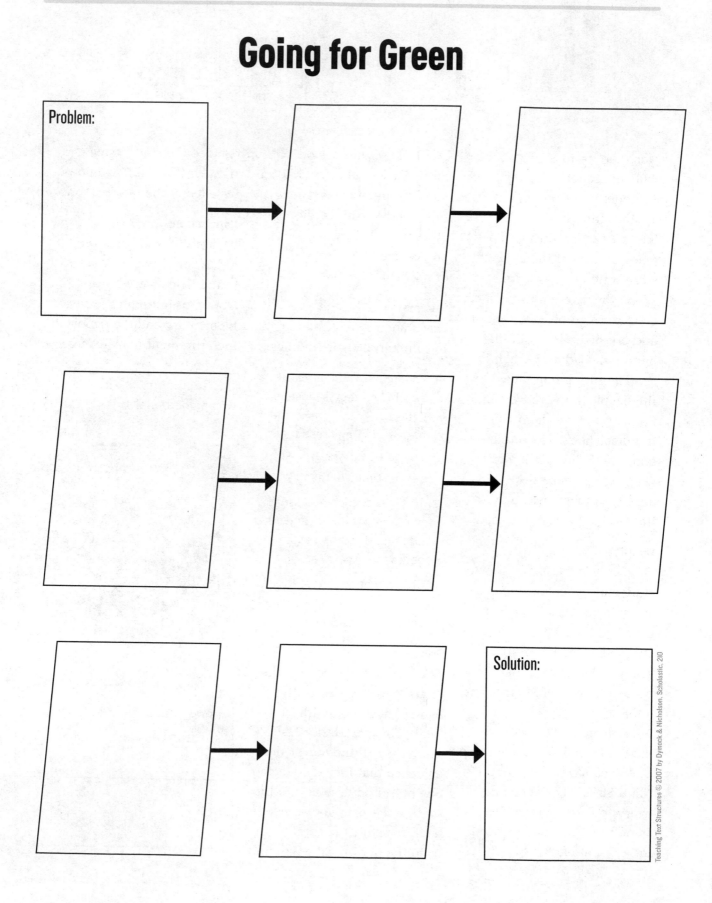

Problem:

Solution:

Get Fit!

by Paul Coco

Stay healthy and have fun by exercising often and eating the right foods

Think about what you do on an average day. When you're in the cafeteria, do you reach for ice cream or an apple? Do you plop in front of the TV after school or ride a bike outside?

Today, many American kids aren't eating healthy foods or spending enough time running, jumping, or even walking. Instead, they're munching on sugary snacks like chocolate and soda, while sitting inside to play video games. Does this sound like your daily routine?

Recent studies show that about 9 million young Americans between the ages of 6 and 19 are overweight. That is about one out of every six kids in the United States. Weight gain caused by a poor diet and lack of exercise can lead to serious health problems, such as heart disease and **diabetes**, when you get older.

Fortunately, you can stay in shape and have fun just by moving your body and eating the right foods. So, head outside to exercise and keep your body healthy.

A Big Problem

What makes people overweight? Weight gain can occur when the body takes in more calories from food and drinks than it uses up through physical activity. The more you move around, the more calories you burn off.

Unfortunately, many kids today aren't moving. Instead, they're using computers, watching TV, and playing video games. A recent study by the U.S. Department of Health and Human Services found that the percentage of kids ages 6 to 11 who are seriously overweight has

Fitness Fun!

Some health experts recommend that kids get an hour of exercise each day, or on most days. It's easy to get moving. Once you get hooked on exercising, you'll have more energy, build muscle, and make your heart stronger. Here are some fun ways to get active:

- Ride a bike or go for a jog.
- Get involved in a game of tennis, volleyball, or kickball.
- Jump rope.
- Dance along to your favorite music.
- Take a long walk with a friend or relative.

- Hit the pool for a swim.
- No matter what exercise you do, experts agree that it's best to set up a fitness plan. Keep track of how often you do an activity so you can see how much progress you've made and reward yourself for your hard work.

GET MOVING! Going for a run or taking a long walk are great ways to exercise and stay healthy.

more than tripled since the 1970s. According to the U.S. **Surgeon General**, one in seven American kids does not regularly participate in any physical activity.

To fight the problem, the U.S. government recently issued new guidelines for healthy living. The guidelines recommend that all kids—not just those who are overweight—should get one hour of exercise on most days *(see Fitness Fun!)*.

Getting active helps you to be healthy, but you also need to eat the right foods. Eating smart means that you feed your body more fruits, vegetables, dairy, and whole grains *(see sidebar, far right)*.

Be Good to Your Body

Today, families, schools, and health experts are working hard to keep kids fit. Public schools in Maryland have cracked down on fattening food. Ice cream has been taken out of some school cafeterias in that state, while snack carts sell only foods low in fat and sugar. Schools in other states such as Texas and California have removed sugary soda and junk food from cafeterias and vending machines.

Kids are also getting into the workout action.

Many schools across the country are creating physical fitness programs to get kids excited about exercise. In January, students in Medina, Tennessee, began a 90-day fitness program called Power 90. As part of the program, students do jumping jacks, situps, and yoga in their physical education classes.

Are these programs helping kids get fit? Medina student Madison Morris, 12, believes they are. "You can definitely feel the exercises working on your body," Madison says. "They make me feel better about myself."

Back to You

March is National Nutrition Month, a good time to think about eating healthy foods.

Make a list of the foods you eat that are high in fat and sugar. Then make another list of healthy foods you could eat instead. Try to eat more items from the list of healthy foods.

word wise

diabetes: (dye-uh-BEE-teez) noun. A disease in which there is too much sugar in the blood.

Surgeon General: (SUR-juhn JEN-ur-uhl) noun. The nation's top doctor.

EAT SMART!

Follow some of the tips below to stay healthy.

FRUITS & VEGETABLES
Oranges, bananas, and carrots make great snacks and are packed with vitamins and minerals. Experts suggest that kids like you eat five servings of fruits and vegetables each day.

POWERFUL PROTEIN Meats, chicken, turkey, fish, eggs, and nuts are super sources of protein. Protein builds body tissue and helps protect you from diseases.

DYNAMITE DAIRY Milk, yogurt, and cheese contain vitamin D and calcium, which helps build strong bones and muscles. Drinking skim or 1 percent milk is a healthy way to get your protein.

GREAT GRAINS Bread, pasta, cereal, and rice fuel the body with energy to help keep you going during exercise.

HEALTHY CHOICES Skip soda and drink water instead. Ask for a salad or baked potato instead of french fries.

COLORFUL Eat fruits and veggies that are different colors so your body absorbs nutrients from each color group.

Get Fit

Problem	Solution
Children are eating more calories than they are losing.	

Teaching Text Structures © 2007 by Dymock & Nicholson, Scholastic, 213

Koala Chaos

by Mona Chiang

KOALAS LIVING ON AN AUSTRALIAN ISLAND ARE AT THE HEART OF A HEATED DEBATE

Each year, thousands of tourists flock to scenic Kangaroo Island in Australia. For many, the trip's highlight is spotting a fuzzy koala. But for many of the 4,000 residents of Kangaroo Island, as well as conservationists, these furry creatures are far from cute. They are giant pests.

A plan to help rebuild Australia's koala population by bringing the animals to Kangaroo Island has been too successful, some conservationists say. They say that the island's 27,000 koalas are more than it can handle. The koalas are eating so many eucalyptus tree leaves that the trees are dying, which puts the island's **ecosystem** in danger, conservationists argue. Because of this, many scientists and residents are calling for a massive koala cull, or controlled killing.

But this idea has some people, including the Australian Koala Foundation (AKF), protesting. AKF says poor land management—not koalas—is to blame for the island's ecosystem problems. Also, many people don't want the cuddly creatures harmed.

How did the koala, an animal that does little besides eat and sleep, wind up at the center of this tug-of-war?

Moving Koalas

Koalas are marsupials, a group of animals in which the females carry and nurse their young in pouches. The cuddly creatures once **thrived** all over Australia *(see map)*. But when European settlers arrived in the late 1700s, they hunted millions of the animals for their fluffy fur. They also destroyed as much as 80 percent of the koalas' forest habitat for farmland. Due to

MUNCH MUNCH Koalas eat eucalyptus tree leaves, which have little nutritional value. That's why they sleep up to 20 hours a day!

limited living spaces and its sole food source—eucalyptus tree leaves—drastically reduced, the koala population tumbled.

"People were concerned that the koalas would go extinct," says David Paton, a biologist at the University of Adelaide in Australia.

So during the 1920s, scientists introduced 18 koalas to Kangaroo Island. The population did not just thrive there, it exploded.

Picky Eaters

Such a koala boom may not seem like bad news. But

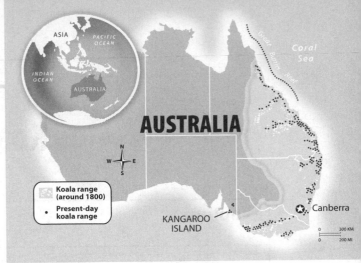

AUSTRALIA

Koala range (around 1800)
• Present-day koala range

KANGAROO ISLAND

Canberra

koalas have big appetites. A koala must eat approximately 1,000 eucalyptus leaves each day to survive. When koalas keep stripping a eucalyptus tree branch of its leaves, the branch dies. If too many branches die, the tree dies. "Koalas can kill a tree bit by bit," says Paton. When that happens, all the animals that depend on the tree for survival—including the koalas—suffer.

Losing eucalyptus trees also affects the island's farming industry. Tree roots deep in the land keep soil in place. Without eucalyptus trees, rain washes away soil, reducing the quality of farmable land.

But not everyone believes that koalas are to blame for tree and soil loss on Kangaroo Island. Deborah Tabart, who runs AKF, says industries, including farming, are the culprits because they have cleared large areas of eucalyptus forests. Tabart says better land management will help repair the ecosystem and sustain koalas and other island species.

Chaos Control

Tabart and the AKF say Australia's way of dealing with the koalas is inhumane.

The government has relocated hundreds of island koalas to parts of mainland Australia. However, koalas get stressed easily, so they don't adapt well to new surroundings and often get sick. In addition, the government recently announced a plan to perform medical operations on 8,000 island koalas. The surgeries would prevent the koalas from having babies.

Paton believes this plan won't lead to a major reduction in the koala population. He believes that the most effective way to control Kangaroo Island's koala population is to cull 20,000 of the animals. But that will be hard to do. Koalas are protected by the law. The Australian government has struck down proposals to allow a koala cull, in part out of concern that a cull would create negative images that would drive away the tourists Australia depends on.

In the meantime, Paton and other scientists estimate that the koala population on Kangaroo Island will double within five years. Paton fears that without a sound solution soon, "the koalas may eat their way out of a home."

word wise

ecosystem: (ee-koh-SISS-tuhm) noun. A community of animals and plants, interacting with their environment

thrive: (thrive) verb. To do well and flourish

SAY CHEESE This photo may make you think that koalas are social beings, but these animals usually keep to themselves

Koala Chaos

Problem	Solution
Residents of Kangaroo Island say 27,000 Koalas have become a giant nuisance.	

CHAPTER 9

Teaching Persuasion/ Argument Structures

Students are often asked to argue the case for or against something, both in their lives and in school, through class debates or writing on topics of interest, such as whether we should only eat organic food, whether cars should be taxed to pay for freeways, whether performance-enhancing drugs should be allowed in sports, whether cell phones should be banned in schools, and so on.

Articles can be a useful way to see how writers handle these issues. They give students some models of how this kind of writing is done, as do opinion columns in magazines and newspapers. School magazines are another source for discussion of these issues.

A persuasive/argument text makes a claim and then presents evidence to support the claim (Chambliss & Calfee, 1998). A claim is something like the theme or message of the article. Argument texts seem to be more easily understood than other texts and perhaps this is because they have a simple structure: a claim, and then evidence to support the claim.

In a persuasion/argument text, an idea is put forward and then facts and opinions are given to support it. The writer makes the case for, against, or both. Advertisements are typical persuasion texts. They make claims and give arguments to support the claim. Claims like "Now is the time to...," "Christmas is for giving...," "Outstanding offer...," "People love to...," and "Why you should vote for me..." signal that you are reading an ad.

Discussion texts give facts and opinions both for and against. The "for-against" argument text is triggered by words like "debate" and "discuss," which require the writer to give information that supports both sides of the question. Words like "Should we...," "The question of...," "A difficult issue...," and so on signal to readers that it is a discussion text. The text offers arguments for and against, along with a conclusion that restates the main message.

For	Against

The design of the persuasion/argument text is simple: it gives arguments for and against, or both. The topic of the text is the "claim," which can be in the form of a definite statement such as "Fossil fuels should be banned" or in the form of a question such as "Should schools have prize-giving ceremonies at the end of the year?"

Persuasion/Argument Articles

The two articles in this chapter have a persuasion/argument structure. In the article "War: Who Wants to Remember It?" the writer asked school students to make arguments both for and against remembering war. In "The Freeway Debate," the City Council asked the public for its opinion on whether a freeway should be extended through the city. The public came up with arguments both for and against.

At the end of the chapter you will find the articles and diagram templates to photocopy and distribute to students to use in small groups or in a whole-class setting. The table below provides an overview of the articles, giving you a quick guide to their content. We suggest that it might be better to start with the article "War: Who Wants To Remember It?" since it is simpler than "The Freeway Debate."

Summary of Persuasion/Argument Articles

Title	Topic	Content Area	Grade Level
War: Who Wants to Remember It?	Arguments for and against remembering wars	Social Studies	6
The Freeway Debate	Arguments for and against building freeways into cities	Social Studies	6+

How to Teach the Persuasion/Argument Structures

When you introduce the passages to students, we suggest using the CORE model (explained in Chapter 3) to tap into students' prior knowledge, discuss unfamiliar concepts, and pronounce words that are hard to decode—before students start reading for themselves.

Before you start the lesson, be sure to check the readability of the passages. If the passage is above the assigned grade level in reading difficulty, spend time going over possible sticking points in the text.

For example, "The Freeway Debate" is quite long and contains many words that are hard to decode and probably unfamiliar, such as "emissions," "chasm," "upheaval," and "Ngauranga Gorge." You may also want to point out Auckland and Wellington on a map of New Zealand, as well as Portland, Oregon, and Los Angeles, California, to help put the places discussed in this article into some context.

It's much easier typically to make links between a topic in a persuasion/argument text and students' lives because students have their own opinions about things that they often want to share. Invite students to discuss some of the topics they think are currently important and why.

Lessons

War: Who Wants to Remember It?

Rationale This is an argument text. In an argument text, facts, emotions, and opinions both for and against are given. In this text the argument design is signaled by the topic: "War: Who Wants to Remember It?" It implies that some will want to remember and some will not. There are also some clues to the text design in the first paragraph. There is a sentence that suggests a possible debate: "Is Anzac Day something we should continue to commemorate or are past conflicts best forgotten?" The words in the text suggest two options. This "either-or" pattern offers two alternatives. We can use this pattern to present arguments for and against remembering wars.

An argument text of this kind will also bring out emotions that do not necessarily relate to the facts. Calfee and Chambliss (1987) state that emotional arguments "rely on background knowledge and beliefs shared by author and reader" (p. 368).

Summary The topic of "War: Who Wants to Remember It?" allows for arguments for and against wars. The arguments in this article are:

FOR

1. Soldiers in the war thought they were doing the right thing.

2. The families of the soldiers who fought and died need a way to remember them.

3. The people who fought in wars, helped us to have a free life.

4. Many people have relatives who died in wars, and they want to remember them.

5. When we remember wars, we remember how awful they are and this will stop us from rushing into new wars.

AGAINST

1. Remembering wars only glorifies them.

2. Old wars mean nothing to today's children and teenagers.

3. Many people who opposed past wars were punished—we should respect their feelings against wars.

4. Many of our old "enemies" are now our friends. Remembering old wounds can hurt feelings.

5. It is morally wrong to support wars by remembering them.

CORE Teaching Ideas

Connect to the Content (before reading)

TEACHER: In New Zealand, there is a special holiday on the 25th of April called Anzac Day. Anzac stands for Australia and New Zealand Army Corps. Many families attend special remembrance ceremonies around the country. The ceremonies are to remember a war. On Anzac Day, people wear paper poppies on their shirts as a sign that they remember that day. The ceremonies remember soldiers who fought in the Battle of Gallipoli during World War I, nearly 100 years ago. In this battle, England and its allies invaded the Turkish peninsula called Gallipoli. Many Australian and New Zealand soldiers died in this battle. This was just one of the many areas of fighting in a larger, European war that took place from 1914 to 1918. It involved soldiers from more than 40 countries including the United States. More than 8 million soldiers were killed.

What is unusual about this ceremony is that every year more and more families turn up to remember these old soldiers, who are nearly all dead. Do you think this is a good idea, to remember wars like this? Should little children be going along to ceremonies that remember old battles?

STUDENT 1: The Battle of Gallipoli happened a long time ago. Who cares nowadays? It is old, it should be forgotten.

STUDENT 2: Yes, but what is wrong with going to a ceremony like that? It shows that you feel something for these old soldiers.

STUDENT 3: You can get caught up in the emotion of a ceremony like that. It can make you feel like you want to go to war yourself, to fight people.

STUDENT 4: I wouldn't feel like that. I don't want to go to war and get shot at or blown up. I think it's a good idea to have these ceremonies. It makes you remember that wars are very serious—you can get killed!

STUDENT 5: I'm absolutely against wars. My grandfather was killed in a war. The idea of a special ceremony to glorify an old war makes me feel sick.

STUDENT 6: Is it necessary to have these ceremonies? What are they saying to people? That we should never forget wars? Isn't it making soldiers into heroes? Is it a good idea to be doing this? I can't see the point of going to such a fuss to remember wars.

TEACHER: Well, I am hearing lots of arguments for and against remembering wars. Are your arguments based on facts or emotions?

STUDENTS: Well, there are some facts. People do get killed in wars. But some of our arguments are based on our beliefs about what is right and wrong. There are arguments for and against.

TEACHER: I agree that we have an argument here. An argument is not a bad thing. If it is done properly then we are able to hear opinions for and against. This article I am handing out to you is about remembering wars. It relates to Anzac Day in New Zealand but it could relate to special holidays about old wars in any country. In Australia and New Zealand there is an Anzac Day. In the United States, there is Veterans Day. So this article is relevant to other countries. How strong are the arguments for and against—that is the question we need to look at.

STUDENTS: Do you think we should? There will always be differences of opinion about anything, including wars. How can we settle an argument like this one?

TEACHER: Maybe we can't settle it. We might have to accept that there is no black-and-white answer to some questions. Let's have a quick look at this article. It has a bunch of quotations that are comments made by school students in New Zealand schools. What strikes you about some of the statements?

STUDENTS: Well, some are for, some are against.

TEACHER: Yes—let's organize the information so that it fits an argument structure. I want you to list the student opinions as either for or against remembering wars.

Organize (After reading)

TEACHER: What did you think of the article?

STUDENTS: It's interesting to hear the different opinions. We thought that students would all agree because we are a new generation and we have our own new ideas.

TEACHER: Well, there you are. It shows that if you ask enough people you will get different opinions to your own. There are many ways of looking at the same issue, ways that you might not have thought about yourself.

Review

TEACHER: Any lessons learned today?

STUDENTS: Yes—we found out that you can remember wars in different ways. You can glorify war if you want to, but most people are just sad that wars have to happen.

TEACHER: I agree. Most of us are against war. We do not want them to happen unless absolutely necessary. Remembering old wars can make us more sensitive to the fact that going to war is a last resort, and that you can pay a terrible price for going to war.

Extend Ask students to find out more about the arguments for and against war. They could visit a rest home for the elderly and interview old soldiers. What did they think about the war they fought in? Why did they go to war? Do they still believe in war or do they think it is a terrible thing? Students could also ask the wives and children of old soldiers what they think. Do their relatives like the idea of having Anzac Day or Veterans Day? It would be good to locate some old photos of soldiers or of previous wars—to give some idea of what it was like to be a soldier then. Students could do some searching on the Internet for photos. Then students can make up a new list of arguments for and against, based on the information they gained from their interviews and internet research.

War: Who Wants to Remember It? Answers

Arguments FOR	Arguments AGAINST
1. These people believed they were doing the right thing	1. Worry about wars today, not yesterday
2. We should remember the war, but also remember the mothers who had to stay at home and look after their families by themselves	2. This old war means nothing to children today. They were not part of that war.
3. We should remember the war. These soldiers helped us to have a better life.	3. Yes, remember the soldiers who died but also remember those who believed that war was wrong and who were punished because of their beliefs
4. We should remember because many of our relatives died during that war	4. Our "enemies" in that war now live in our country. We should respect their feelings.
5. When we remember the war we remember the fighting and those killed—and we will not want to go to war again	5. It is morally wrong to remember war and glorify it
Conclusion: There are good arguments to remember old wars but there are also good arguments not to remember these wars. It is not a clear-cut question that we are trying to answer. An argument text like this presents the reader with arguments for and against, and readers have to make up their own minds.	

The Freeway Debate

Rationale This nonfiction article gives facts, opinions, and emotions about whether or not to extend freeways into the inner city. It gives arguments for and against. It is a good example of the argument structure because it summarizes the submissions made by the public to the city council both for the freeway and against it. The argument structure is signaled by the topic of the article, "The Freeway Debate." The concept of a debate implies arguments for and against.

Summary The Freeway Debate gives arguments for and against extending the freeway into the city.

The arguments in favor:

1. Traffic will be able to bypass the congestion of the city.

2. Public transportation could not cope if everyone stopped driving cars.

3. It will take less time to get to work.

4. Future cars, such as electric, will be less damaging to the environment.

5. Freeways can be ugly but with proper landscaping they can be works of art.

6. People should be able to live the lifestyle they want. If they want to drive their cars, we should let them.

The arguments against:

1. Extending the freeway into the inner city will encourage more cars and cause more congestion.

2. Drivers should pay more taxes to pay for public transportation.

3. Is saving a few minutes of time worth all the expense and destruction?

4. More cars mean more pollution.

5. The environment will suffer because of noise and destruction of buildings that would have to make way for the freeway.

6. Why should the rights of car drivers be more important than everyone else's?

CORE Teaching Ideas

Connect to the Content (before reading)

TEACHER: How did you get to school today?

STUDENT 1: My dad drove me.

STUDENT 2: I caught the bus.

STUDENT 3: I rode my bike.

STUDENT 4: I rode my scooter.

STUDENT 5: I walked.

TEACHER: Did anyone come to school on the freeway?

STUDENTS: Yes. My dad says that we get to school much more quickly on the freeway.

TEACHER: Yes—but are there other ways you could get here?

STUDENTS: Of course—but why not take the quickest way?

TEACHER: Well, some people would argue that the quickest way is not always the best way for the city as a whole. Freeways cost a lot of money to build, and only drivers get the benefits from them, and they cause a lot of destruction in building them.

STUDENTS: Yes, but they also make life a lot easier for the people.

TEACHER: Yes—but which people? And who should decide? Are the rights of car drivers more important than the well-being of the people as a whole?

STUDENTS: Well, everyone has their own opinion on that. If we asked everyone for an opinion we would never do anything.

TEACHER: Yes—but what if there are downsides that you are not aware of? Wouldn't you want to know all the facts before you made a decision?

STUDENTS: Well—probably.

TEACHER: This is exactly what we are doing today. We are studying a nonfiction article that present arguments—both in favor and against building a freeway that goes through a city. Let's read the text together. Then I want you to break into small groups and write a short summary of the arguments for and against extending the freeway through the city. I will give you some thick paper to write the arguments. Divide the page into two halves and then list the arguments for and against.

Organize (After reading)

TEACHER: What did you think of the article?

STUDENTS: We thought it would be a good thing to extend the freeway because it would mean we could get up later in the morning because it would take less time to get to school. But the issue is a bit complicated. We didn't realize that some people would be against building the freeway. We didn't realize that some people would have to give up their homes to make way for the freeway. That makes it a bit harder to decide for or against.

TEACHER: Well yes, that is the whole point of an argument text. It makes you more aware of the arguments for and against.

STUDENTS: Maybe we need to think more about other ways to get somewhere than taking a car. Public transportation is more efficient. Even walking or riding a bike is good because it does not pollute the environment.

TEACHER: What kind of structural design did you come up with?

STUDENTS: It was an argument design. We listed the arguments for and against. We thought that freeways would be helpful because they meant less congestion in the city. But some said that freeways only make it easier to use cars so we will end up with even more cars than we had before, with even more pollution. We hadn't thought of that.

TEACHER: The text design that you just completed is a good way to summarize the arguments for and against a topic. It will be really helpful when you need to write an argument essay. You can write three or four arguments in favor, and then three or four arguments against. Then you write a conclusion where you give your own opinion, based on the arguments.

Review

TEACHER: Any lessons learned today?

STUDENTS: Yes—it seems that every time you try to make things better you can make things worse.

TEACHER: Yes—an argument article can make you feel that way because it gives both sides of the question. What was the message of the article?

STUDENTS:	Probably the message is that there will be benefits to change but there will be costs as well. That is probably why some people like change and others do not. Change will help some and not others.
TEACHER:	That is very insightful. And did you learn anything about text structure?
STUDENTS:	Yes—it is a good idea to list the arguments for and against when you are thinking about the meaning of an article. If there are no arguments against something, then maybe there is something wrong, maybe the author is not telling us the whole truth. There are probably arguments for and against any kind of change.

Extend Ask students to think of another topic closer to home that might be difficult to decide on. For example, Calfee and Patrick (1995) asked students to write arguments for and against having lockers in the school. Students already know that lockers give privacy and security, but from the principal's point of view, lockers are expensive to buy and school funds are limited. Perhaps students can suggest a similar topic, such as whether mobile phones should be allowed into the school, and give arguments for and against. They could interview all the stakeholders in the issue, such as other students, parents, and teachers.

The Freeway Debate Answers

For	Against
1. Less congestion in the city	1. More cars, more congestion
2. Cars help. Need less public transportation	2. Drivers should pay taxes to get better public transport
3. Freeways are quicker	3. Is saving a few minutes that important?
4. Cars will soon be eco-friendly	4. Cars will always be unfriendly to the environment
5. Artists can make freeways beautiful to look at, get rid of ugly houses	5. Why should people have their houses destroyed to make way for a freeway?

WAR: Who Wants to Remember It?

More than 2,700 New Zealand soldiers died as a result of a horrific World War I battle at Gallipoli Peninsula, Turkey, on April 25, 1915. Ever since, on Anzac Day, people from New Zealand have been re-membering them and all the other New Zealand ser-vicemen and women who have died in wars since.

Is Anzac Day something people should continue to commemorate, or are past conflicts best forgotten? *School Journal* asked its readers—middle and high school students in New Zealand—for their thoughts on the Anzac debate.

We still have wars today. We should be worrying about them rather than thinking about the past.

—Caroline Slater, Clyde Quincy School

It's important to hold Anzac Day because so many people died fighting for what they believed, at that time, was right.

—Kieran Blogg, Geraldine High School

It's good to have a ceremony that remem-bers soldiers, but we shouldn't forget paci-fists who were put in jail because of what they believed in or the mothers who stayed behind to look after children by themselves.

—Amanda Sweeney, Anderson's Bay School

We should continue to hold Anzac Day. War anniversaries don't celebrate war; they com-memorate the part soldiers played in the war so that we could have a better life.

—Tim Landreth, Catlins Area School

Anzac Day has meaning for the young people of today because so many lost grandparents or great-aunts and great-uncles during the war.

—*Anna Bray-Sharpin,*
Nelson Intermediate School

Anzac Day means nothing to today's kids. They didn't fight in the battle of Gallipoli.

—*Zara Webb Pullman,*
Clyde Quincy School

It's good to commemorate Anzac Day, but I think we should also remember the civilians who died in the war. They suffered just as much as the soldiers.

—*Ora Simpson,*
Tahuna Normal Intermediate

Anzac Day is important. It's when we remember those who died for us and when survivors of the war remember their old friends.

—*Benjamin McGill,*
Catlins Area School

Many descendants of wartime "enemies" now live in New Zealand. We should recognize the feelings of these people when we commemorate Anzac Day.

—*Nick Chalmers,*
Nelson Intermediate School

If we stop having Anzac Day, we'll forget about the fighting, and we might choose war again.

—*Melissa Holloway,*
Anderson's Bay School

It's pointless to remember war and morally wrong to honor and glorify it.

—*Zara Webb Pullman,*
Clyde Quincy School

War: Who Wants to Remember It?

Arguments FOR	Arguments AGAINST
Conclusion:	

The Freeway Debate

by Pat Quinn

Background

In New Zealand, the Wellington City "Western Foothills Motorway" was designed as a full freeway from Ngauranga Gorge to the Mt. Victoria tunnel.

It was a 20-year construction plan, due for completion in 1992. By 1978, all but the last 1.6 kilometers had been completed.

Construction then "paused," and the remaining part of the plan, the Central City Bypass, was reconsidered. A revised plan, less complex than the original, was drawn up for the remaining section, but meanwhile people had changed their ideas about freeways.

1 kilometer = .62 miles
1 meter = 3.28 feet

The Problem

Freeways were once seen as the most up-to-date and efficient way to move traffic in and out of a city. By the time of this debate people had become more aware of the pollution that traffic brings into the city, and the noise and upheaval that big road construction causes.

Even the City Council, which had originally approved the idea of the freeway found itself unable to agree on whether to continue with the plan.

So the council and the freeway builders, Transit New Zealand, asked members of the public to let them know what they thought about the motorway extension. People attended public meetings, telephoned in their opinions, and wrote letters and submissions.

FOR	AGAINST
Cars, trucks, buses, motorcycles, and emergency services use the existing freeway to get into the city, to cross town to the suburbs on the other side, and to get to the airport and the hospital. But at the moment, the freeway stops at a city intersection. This means that all freeway traffic has to come into the city. The city streets were never designed to take a high volume of traffic, and at peak times, especially in the mornings, there are traffic jams and long delays. Traffic surveys show that between 7 A.M. and 9 A.M., 37 percent of the vehicles using the freeway are going to and from areas outside the city. They don't need, or want, to have to travel through town. The extension will let this traffic bypass the city center.	An extension of the freeway might make it easier to get across town, but it will also encourage more people to bring their cars into the city. More cars mean more city traffic, more parking problems, and more accidents. The traffic jams won't go away, they'll just move to different parts of the city.
Our city populations in New Zealand are relatively small. In Auckland there are about 1,300,000 people, in Wellington 424,000, whereas Los Angeles County has a population of about 9,948,000, twice as many as the whole of New Zealand. In cities our size, it would be uneconomic to have a public transportation system that would get everyone quickly to where they want to go.	We should learn from other cities. Portland, for instance, in Oregon, where they scrapped plans for a new motorway and instead spend $450 million on upgrading their bus fleet and building a light rapid-transit railway. Or Los Angeles, where the roads have become so clogged with traffic that they've decided to invest *$7 billion* on a light-rail commuter system. Another option would be a park-and-ride system where drivers leave their cars at parking areas outside the city, then catch a bus shuttle service into town. The average bus carries about 40 people at peak hours, compared with the 1.33 that travel by car.
If the freeway is completed, people can more easily go where and when they want. The time it takes to get across the city will be reduced from nine minutes to about two minutes. It might not seem much for a day, but it adds up over a year. And there are savings for vehicles, too. With less time on the road and a clearer path, vehicle maintenance and running costs will be lower.	If people had to pay more for the right to bring their cars into the city at toll gates (with an extra charge on cars with only one person aboard), or through higher parking fees, there would be more money available for a better public transportation system.
	Is it really worth building a freeway extension to save a few minutes of travel time? People will just leave home later, or spend the extra minutes at the office.

FOR

With advances in car technology, cars of the future will be less damaging to the environment. In Japan during the 1970s, carbon monoxide emissions were halved, and lead emissions in the U.S. dropped by 94 percent after lead-free gas was introduced. In New Zealand, we have regulations stating that by 1996 only unleaded gas will be on sale, and carbon dioxide emissions are targeted to drop 20 percent by 2005. Anyway, once the extension is in place, exhaust pollution could decrease slightly with improved traffic flows. At higher speeds, vehicles are burning fuel more efficiently, with less toxic emission than if they're stopping and starting in a traffic jam.

Working on an average growth in traffic of 2 percent per year over the next 25 years, the council has used a computer-based-model to work out traffic volumes and delays on the present motorway. Engineers have compared that with what would happen if an extension was built. They found that an extension would improve traffic flow around the city.

Admittedly, there is a problem with the tunnels. One tunnel, at the city end of the freeway, is three lanes wide; the other tunnel, where the extension will end, has two lanes. The freeway is four lanes wide so traffic will have to slow down and merge for each of the tunnels. To make it really worthwhile, new tunnels would have to be built.

It's also true that some freeways can be unsightly, but with good design, and with tree and shrub planting, they can be beautiful in their own way. Overbridges and

AGAINST

More cars have always meant more pollution. Car exhaust fumes produce toxic substances including lead, carbon, monoxide, carbon dioxide (the "greenhouse gas"), and nitrous and sulphor oxides that cause acid rain, which has already killed forests in Europe. Also, the gas and oil that vehicles use is a limited resource, so wouldn't it be wiser to look at alternatives to car travel? The average diesel bus uses only a third as much energy per passenger per kilometer as the average car. Rail and trolley buses run on electricity, which is abundant in New Zealand because of hydroelectric power.

What about the fact that the proposed extension ends at a narrow tunnel? This will create a bottleneck, and new traffic jams. Are we going to have to build a new tunnel?

Think of the cost! The cost of the freeway extension alone is up to $110 million and rising all the time. How many more million for tunnels? This is money that would be better spent on an improved public transportation system so that people don't need to use cars so much. Following this option would also avoid the mess that a motorway would cause.

However much the freeway is beautified, the air pollution and noise pollution will be considerable. The plans for the extension show it as a seven-meter-deep "trench" style freeway—a four-lane chasm separating inner-city suburbs from the city and from each other.

FOR

pedestrian walkways can link people on either side, and by having the freeway below street level, traffic noise will be reduced. At the moment, some of the areas that the extension will pass through look a mess, but they'll be tidied up if the freeway goes in. And buildings that are historically important can be moved to another site.

Perhaps it comes down to a lifestyle choice. Many people *prefer* to use their cars. To some, a car is more than just a convenience; it's a status symbol, a sign of independence, a place where you can be warm, dry, and listen to music. People have a right to this.

AGAINST

A hundred houses and apartments, five schools, a dental clinic, a synagogue, and a church are in the path of the new section of the freeway. They'll be affected by the traffic noise once the extension is built—that's apart from the mud, noise, dust, and road work during the five years of construction.

Are the rights of the people who want driving convenience more important than the rights of those who want less traffic and less pollution in their city?

The debate goes on: convenience versus conservation. Similar arguments are being raised over sewage outfalls, historic buildings, national parks, mining, defense spending, and nuclear energy. There is seldom a clear-cut right answer. It is a matter of people thinking about the issues, discussing them, and making their feelings known to those in authority. The outcome may or may not be what they wanted, but at least they have had a chance to influence the decision. They haven't allowed things to "just happen."

The Freeway Debate

For	Against

CHAPTER 10

Conclusion

We have focused on expository text because it is the one kind of text that students do not intuitively grasp. In fact, it is the kind of text that paralyzes many students. When they read about things like armadillos, or climate change, or endangered species, or stem cell research, they find it hard to bring together the key ideas in a verbal summary or written report. It is as if there are too many things to remember. And there are.

This is where text structure awareness comes in. The lessons we have provided in our book show students how to see the forest for the trees, how to organize small points by putting them into categories that are easy to remember. An awareness of text structure makes the text much simpler to remember and write about. This kind of mental organization of ideas fits well with our mental processes because our minds like to be organized. To illustrate, I remember reading a children's story about a boy whose room was always untidy and it drove his parents crazy. One day, his mother decided to put all his toys in different places—for example, she put his toy truck on top of the wardrobe. When her son came home he couldn't find his toys. What did he do? He decided to organize his room so that he knew where everything was. It's a fun story and it does illustrate our human need to organize.

We like to organize because our short-term memory is limited. We can't remember all the information that we read. We can remember four or five main points but that is all. So the key is to break down the information into categories and then put the minor facts and details into each category. The text structures in this book are all essential strategies for summarizing the main points.

The text structure lessons in the book will help students to go beyond the norm so they can build on their prior knowledge, capture the main ideas, learn to summarize, visualize, come to grips with new vocabulary, and put on one page what took the writer of the text many pages.

The text structures will also be useful if the student is asked to write about the text, a short summary or even a detailed report. From a writing point of view, each text structure has within it a few simple subheadings followed by details that can flesh out the subheadings.

The structures tackled in this book can be used for oral language activities as well. For example, an oral language task might be to imagine you have problems with the neighbor's dog. It barks all day while your neighbors are at work. The class might decide to use a problem-solution structure for acting out this scenario. Everyone might agree that the neighbors probably love their dog so it is best to argue the pros and cons, even though we would like to give an ultimatum (e.g., "put a muzzle on that dog!"). In talking out this problem-solution structure, the students acting out the dialogue could say some positive things to begin with (e.g., you have a nice-looking dog) before going to the problem (e.g., he barks all day) and a possible solution (e.g., have you tried a dog-psychologist?).

Some readers may wonder why we have focused so much on text structure even though text structure is only one part of the comprehension puzzle. We believe it is the most important part. After all, the goal of reading is to understand what one reads. Vocabulary, grammatical structure, and main ideas are all important of course, but teaching about text structure entails covering these areas as well.

It has been said many times that there is nothing more practical than a good theory. The theory that drives this book is the simple view of reading, which says that to understand a text you need to be a fluent decoder and have good comprehension skills. Fluent decoding means being able to read the words accurately and effortlessly so that all mental energy can be reserved for comprehension. Good language comprehension requires a good vocabulary, grammatical knowledge, the ability to pinpoint the main ideas of paragraphs, and the ability to pull all the ideas in a text in order to see the "big picture." It is the "big picture" part of language comprehension that we chose to work on in this book. Students will acquire other components through classroom instruction. They will learn to use a dictionary to build vocabulary, and learn to find the main ideas in paragraphs. It is the big-picture part of the puzzle, capturing all the main ideas in one structure, that our text structure lessons are designed to reinforce.

To conclude, the text structure lessons in this book are a great preparation for the academic demands of grades 4 through 6, and will be especially useful in high school. Teaching them now will provide your students with excellent strategies that will have long-lasting effects. As one college student said to us, "Why did we have to wait till now to learn about these structures?" Now that you have read this book and used the lessons with your class, you will not have to worry about your own students. They will have acquired essential study skills for success.

References

Anderson, R. C., & Freebody, P. (1981). Vocabulary knowledge. In J. T. Guthrie (Ed.), *Comprehension and teaching: Research reviews* (pp. 77–117). Newark, DE: International Reading Association.

Beck, I. L., McKeown, M. G., Hamilton, R. L., & Kucan, L. (1998). Getting at the meaning. *American Educator, 22* (1), 66–71, 85.

Block, C. C., & Pressley, M. (2003). Best practices in comprehension instruction. In L. M. Morrow, L. B. Gambrell, & M. Pressley (Eds.), *Best practices in literacy instruction* (2nd ed., pp. 111–126). New York: Guilford Press.

Block, C. C., & Pressley, M. (2007). Best practices in teaching comprehension. In L. B. Gambrell, L. M. Morrow, & M. Pressley (Eds.), *Best practices in literacy instruction* (3rd ed., pp. 220–242). New York: Guilford Press.

Block, C. C., & Pressley, M. (Eds.). (2002). *Comprehension instruction: Research-based best practices.* New York: Guilford Press.

Brown, R. (2002). Straddling two worlds: Self-directed comprehension instruction for middle schoolers. In C. C. Block & M. Pressley (Eds.), *Comprehension instruction: Research-based best practices* (pp. 337–350). New York: Guilford Press.

Brown, S. L., & Day, J. D. (1983). Macrorules for summarizing text: The development of expertise. *Journal of Verbal Learning and Behavior, 22,* 1–4.

Calfee, R. C. (1994). *Implications of cognitive psychology for authentic assessment and instruction.* Technical Report No. 69, University of California at Berkeley & Carnegie Mellon University.

Calfee, R. C., & Associates (1984). *The book: Components of reading instruction.* Unpublished manuscript, Stanford University, Stanford, CA.

Calfee, R. C., & Chambliss, M. J. (1987). The structural designs of large texts. *Educational Psychologist, 22,* 357–378.

Calfee, R. C., & Curley, R. G. (1984). Structures of prose in the content areas. In J. Flood (Ed.), *Understanding reading comprehension* (pp. 161–180). Newark, DE: International Reading Association.

Calfee, R. C., & Drum, P. A. (1986). Research on teaching reading. In M. Wittrock (Ed.), *Handbook of research on teaching* (pp. 804–849). New York: Macmillan.

Calfee, R. C., & Patrick, C. L. (1995). *Teach our children well: Bringing K–12 education into the 21st century.* Stanford, CA: Stanford Alumni.

Calfee, R. C., Henry, M., & Funderburg, J. (1988). A model for school change. In S. J. Samuels & P. D. Pearson (Eds.), *Changing school reading programs* (pp. 121–141). Newark, DE: International Reading Association.

Calfee, R., Chambliss, M. J., & Beretz, M. M. (1991). Organizing for comprehension and composition. In R. Bowler & W. Ellis (Eds.), *All language and the creation of literacy* (pp. 79–93). Baltimore, MD: Orton Dyslexia Society.

Chall, J. S. (1983). *Stages of reading development.* New York: McGraw-Hill.

Chall, J. S., & Jacobs, V. A. (2003). The classic study on poor children's fourth-grade slump. *American Educator, 27* (1), 14–15, 44.

Chambliss, M. J. (1993). Assessing instructional materials: How comprehensible are they? In C. J. Gordon, G. D. Labercane, & W. R. McEachern (Eds.), *Elementary reading: Process and practice* (2nd ed., pp. 319–340). Needham Heights, MA: Ginn.

Chambliss, M., & Calfee, R. C. (1998). *Textbooks for learning: Nurturing children's minds.* Malden, MA: Blackwell.

Dickson, S. V., Simmons, D. C., & Kameenui, E. J. (1998). Text organization: Research bases. In D. C. Simmons & E. J. Kameenui (Eds.), *What reading research tells us about children with diverse learning needs* (pp. 239–277). Mahwah, NJ: Lawrence Erlbaum.

Duke, N. K. (2000). 3.6 minutes per day: The scarcity of informational texts in first grade. *Reading Research Quarterly, 35,* 202–224.

Duke, N. K. (2004). The case for informational text. *Educational Leadership, 61* (6), 40–44.

Durkin, D. (1978–1979). What classroom observations reveal about reading comprehension instruction. *Reading Research Quarterly, 15,* 481–533.

Dymock, S. J. (1993). Reading but not understanding. *Journal of Reading, 37,* 86–91.

Dymock, S. J. (1998). A comparison study of the effects of text structure training, reading practice, and guided reading on reading comprehension. In T. Shanahan & F. V. Rodriguez-Brown (Eds.), *National Reading Conference Yearbook* (Vol. 47, pp. 90–102). Chicago, IL: National Reading Conference.

Dymock, S. J. (1999). Teaching text structures. In G. B. Thompson & T. Nicholson (Eds.), *Learning to read: Beyond phonics and whole language* (pp. 174–192). New York: Teachers College Press.

Dymock, S. J. (2005). Strategies for improving children's comprehension of expository texts. *The Reading Teacher, 59*, 177–182.

Dymock, S. J. (in press). Comprehension strategy instruction: Teaching narrative text structure awareness. *The Reading Teacher, 61*.

Dymock, S. J., & Nicholson, T. (1999). *Reading Comprehension: What is it? How do you teach it?* Wellington, New Zealand: New Zealand Council for Educational Research.

Dymock, S. J., & Nicholson, T. (2001). *Reading comprehension: What is it? How do you teach it? Supplementary material: Narrative. Teacher's guide and student worksheets.* Wellington, New Zealand: New Zealand Council for Educational Research.

Dymock, S. J., & Nicholson, T. (2002). *Reading comprehension: What is it? How do you teach it? Supplementary material: Transactional. Teacher's guide and student worksheets.* Wellington, New Zealand: New Zealand Council for Educational Research.

Gaskins, I. W. (2003). Taking charge of reader, text, activity, and content variables. In A. P. Sweet & C. E. Snow (Eds.), *Rethinking reading comprehension* (pp. 141–165). New York: Guilford Press.

Gough, P. B., & Tunmer, W. E. (1986). Decoding, reading, and reading disability. *Remedial and Special Education, 7*, 6–10.

Graves, M. F., Juel, C., & Graves, B. B. (Eds.). (2004). *Teaching reading in the 21st century* (3rd ed.). Mahwah, NJ: Erlbaum.

Hare, V. C., Rabinowitz, M., & Schieble, K. M. (1998). Text effects on main idea comprehension. *Reading Research Quarterly, 24*, 72–88.

Harris, T. L., & Hodges, R. E. (Eds.) (1995). *The literacy dictionary: The vocabulary of reading and writing.* Newark, DE: International Reading Association.

Hirsch, E. D. Jr. (2006). Building knowledge: The case for bringing content knowledge into the language arts block and for a knowledge-rich curriculum for all children. *American Educator, 30* (1), 8–29.

It's snowing! (2005, January). *Weekly Reader*, Grade 1, Week 4.

Jorgenson, G. W. (1977). Relationship of classroom behavior to the accuracy of the match between material difficulty and student ability. *Journal of Educational Psychology, 69*, 24–32.

Juel, C. (1988). Learning to read and write: A longitudinal study of 54 children from first through fourth grades. *Journal of Educational Psychology, 80*, 437–447.

Meyer, B. J. F. (1975). *The organization of prose and its effects on memory.* Amsterdam: North-Holland.

Meyer, B. J. F. (1981). Basic research on prose comprehension: A critical review. In D. F. Fisher & C. W. Peters (Eds.), *Comprehension and the competent reader: Inter-speciality perspectives* (pp. 8–35). New York: Pracger.

Meyer, B. J. F., & Poon, L. W. (2001). Effects of structure strategy training and signaling on recall of text. *Journal of Educational Psychology, 93*, 141–159.

Meyer, B. J. F., & Rice, G. E. (1984). The structure of text. In P. D. Pearson, R. Barr, M. L. Kamil, & P. Mosenthal (Eds.), *Handbook of reading research* (Vol. 1, pp. 319–351). New York: Longman.

Meyer, B. J. F., Brandt, D. M., & Bluth, G. J. (1980). Use of top-level structure in text: Key for reading comprehension of ninth-grade students. *Reading Research Quarterly, 16*, 72–103.

Meyer, B. J. F., Young, C., & Bartlett, B. J. (1993). Reading comprehension and use of text structure across the adult life span. In S. R. Yussen & M. C. Smith (Eds.), *Reading across the life span* (pp. 165–192). New York: Springer-Verlag.

Nagy, W. E. (1988). *Teaching vocabulary to improve reading comprehension.* Newark, DE: International Reading Association.

Nagy, W. E., & Scott, J. A. (2000). Vocabulary processes. In M. L. Kamil, P. B. Mosenthal, P. D. Pearson, & R. Barr (Eds.), *Handbook of reading research* (Vol. 3, pp. 269–294). Mahwah, NJ: Lawrence Erlbaum.

National Center for Education Statistics. (2004). *Report on National Assessment of Educational Progress. The nation's report card: Reading highlights 2003.* Washington, DC: United States Department of Education.

National Reading Panel. (2000). *Teaching children to read: An evidence-based assessment of the scientific research literature on reading and its implications for reading instruction. Reports of the subgroups* [NIH Publication No. 00-4754]. Washington, DC: National Institute of Child Health and Human Development.

Neuman, S. B. (2006). How we neglect knowledge—and why. *American Educator, 30* (1), 24–26, 51.

Newman, J. (1995) Moving house. *School Journal 2*, (3), 32–33. Wellington, New Zealand: Learning Media.

Nicholson, T. (1984). Experts and novices: A study of reading in the high school classroom. *Reading Research Quarterly, 19,* 436–451.

Nicholson, T. (1989). Research revisited: A study of reading and learning in the secondary school classroom. *Language and Education, 3,* 1–11.

Nicholson, T. (1999). Reading comprehension processes. In G. B. Thompson & T. Nicholson (Eds.), *Learning to read: Beyond phonics and whole language* (pp. 127–149). New York: Teachers College Press.

Nicholson, T. (2006). *Phonics handbook.* Chichester, England: Wiley.

Ogle, D., & Blachowicz, C. L. Z. (2002). Beyond literature circles: Helping students comprehend informational texts. In C. C. Block & M. Pressley (Eds.), *Comprehension instruction: Research-based best practices* (pp. 259–274). New York: Guilford Press.

Pearson, P. D. (1996). Reclaiming the center. In M. F. Graves, P. van den Broek, & B. M. Taylor (Eds.), *The first R: Every child's right to read* (pp. 259–274). New York: Teachers College Press.

Pearson, P. D., & Duke, N. K. (2002). Comprehension instruction in the primary grades. In C. C. Block & M. Pressley (Eds.), *Comprehension instruction: Research-based best practices* (pp. 247–58). New York: Guilford Press.

Pearson, P. D., Roehler, L. R., Dole, J. A., & Duffy, G. D. (1992). Developing expertise in reading comprehension. In S. J. Samuels & A. E. Farstrup (Eds.), *What research has to say about reading instruction* (2nd ed., pp. 145–199). Newark, DE: International Reading Association.

Perfetti, C. A., Marron, M. A., & Foltz, P. W. (1996). Sources of comprehension failure: Theoretical perspectives and case studies. In C. Cornoldi & J. Oakhill (Eds.), *Reading comprehension difficulties: Process and intervention* (pp. 137–165). Mahwah, NJ: Lawrence Erlbaum.

Pressley, M. (2000). What should comprehension instruction be the instruction of? In M. L. Kamil., P. B. Mosenthal, P. D. Pearson, & R. Barr (Eds.), *Handbook of reading research* (Vol. 3, pp. 545–561). Mahwah, NJ: Lawrence Erlbaum.

Pressley, M. (2002). Comprehension strategies instruction. In C. C. Block & M. Pressley (Eds.). *Comprehension instruction: Research based practices* (pp. 11–27). New York: Guilford Press.

Pressley, M. (2006a). *Reading instruction that works: The case for balanced teaching* (3rd ed.). New York: Guilford Press.

Pressley, M. (2006b, April). *What the future of reading research could be.* Paper presented at the meeting of the International Reading Association, Chicago, Illinois.

Pressley, M., & Block, C. C. (2002). Summing up: What comprehension instruction should be. In C. C. Block & M. Pressley (Eds.), *Comprehension instruction* (pp. 383–392). New York: Guilford Press.

Pressley, M., Wharton-McDonald, R., Mistretta-Hampston, J., & Echevarria, M. (1998). Literacy instruction in 10 fourth- and fifth-grade classrooms in upstate New York. *Scientific Studies of Reading, 2,* 159–194.

RAND Reading Study Group (2002). *Reading for understanding: Toward an R & D program in reading comprehension.* Washington, DC: RAND Corporation.

Rosenblatt, L. M. (1978). *The reader, the text, the poem: The transactional theory of the literary work.* Carbondale, IL: Southern Illinois University Press.

Smith, B. D. (1991). *A descriptive analysis of the content in three basal readers.* Unpublished doctoral dissertation, The University of Arizona.

Smolkin, L. R., & Donovan, C. A. (2002). "Oh excellent, excellent question!" Development differences and comprehension acquisition. In C. C. Block & M. Pressley (Eds.), *Comprehension instruction: Research based best practices* (pp. 140–57). New York: Guilford Press.

Stanovich, K. E. (1986). Matthew effects in reading: Some consequences of individual differences in the acquisition of literacy. *Reading Research Quarterly, 21,* 360–406.

Stanovich, K. E. (2000). *Progress in understanding reading.* New York: Guilford Press.

Sweet, A. P., & Snow, C. E. (2003). (Eds.). *Rethinking reading comprehension*: NY: Guilford Press.

Thomas, L. (2002). The food detectives. In *A mystery to me* (pp. 20–25). Wellington, New Zealand: Learning Media.

Vacca, R. (1998). Let's not marginalize adolescent literacy. *Journal of Adolescent and Adult Literacy, 41,* 604–609.

Weaver, C. A., & Kintsch, W. (1991). Expository text. In R. Barr., M. L. Kamil, P. B. Mosenthal, & P. D., Pearson (Eds.), *Handbook of reading research* (Vol. 2, pp. 230–245). New York: Longman.

Williams, J. P. (2005). Instruction in reading comprehension for primary-grade students: A focus on text structure. *Journal of Special Education, 39,* 6–18.

Wulsin, H. W. (2004, December 17). Professor popsicle. *Current Science, 90* (8), 6–7.